# rachael ray
# just in time!

# rachael ray
# just in time!

ALL-NEW
30-MINUTE MEALS,
PLUS SUPER-FAST
15-MINUTE MEALS
AND SLOW-IT-DOWN
60-MINUTE MEALS

clarkson potter/publishers
new york

Other Books by Rachael Ray

*Rachael Ray Get Real Meals*
*Rachael Ray 365: No Repeats*
*Rachael Ray Express Lane Meals*
*Rachael Ray 2, 4, 6, 8*

Copyright © 2007 by Rachael Ray
Photographs copyright © 2007 by Tina Rupp

Published in the United States by CLARKSON POTTER/PUBLISHERS,
an imprint of the CROWN PUBLISHING GROUP, a division of
RANDOM HOUSE, INC., New York.
www.crownpublishing.com
www.clarksonpotter.com

Clarkson N. Potter is a trademark and Potter and colophon are registered
trademarks of Random House, Inc.

Library of Congress Cataloging-in-Publication Data is available upon request

ISBN 978-0-307-38318-1

Printed in the United States of America

DESIGN BY JENNIFER K. BEAL

10  9  8  7  6  5  4  3  2  1

First Edition

# acknowledgments

Special thanks to all the readers and viewers of *30-Minute Meals* who continue to inspire me and who keep my appetite to write and to cook strong, even after all these years. Stay hungry for more!

Love and thanks to my family and my sweet Isaboo for being such good eaters and great cooks, too. Their recipes have helped to fill many pages of the *30-Minute Meal* cookbooks.

Many thanks to Em, for all her tasty ideas. And last, but certainly not least, many thanks to Pam Krauss and Michelle Boxer for organizing my brain.

*Just in Time* is dedicated
to those who believe
there's *always* time for
a good meal.

# contents

# the just in time breakdown

## Chicken, Turkey, and Eggs

## Beef, Pork, and Lamb

# 30-minute meals

## Sandwiches, Pizzas, and Burgers

## Chicken, Turkey, and Eggs

## Beef, Pork, and Lamb

# 60-minute meals

## Sandwiches, Pizzas, and Burgers

## Stoups, Stews, and Chilis

## Pasta and Grains

## Salads and Vegetable Entrées

# introduction

People stop me all the time, especially in the grocery store, and ask how I keep coming up with new 30-Minute Meals after writing so many. They want to know, do I ever get recipe block?

Nope. 30-Minute Meals have developed a personality and life of their own. Now, the menus speak to *me*. The conversations go something like this: "Hey, Rach, you haven't written a burger in a while; what about a fish burger? Maybe with swordfish? Tasty idea."

The concept of 30-Minute Meals has become so ingrained in my very being that I write them in my sleep. I keep notebooks on the bedstand whether I'm at home or traveling, for the 3 A.M. call from the kitchen in my head. When I look at ingredients I see increments of time. When I walk through the grocery store, I don't see red peppers and green beans, I see 5 to 6 minutes in a sauté pan and 2 minutes in boiling salted water.

There are a lot of great new 30-MM here, in all the top categories: new pasta recipes you can feel really good about eating, like the super healthy Whole-Wheat Pasta Arrabbiata with Fire-Roasted Tomatoes and Arugula. There's a lot of new MYOTO (Make-Your-Own Take-Out) like Grilled Chicken Shawarma and figure-friendly Tex-Mex like Charred Chili Rellenos. There are burgers made from more than ground beef, including the aforementioned swordfish burger and a French tuna burger, and there are tons of new meals to entice the pickiest of eaters into eating better and broader choices when it comes to food—check out the Sloppy Dude recipe that combines 99% fat-free turkey breast with ground tomatillos for a heaping portion of lean protein that tastes like salsa and chips. There are fancy meals for romantic suppers and family fare for big eaters and, as always, I write with the goal of using all types of ingredients—but in moderation. These meals are filled with color—lots of fresh fruits, veggies, and herbs mixed up with lean proteins and grains. Sure, there are a few guilty pleasures, like a couple of new comfort food faves like Mac and Cheese Lorraine. But as long as these are the exception rather than the rule, what's the harm? Look at it this way, comfort food drives us to go back to the gym, right?

In this book you'll also find two *new* categories of recipes, recipes that break the 30-minute mold but are every bit as easy and delicious.

## 15-Minute Meals

Sometimes there are just not enough hours in the day.

Even on a rainy weekend when I get up and have no plans beyond cleaning out the closets or the refrigerator, somehow it can get to be 8:00 at night, my husband and I are hungry, tired, and cranky, and there's no food in the house. Even I don't have the patience for a 30-Minute Meal. That's why I came up with a whole bunch of 15-Minute Meals, quick and tasty recipes that are designed to be easy to shop for, easy to prepare, and satisfying to your senses and your stomach when you are as hungry as you are tired and you have simply run out of time. Your jaw will drop when you see the quality—and quantity—of the food you can cook up in about 15 minutes. The 15-minute paella is the biggest show stopper, but there are plenty of other delicious options that have a can of soup or PB&J beat hands down, with not a lot more effort.

You can do it. You have time and you should cook, *tonight*. It's good for you, body and soul, and it's quicker than pizza delivery.

## 60-Minute Meals

On the other hand, in every week there's a day when you just slow down. For me, it's Sunday (maybe because my middle name, *Domenica*, is Sunday in Italian). Sometimes I have to wait a month to get a Sunday off, but even when

I'm working my body always knows when it's Sunday. I walk, talk, move and even breathe a little slower. I let the events of the day take their own course, rather than tackle the marathon tasks I try to cram into a normal day.

For these days, I have even slowed down the 30-Minute Meal. 60-Minute Meals have no more work or steps than 30-Minute Meals, they just take their own sweet time getting to the table. They're like a mellow friend you could watch movies with on the sofa in the rain—comforting and cozy. Our family faves from this group include Elsa's Cider Beef, Mom's Baked Stuffed Sole, Curried Vegetable Stoup, Spanish-Style Stuffed Peppers, and Oven-Roasted Cioppino. So the next time you want to slow down a bit, try out a 60-Minute Meal and see how satisfying an hour can be!

**So whether you need dinner on the table NOW or you can make a lazy afternoon of it, you've got plenty of options to choose from. Speed it up or slow it down, it's your call. And either way, chop on! Cook on! Eat well! Be Well! Enjoy.**

**Note: All recipes in this book serve four unless otherwise noted.**

Greek Mixed Grill Kebabs
and Pine Nut–Orzo Salad (page 216)

**Harvest Creamy Corn "Choup"
with Parsley (page 76)**

Cornish Hens and Citrus-Scented
Roasted Vegetables (page 268)

Roasted Pork Loin and Gravy with
Roasted Veggies and Potatoes (page 318)

Roll-over Supper:
Roasted Pork and Black Bean Chili
(page 321)

Panzanella Stoup (page 80)

Pasta Shells with Pancetta, Peas, and
Shrimp (page 116)

Lamb Meatballs in Tomato Mint Sauce with Pine Nut Couscous (page 308)

From Top:
Sloppy Dude
(page 48)

Italian
Barbecue
Sliced Steak
Sammies
(page 56)

Grilled Fish
Sammies with
Garlic Tartar
Sauce and
Baked Waffle
Fries with Spicy
Bloody Ketchup
(page 26)

# rachael ray
# just in time!

# Sammie Night

## Burgers, Heroes, Clubs, Wraps and Pizzas

(continued)

# How much do I love sandwiches? Let me count the ways.

They're the ultimate all-in-one meal, with protein, carbs, and veggies all in one tidy (or not so tidy) package; they're easy on the pocketbook, and you don't even need a fork and knife to eat them! Whether it's a burrito, Stromboli, quesadilla, hero, or a slice of pizza, I end up serving some variation of dinner-on-bread at least once a week. Of course it's a well-known fact that I love burgers. I even call myself the Queen of Burgers and by now I could make a different one every night for a year. If you like to mix it up and swap out a club sandwich or a slice of pizza for the burger every now and then (or if EVERY night is sammie night at your house) you'll find plenty of new go-to's here. If you've only got 15 minutes you can still make a super-fast tuna melt or chicken tostada. Want to slow it down? Caramelize a savory mess of onions to pile onto a French Onion Burger with super crispy fries that are worth every minute of the extra 15 you'll need to let them bake and Dijon Gravy to dunk them in. Either way, you'll leave the table happy.

# Deli-Stuffed Eggwiches

My friends all make this one when they're eating in front of the TV in their socks. It's fun to make for lazy weekend mornings, too.

2 **eggs**
  Splash of **milk** or cream
  **Salt** and **black pepper**
2 tablespoons **honey**
2 rounded tablespoons **apricot** or **raspberry preserves**
2 rounded tablespoons **grainy Dijon mustard**
8 slices **white** or **wheat bread**
4 slices **boiled ham**
4 slices **Swiss cheese**
4 slices **herb-roasted turkey**
2 tablespoons **butter**

In a shallow bowl, beat the eggs and milk or cream with salt and pepper to taste. Set aside. Mix together the honey, preserves, and mustard in a small bowl, and spread the mixture on one side of each bread slice. With the spread sides facing in, make sandwiches of ham, cheese, and turkey, folding the meat and cheese as needed to fit the bread.

Melt the butter in a skillet over medium heat. Dip each sandwich in the egg mixture and place in the skillet. Cook for 3 minutes on each side, or until deeply golden and warm through. Halve the sandwiches corner to corner and serve hot.

# Provençal Tuna Melts

Too pooped to cook? We make this sammie on hot nights after long days and we wash it down with crisp, cold French rosé. Ooo-la-yum-o!

1 **baguette**
4 tablespoons (½ stick) **butter**, softened
3 (6-ounce) cans **white tuna** packed in water, drained and flaked
6 fresh **tarragon sprigs**, leaves only, chopped
½ cup fresh **basil leaves** (about 10 leaves), chopped or thinly sliced
¼ cup fresh **flat-leaf parsley**, a generous handful, chopped
½ cup pitted good-quality **black** or **green olives**, chopped
2 **shallots**, finely chopped
3 tablespoons **capers**, drained
   Juice of 1 **lemon**
3 tablespoons **EVOO** (extra-virgin olive oil)
   **Black pepper**
8 slices **Gruyère** cheese

Split the baguette horizontally and cut into 4 pieces. Open each piece and slather with butter. Place a large skillet over medium heat; add the toasted bread, buttered side down, and toast until deep golden brown, 3 to 4 minutes. Work in 2 batches if the pan is not large enough.

Preheat the broiler.

In a bowl, combine the tuna with the herbs, olives, shallots, capers, lemon juice, and EVOO. Mix well and season with pepper to taste.

Working on a baking sheet, fill the toasted baguettes with tuna. Cover the mounded tuna with 2 slices of Gruyère and place the sammies under the broiler until the cheese is bubbly, 2 minutes. Serve hot.

# Fresh Tuna BLT

High in protein and packed with fiber, too, this is fit for a champ, Laila Ali. You'll think it's a knockout, too!

2 tablespoons **EVOO** (extra-virgin olive oil), plus some for drizzling
8 slices **turkey bacon**
4 (6-ounce) fresh **tuna steaks**, each steak halved horizontally to make 8 thin steaks
1 tablespoon **chipotle chili powder** for a spicy club, or 1 tablespoon smoked sweet paprika for a mild club
**Salt** and **black pepper**
2 **avocados**, halved, pitted, and scooped from their skins
Juice of 1 **lime**
8 slices **whole-grain bread**, toasted
8 **lettuce leaves**, such as butter or Bibb lettuce
2 ripe **tomatoes**, sliced
**Fancy potato chips** to serve alongside

Preheat a skillet over medium-high heat with a drizzle of EVOO. Cook the bacon until crisp, about 5 minutes. Remove from the skillet and break each slice in half.

While the bacon cooks, season the tuna steaks by rubbing with equal amounts of the chili powder or paprika, then season with salt and pepper.

In a large skillet, heat 2 tablespoons EVOO, twice around the pan, over medium-high heat until it ripples. Add the tuna and cook for 1 minute on each side for rare, 3 minutes on each side for fully cooked. Cook the tuna in batches if your pan is not large enough to accommodate all of the steaks, dividing the EVOO between the pans. Transfer the tuna to a plate.

Place the avocados in a bowl along with the lime juice and some salt and pepper. Smash with a fork until somewhat smooth.

Toast the bread.

To assemble the sandwich, spread some avocado mash on a slice of bread. Top with a tuna steak, 2 half-pieces of crispy bacon in an X, a lettuce leaf, a slice of tomato, a second piece of tuna, 2 more half-pieces of bacon, lettuce, and a slice of tomato. Slather some more avocado mash on the second slice of bread and set in place. Insert a toothpick in each of the 4 corners, then cut the club into 4 triangles. Serve with some potato chips.

# Grilled Fish Sammies with Garlic Tartar Sauce and Baked Waffle Fries with Spicy Bloody Ketchup

Fish and chips is a staple of pubs across the United Kingdom, but this fishy is swimming uptown to the "gastro-pub"—which means it's a bit updated and a lot delicious.

1-pound bag **frozen waffle fries**

¾ cup **mayonnaise**

1 **garlic clove**, grated

3 tablespoons drained **capers**

¼ cup pitted **green olives**, chopped

A handful of fresh **flat-leaf parsley**, finely chopped

1 cup **ketchup**

2 teaspoons **Worcestershire sauce** (eyeball it)

1 teaspoon **hot sauce**

1 tablespoon **prepared horseradish**

4 **crusty rolls**, split

4 (6–8 ounce) skinless **white fish fillets**, such as halibut

**Salt** and **black pepper**

1 tablespoon **EVOO** (extra-virgin olive oil)

1 **lemon**, halved

**Celery salt**

8 **green or red leaf lettuce** leaves

½ **red onion**, very thinly sliced

Preheat the oven to 425°F.

Spread the fries on a rimmed baking sheet and bake for 20 minutes, turning once.

In a small bowl, combine the mayo with the grated garlic, capers, olives, and parsley. In a separate bowl, combine the ketchup with the Worcestershire, hot sauce, and horseradish. Toast the rolls on the grill or heat the broiler and set them in the middle of the oven to brown for a few minutes until golden.

While the fries bake, heat a skillet, grill, or grill pan over medium-high heat. Season the fish with salt and pepper and drizzle on both sides with the EVOO. Cook the fish for 3 to 4 minutes on each side until firm and opaque and cooked through. Squeeze the lemon over the cooked fish.

Remove the fries from the oven and season with celery salt and black pepper.

Place the fish on the toasted rolls and top with lettuce, red onion, and tartar sauce. Serve the fries alongside with the bloody ketchup.

# Saltimbocca Burgers

*Saltimbocca* means "jump in your mouth," and you won't be able to get this burger in your mouth fast enough. Traditionally saltimbocca is made with veal scallopini, but this burger version is a much less formal way to get the same great flavors.

1½   pounds **ground veal** or chicken
3   to 4 large **garlic cloves**, grated or finely chopped
15   to 16 fresh **sage leaves**, thinly sliced
    **Salt** and **black pepper**
4   tablespoons **EVOO** (extra-virgin olive oil)
2   cups **baby romaine leaves** or 6 to 8 leaves from the center of a romaine heart, chopped
    Juice of ½ **lemon**
8   1-inch-thick slices good-quality **semolina bread** cut on an angle
8   slices **prosciutto di Parma**
8   thin slices **Italian Fontina** cheese
8   **celery sticks**, from the heart, trimmed
1   sack **fancy potato chips**, such as Terra's Garlic and Onion Yukon Chips

Preheat the broiler.

In a bowl mix the ground meat with the garlic, sage, salt, and pepper. Score the meat with the side of your hand into 4 equal parts. Form each portion into a large patty and make a divot at the center of each to prevent burger bulge while cooking.

Heat 2 tablespoons of the EVOO, twice around the pan, in an oven-proof nonstick skillet over medium-high heat. Cook the patties for 3 to 4 minutes on each side, turning once. Leave the burgers in the skillet.

While the burgers cook, dress the greens with the lemon juice, the remaining 2 tablespoons EVOO, and salt and pepper. Toast the bread on both sides under the broiler. Remove the bread slices but keep the broiler on.

Top each burger with a couple slices of folded prosciutto and Fontina cheese. Slide the skillet under the broiler to melt the cheese.

Place the burgers on 4 toasted bread slices and top with romaine salad and a second slice of toasted bread. Serve with a couple of celery sticks and a few potato chips.

## tidbit

If your skillet does not have an ovenproof handle, wrap the handle in 2 layers of heavy-duty aluminum foil before slipping it under the broiler.

# Red, Wine, and Blue Burgers with Baked Jalapeño Poppers

Here's a Fourth of July menu that will set off fireworks in your mouth all year long!

- 12 large **jalapeños**
- 4 ounces **cream cheese**, softened
- 4 ounces **manchego cheese**, grated
- 2 to 3 tablespoons **green olives** with pimientos, finely chopped
- 2 tablespoons chopped fresh **flat-leaf parsley** or cilantro
  **Salt** and **black pepper**
- 2 pounds **ground sirloin**
- 3 **scallions**, white and green parts, chopped
- 2 teaspoons **grill seasoning**, such as McCormick's Montreal Steak Seasoning, ½ palmful
- 2 teaspoons **Worcestershire sauce**
- ½ cup **dry red wine**
- 2 tablespoons **EVOO** (extra-virgin olive oil), 2 times around the pan
- 1 cup **buttermilk**
- 1 cup **blue cheese**, crumbled
- 1 teaspoon **hot sauce**
- 4 **kaiser rolls**, split
- 2 bunches of **watercress**, trimmed of any thick stems
  **Fancy potato chips**, such as rosemary flavor
- 6 **celery ribs**, cut into 3-inch sticks

Preheat the oven to 425°F.

Working lengthwise, slice off the top quarter of each jalapeño and set aside. Use a small spoon or paring knife to scrape the seeds out of each jalapeño, making little jalapeño canoes.

Finely chop the reserved pepper trimmings and place in a mixing bowl. Add the cream cheese, manchego, olives, parsley, salt, and pepper and combine thoroughly. Use a small spoon to fill the canoes or transfer the mixture to a resealable plastic bag, snip off the corner, and squeeze the mixture into the hulls of your jalapeño canoes. Arrange the poppers on a baking sheet and bake for 15 minutes.

While the poppers bake, make the burgers. Combine the ground sirloin, scallions, grill seasoning, Worcestershire, and red wine in a bowl. Mix until thoroughly combined. Using the side of your hand, score the meat into 4 equal portions, then form each portion into a large 1-inch-thick patty. Make an indentation at the center of each patty so that as the burgers cook and plump the tops will remain flat and even.

Preheat a large skillet over medium-high heat with the EVOO. Once you see ripples in the oil add the patties and cook for 4 to 5 minutes on each side for medium, or until they reach your desired doneness.

While the burgers are cooking, put together the blue dressing. In a mixing bowl combine the buttermilk, blue cheese, hot sauce, and a little salt and pepper. Blend until thoroughly combined. Toast the split rolls in the oven until lightly golden.

Place a burger on top of each toasted roll bottom. Top the burgers with some watercress and a couple dollops of the blue cheese sauce. Serve with the poppers, fancy chips, and celery sticks.

# Meat and Potatoes Burger

Craig Ferguson gave me my schooling in mashed potatoes, "the only thing he makes." He adds an egg to his mashers and it makes all the difference. I wrote this recipe for him. He rewrote the potatoes for us all—giving the world the perfect meat and potatoes supper. Kudos, baby!

2 large **baking potatoes**, peeled and cut into chunks
   **Salt**
1 tablespoon **butter**
   Splash of **whole milk** or half-and-half
1 **egg**, lightly beaten
   A couple of tablespoons snipped **chives**
   **Black pepper**
2 pounds lean **ground sirloin**
2 tablespoons **Worcestershire sauce** (eyeball it)
3/4 cup flat-leaf **parsley leaves**, a generous handful, finely chopped
1 small **onion**, peeled
2 tablespoons **EVOO** (extra-virgin olive oil)
4 poppy seed or plain **kaiser rolls**
   **Dijon mustard**
1 bunch **watercress**, trimmed of thick stems

Place the potatoes in a sauce pot with water to cover by one inch. Bring to a boil over high heat, add some salt, and cook the potatoes until tender, 12 minutes. Turn off the heat. Drain the potatoes and return to the pot, and let them sit for a minute to dry out. Add the butter and milk or half-and-half—just a splash. Add the egg and mash with a potato masher or fork. Add the chives and salt and pepper and continue to mash until fairly smooth.

Preheat the broiler.

While the potatoes are cooking, start on the burgers. In a bowl, combine the sirloin, Worcestershire, and parsley. Grate about 2 to 3 tablespoons of the onion directly into the bowl; wrap up the remainder of the onion and save for another use. Season the meat with salt and pepper and mix to combine. Score the meat with the side of your hand into 4 equal portions. Form each portion into a patty about 1 inch thick and press a slight indentation into the center of each. This dent will promote more even cooking and prevent the burger from bulging.

Preheat a large skillet over medium-high heat with about 2 tablespoons of EVOO, twice around the pan. Once the oil ripples, add the patties and cook on each side for 7 to 8 minutes for rare to medium rare, 11 to 12 minutes for medium to medium well done, turning once.

While the burgers are working, split the buns and toast lightly under the broiler.

To build your burger, slather the bun bottoms with Dijon mustard and top with watercress. Place a burger on each bun and place a pile of mashers on top of each. The mashers will hold the bun tops in place.

This is a real square meal in round form. Nice!

# French Onion Burgers with Oven Fries and Dijon Gravy

This could be a 30-minute meal but getting the oven fries extra crispy takes 45 minutes and they're worth the wait. Whet your appetite with a glass of Bordeaux while these bake.

- 4 large **baking potatoes**, scrubbed and dried
- 7 **garlic cloves**, 4 crushed, 3 grated or finely chopped
- ½ cup **EVOO** (extra-virgin olive oil)
  **Salt** and **black pepper**
- 4 tablespoons **butter**
- 2 large **onions**, thinly sliced
- 1 fresh or dried **bay leaf**
- 1 teaspoon **ground thyme**
- ½ cup good-quality **dry sherry**
- 2 pounds **lean ground sirloin**
- 3 tablespoons **Worcestershire sauce** (eyeball it)
  A generous handful of fresh **flat-leaf parsley**, finely chopped
- 1 large **shallot**, finely chopped or grated
- 2 tablespoons all-purpose **flour**
- 2 cups **beef stock**
- 2 rounded tablespoons **Dijon mustard**
- 8 1-inch-thick slices of fat **French bread**—bigger than a baguette
- ½ pound **Gruyère cheese**, shredded
- 2 hearts of **romaine lettuce**, chopped
  Juice of 1 **lemon**

Preheat the oven to 425°F.

Halve the potatoes lengthwise, then cut each half into 5 thin wedges. Place the potatoes and 4 crushed garlic cloves on a rimmed baking sheet and coat with about 3 tablespoons of the EVOO. Season liberally with salt and pepper and roast for 45 minutes, turning once, until deeply golden in color and crispy.

Once the fries have had a 15-minute head start, heat a skillet over medium heat with 1 tablespoon of the EVOO and 2 tablespoons of the butter. Add the onions, the grated or chopped garlic, the bay leaf, thyme, salt, and pepper. Cook until the onions caramelize, 20 minutes or so. Add the sherry and deglaze the pan, scraping up any bits from the bottom, and cook for a couple of minutes longer.

While the onions are cooking, preheat a grill pan or large skillet over medium-high heat. In a bowl combine the sirloin with the Worcestershire sauce, parsley, salt, and pepper. Divide the mixture into 4 portions, then form each portion into a large patty. Coat the patties in a little EVOO and cook for 5 minutes on each side for pink centers, a minute or so less for rare and 2 minutes longer for well done.

Melt 2 tablespoons of the butter in a small saucepot over medium heat. Add the shallots and cook for 2 to 3 minutes, then whisk in the flour and cook for another minute. Whisk in the stock and cook, stirring, for a couple of minutes to thicken. Season the gravy with pepper and stir in the Dijon mustard. Set aside.

When the fries have cooked for about 40 minutes, turn the oven to broil. Place the bread on a baking sheet and and toast on both sides 6 inches from the broiler until lightly golden. Set 4 pieces of bread aside, then mound the Gruyère onto the remaining bread rounds—just like the large croutons that top French onion soup. Return to the oven to melt the cheese, 1 to 2 minutes.

Dress the greens with the lemon juice, the remaining 3 tablespoons of EVOO, and salt and pepper.

Place the burgers on the plain toasts and top with mounds of the French onions. Take the cheesy bread and set in place on top of the onions, cheesy side down, of course. Serve a little green salad alongside. Serve the fries piled high on a platter and pour the gravy over them, or pour the gravy in a bowl and dip as you go.

# Chicken Sausage Burgers with Balsamic Onion Barbecue Sauce

Here's some tasty proof that chicken can pack just as much punch as beef can in a burger. The balsamic onion barbecue sauce is so addictive it could easily find its way into some of your own creations!

4 tablespoons **EVOO** (extra-virgin olive oil), plus more for liberal drizzling

¼ pound **pancetta**, chopped

2 **red onions**, chopped, and ½ small **red onion**, very thinly sliced

**Salt** and **black pepper**

1 fresh or dried **bay leaf**

2 pounds **ground chicken**

1½ tablespoons **fennel seed**, lightly toasted

1 teaspoon **red pepper flakes**, or more if you want it extra spicy

¼ teaspoon **ground allspice**

Zest and juice of 1 **orange**

3 tablespoons finely chopped fresh **rosemary**, from 4 to 5 sprigs

4 **garlic cloves**, grated with a Microplane or the small side of a box grater

A couple of generous handfuls of grated **Parmigiano-Reggiano** or Romano cheese

2 tablespoons **Worcestershire sauce** (eyeball it)

½ cup aged **balsamic vinegar**

3 tablespoons **honey** or dark brown sugar

2 **ripe tomatoes**, sliced

8 to 10 fresh **basil leaves**, torn

½ **Belgian endive**, chopped

1 cup **arugula leaves**, shredded

½ head of **radicchio**, chopped

4 **crusty rolls**, split, toasted, and drizzled with EVOO or buttered

Preheat a grill pan or outdoor grill to medium-high.

Place 2 tablespoons of the EVOO in a pot over medium-high heat. If you're cooking outside you can put the pot right on the grill. Add the pancetta to the pot and cook and stir to crisp it up, 3 to 4 minutes. Add the chopped onions to the pot and season them with salt and pepper; go heavy on that pepper, because it will really balance out the sweetness of your sauce later on. Add the bay leaf.

While the onions cook, place the ground chicken in a bowl and add the fennel seed, red pepper flakes, allspice, orange zest, rosemary, garlic, salt and pepper, and cheese. Mix the meat with the seasonings and use the side of your hand to score the mixture into 4 equal portions. Form each portion into a large patty. Make a shallow dent in the center of each patty to prevent the burger from bulging as it cooks. Drizzle the patties liberally with EVOO and grill for 6 to 7 minutes on each side.

When the onions are very soft and begin to caramelize, remove the bay leaf and add the Worcestershire sauce, balsamic vinegar, honey or brown sugar, and the orange juice. Let the sauce continue cooking to thicken and sweeten up for 6 to 7 minutes, or until the liquids are syrupy. Add more black pepper to taste.

While the onions cook, arrange the tomato slices on a plate. Sprinkle with the red onion slices and basil leaves and drizzle with the remaining 2 tablespoons of EVOO. Season with salt and pepper.

Mix the chopped endive, shredded arugula, and chopped radicchio together. Pile some of the chopped lettuces on the bun bottoms, then top with the burgers and lots of onion barbecue sauce. Set the bun tops in place and serve with the tomato salad.

# Kentucky Burgoo Burgers and Southern Succotash

Burgoo is a thick meat-and-vegetable stew with a tangy taste. Combining the flavors and ingredients into a burger and succotash transforms any burger night into Derby Day. The stew is traditionally served with a stiff biscuit; here a sammie-size English muffin stands in. Serve with sweetened iced tea, spiked with mint and bourbon if you like!

- 1 pound **ground sirloin**
- 1 pound **ground pork**
- 2 teaspoons **paprika**
- 2 **garlic cloves**, grated or minced
- 1 tablespoon **Worcestershire sauce** (eyeball it)
  A handful of fresh **flat-leaf parsley**, chopped
  **Salt** and **black pepper**
- 4 tablespoons **EVOO** (extra-virgin olive oil)
- 1 small **onion**, finely chopped
- 1 green **bell pepper**, seeded and chopped
- 3 tablespoons **cider vinegar**
- 2 tablespoons **dark brown sugar**
- 1 cup **tomato sauce**
- 1 cup **frozen lima beans**
- 1 cup **frozen corn**
- 1 cup chopped **frozen okra**
- ½ cup chopped **pickled green beans**
- 1 tablespoon **hot sauce**
- 2 tablespoons **chopped thyme**, 5 to 6 sprigs
- 2 to 3 **scallions**, chopped
- 4 sandwich-size **English muffins**, split
- 2 tablespoons softened **butter**

Mix the ground beef and pork with the paprika, garlic, Worcester-shire, parsley, salt, and pepper in a large bowl. Heat a large skillet over medium-high heat with a tablespoon of the EVOO, once around the pan. While the pan heats, use the side of your hand to score the meat into 4 equal portions, then form each portion into a large patty. Make an indentation in the center of each burger to prevent the burger from bulging as the meat cooks. Cook the burgers for 6 minutes on each side, turning once.

Heat a small pot over medium heat with 2 tablespoons of the EVOO (eyeball it). Add the onions and bell pepper and cook for 8 to 10 minutes, then add salt, pepper, the vinegar, and the brown sugar. Stir for a minute to combine, then add the tomato sauce and reduce the heat to low. Simmer for 5 minutes.

Heat a medium skillet over medium-high heat and add the remain-ing tablespoon of EVOO, once around the pan. Add the limas, corn, okra, pickled beans, hot sauce, thyme, and salt and pepper and cook for 5 to 6 minutes to heat through. Toss in the scallions and turn off the heat.

Toast the English muffins and spread with the softened butter. Top each muffin bottom with a burger and spoon on some of the pep-per and onion topping. Serve the succotash alongside.

# BBQ Bacon Burgers and Corn on the Cob with Smoky Cream

Here is a meal for a man's man. I wrote it for one, actor Jeffrey Dean Morgan, and it's a burger adaptation of his own pinwheel steaks.

1 cup **heavy cream**

1 **chipotle pepper** in adobo sauce, minced to a paste

Zest and juice of 1 **lime**

**Salt**

2 tablespoons **EVOO** (extra-virgin olive oil), plus more for drizzling

8 **bacon slices**

1 **red onion**, finely chopped

2 tablespoons **Worcestershire sauce** (eyeball it)

3 tablespoons **dark brown sugar**

1 (15-ounce) can **tomato sauce**

**Black pepper**

2 pounds **ground sirloin**

1 tablespoon **ground cumin**, a palmful

1 tablespoon **chili powder**, a palmful

2 tablespoons **steak seasoning**, such as McCormick's Montreal Steak Seasoning, a couple of palmfuls

2 teaspoons **ground coriander**, 2/3 palmful

2 **garlic cloves**, grated or finely chopped

4 ears of **corn on the cob**, husked

1 pound fresh **spinach**, tough stems removed

4 **kaiser rolls**, split and toasted

½ pound **queso fresco**, asadero cheese, or other white, mild cheese, grated

2 **scallions**, whites and green tops, finely chopped

A handful of fresh **cilantro** or flat-leaf parsley leaves, finely chopped

Preheat an outdoor grill to medium hot or a grill pan over medium-high heat.

Place a small saucepot over medium heat and add the heavy cream, chipotle paste, and lime zest. Bring to a simmer and season with salt. Turn the heat down to low and simmer gently for about 10 minutes.

Heat a skillet over medium-high heat with a drizzle of EVOO. Add the bacon to the pan and cook until crispy, 8 to 10 minutes. Transfer the bacon to a paper-towel-lined plate to drain, and pour off all but a couple of tablespoons of bacon fat from the pan. Add the red onions to the skillet and cook for 5 minutes, still working over medium-high heat. Add the Worcestershire, brown sugar, and the lime juice; stir for a minute; then add the tomato sauce and bring up to a simmer. Season the sauce with salt and pepper and cook for 10 minutes to reduce and thicken a bit.

In a medium bowl, combine the ground meat with the cumin, chili powder, steak seasoning, coriander, and garlic. Using the side of your hand, score the meat into 4 portions, then form each portion into a large patty about 1 inch thick. Make a shallow indentation at the center to prevent the burgers from bulging as they cook. Coat the patties with 1 tablespoon of the EVOO.

Run the husked corn under cold water to wet it down. Place the corn and the patties on the grill. (You could also char the corn on all sides under a hot broiler instead.) Grill the burgers for 10 minutes, turning once, for medium doneness. Baste them with some of the BBQ sauce during the last 2 minutes of cooking.

Just before the burgers and corn are ready to come off the grill, place a medium skillet over medium-high heat and add the remaining tablespoon of EVOO, once around the pan. Add the spinach to the pan and cook for about 1 minute, or until barely wilted.

Place each burger on a kaiser roll and top it with some BBQ sauce, bacon slices, and spinach. Pour the chipotle-cream mixture over the grilled corn and sprinkle with the cheese. Garnish with the chopped scallions and cilantro.

# Caribbean Burgers with Mango Salsa

Can you say *tasty*, mon? This is so full of authentic island flavor you'll wanna play a steel-drum serenade on your pots and pans.

- 2 pounds **ground chicken**, pork, or turkey breast
- 1½ teaspoons **ground allspice**, ½ palmful
- ½ teaspoon **ground cinnamon** (eyeball it)
- ½ teaspoon grated **nutmeg** (eyeball it)
- 1 teaspoon **dried or ground thyme**, ⅓ palmful
- ½ teaspoon **cayenne pepper**
- 1 tablespoon **light or dark brown sugar**
- 5 to 6 fresh **basil leaves** or 2 tablespoons fresh cilantro, your choice, chopped
- **Salt** and **black pepper**
- 2 tablespoons **EVOO** (extra-virgin olive oil), plus some for drizzling
- 1 ripe **mango**, peeled and cut in ¼-inch dice
- 1 small **red bell pepper**, seeded and cut in ¼-inch dice
- 1 **jalapeño pepper**, seeded and finely chopped
- ¼ **seedless cucumber**, peeled and cut in ¼-inch dice
- Zest and juice of 1 **lime**
- 4 **cornmeal kaiser rolls**, split
- **Bibb lettuce leaves**
- **Spicy specialty potato chips**, any brand you like

Preheat the broiler.

Place the ground meat in a mixing bowl. Combine the dry spices and brown sugar in a small dish, then sprinkle evenly over the meat. Add the fresh basil or cilantro and lots of salt and black pepper, and mix with the meat to combine. Form the seasoned meat into 4 large patties. Make a divot in the center of each burger; as the burgers cook the well will swell up and you'll end up with a flat surface—no burger-bulge.

In a large nonstick skillet heat the 2 tablespoons of EVOO, twice around the pan, over medium-high heat. Add the burgers to the skillet and cook until browned and cooked through, about 6 minutes per side.

While the burgers cook, make the mango salsa. In a small bowl, combine the mango, red bell pepper, jalapeño, cucumber, and lime zest and juice. Season with salt to taste.

Toast the rolls lightly under the hot broiler.

Transfer the burgers to the toasted bun bottoms and top with Bibb lettuce, lots of salsa, and the bun tops. Serve with a few chips alongside.

# Gyro Burgers with Village Vegetable Salad

I wrote this one for one tasty Greek guy, John Stamos. (*My* hottie, John Cusimano, likes it, too!)

2 pounds **ground chicken** or ground lamb

2 fresh **oregano sprigs**, leaves stripped and finely chopped, or 1 teaspoon dried

1 tablespoon **ground coriander**, a palmful

½ tablespoon **ground cumin**, ½ palmful

1 teaspoon **cayenne pepper** or 4 teaspoons hot sauce

2 tablespoons **fresh thyme leaves** from 5 to 6 sprigs, chopped

2 **lemons**

¼ cup chopped fresh **flat-leaf parsley** plus ½ cup fresh **flat-leaf parsley leaves**

Salt and **black pepper**

6 tablespoons **EVOO** (extra-virgin olive oil)

1 cup plain **Greek-style yogurt**

1 small **garlic clove**, grated with a Microplane or the small side of a box grater

1 **seedless cucumber**, ¼ cup peeled and finely chopped and the remainder cut into bite-size chunks

4 **plum tomatoes**, halved and lightly seeded and cut into bite-size chunks

8 **Greek hot pickled peppers**, chopped

1 small green **bell pepper**, seeded and chopped

1 small **red onion**, chopped

½ cup pitted **kalamata olives**, coarsely chopped

⅓ to ½ pound **feta cheese**, sliced or crumbled

4 **crusty rolls**, split and lightly toasted

Romaine lettuce leaves

**Specialty chips** in a Mediterranean flavor

Place the meat in a large bowl and add the oregano, coriander, cumin, cayenne or hot sauce, thyme, the zest of 1 lemon, the chopped parsley, salt, and pepper. Mix and form 4 large patties. Using your palm, make an indentation in the center of the patties to prevent dreaded burger bulge when they cook.

Heat 2 tablespoons of the EVOO in a large nonstick pan over medium-high heat. Cook the patties for 6 to 7 minutes on each side.

While the burgers cook, mix the yogurt with the garlic and the juice of ½ lemon. Place the finely chopped cucumber on a paper-towel-lined plate to drain, then add to the yogurt. Season the yogurt with salt and stir to combine.

Place the chunks of cucumber and tomato, the Greek peppers, bell peppers, red onions, and olives in a bowl and add the ½ cup of parsley leaves. Dress the salad with the juice of 1½ lemons, the remaining 4 tablespoons of EVOO, salt, and pepper. Toss the salad and arrange the feta on top.

Serve the burgers with the yogurt sauce and romaine lettuce on crusty toasted rolls. Pile the salad and chips alongside.

# Sloppy Cubanos

A Cuban cousin to Joe; serve with plantain chips.

- 1 tablespoon **EVOO** (extra-virgin olive oil), once around the pan
- ¼ to ⅓ pound **chorizo**, casings removed and finely chopped, about 1 cup
- 1 pound **ground pork**
- 1 **onion**, finely chopped
- 2 **garlic cloves**, grated or finely chopped
- 1 teaspoon **ground allspice**, ⅓ palmful
- 2 teaspoons **paprika**, ⅔ palmful
- 2 teaspoons **ground coriander**, ⅔ palmful
  **Salt** and **black pepper**
- 2 tablespoons **light or dark brown sugar**
- 1 tablespoon **Worcestershire sauce** (eyeball it)
  Zest and juice of 1 **lime**
- 1 cup **chicken stock**
- 1 (8-ounce) can **tomato sauce**
- 4 **Portuguese rolls or sub rolls**, split
- 4 deli-cut slices **Swiss cheese**
- 4 large dill or **half-sour pickles**, chopped

Preheat the broiler.

Heat the EVOO in a large skillet over medium-high heat. Add the chorizo and cook until browned, about 2 minutes, then add the pork. Cook the pork for 3 to 4 minutes, crumbling it with a wooden spoon, then add the onions, garlic, allspice, paprika, coriander, salt, and pepper. Cook for 5 minutes, then add the brown sugar, Worcestershire, and lime zest and juice. Mix well, then stir in the stock and tomato sauce, and simmer for a couple of minutes.

Toast the rolls lightly under the broiler. Load the saucy meat mixture onto the rolls and top each with a slice of Swiss cheese. Return to the broiler for a minute to melt the cheese. Sprinkle with the chopped pickles and add the roll tops.

# Sloppy Joaquins

A Spanish cousin to Sloppy Joe, this mess of beef, mushrooms, garlic, sherry, and tomatoes is worth staining your shirt for!

2 tablespoons **EVOO** (extra-virgin olive oil), twice around the pan
1 pound **ground sirloin**
6 large **garlic cloves**, finely chopped
1 medium **onion**, chopped
24 medium **cremini** or white mushrooms, cleaned, trimmed, and chopped
Coarse **salt** and lots of **black pepper**
½ cup **dry sherry** (eyeball it)
2 tablespoons **Worcestershire sauce** (eyeball it)
1 (14-ounce) can **tomato sauce**
4 **crusty rolls**, preferably ciabatta or Portuguese rolls if available
2 tablespoons softened **butter**
A handful of fresh **flat-leaf parsley**, chopped
A wedge of **manchego cheese**, for shaving

Heat the EVOO in a deep skillet over medium-high. Add the beef and cook until deeply browned, 6 to 7 minutes. Add the garlic, onions, and mushrooms and cook until the mushrooms are dark and the onions tender, 7 to 8 minutes. Season with salt and pepper, then add the sherry and stir to deglaze the pan. Cook for 1 minute to reduce the sherry. Stir in the Worcestershire and tomato sauce, reduce the heat to low, and cook for 5 minutes more.

Preheat the broiler.

Split the rolls and spread with softened butter. Sprinkle heavily with parsley. Toast the rolls under the broiler for a couple of minutes until charred at the edges. Watch them; they can burn quickly! Top the roll bottoms with meat mixture and shaved manchego cheese, then set the roll tops in place. *¡Olé!*

# Sloppy Dude

I wrote this for a really groovy dude, Ty Pennington. Even if you've never picked up a surfboard, this one will leave you stoked!

2 tablespoons **EVOO** (extra-virgin olive oil), twice around the pan
1 pound **ground turkey breast**
16 **tomatillos**, husks removed and rinsed thoroughly, coarsely chopped
1 **onion**, chopped
3 **garlic cloves**, chopped
1 **jalapeño**, seeded and chopped
Zest and juice of 1 **lime**
1 tablespoon **ground cumin**
**Salt** and **black pepper**
1 cup **chicken stock**
2 small ripe **Hass avocados**, pitted and scooped from skins
4 **crusty rolls**, such as kaiser rolls
½ **red onion**, thinly sliced
2 plum or small **vine tomatoes**, sliced
1 bag **specialty tortilla chips**

Preheat the broiler.

Place a large skillet over medium-high heat and add the EVOO. When it's hot, add the ground turkey and get aggressive breaking it up: it's 99 percent lean, so it takes some doing to break it into individual bits. While the turkey is browning up, place the tomatillos in a food processor and pulse to a coarse puree. Add the tomatillos to the browned turkey along with the onions, garlic, and jalapeño and season with the lime zest, cumin, salt, and pepper. Cook for 5 minutes, then add the stock and simmer for 5 minutes more.

While everything is simmering away and getting "sloppy," use a fork to mash the avocados with the lime juice.

Split and toast the rolls under the broiler until light golden brown, 2 or 3 minutes.

To assemble the Sloppy Dudes, spoon some of the turkey filling onto each bun bottom. Top with red onion and tomato slices and slather the bun tops with mashed avocado before setting in place. Accompany each serving with a few tortilla chips.

## tidbit

When it comes to corn chips these days, your choices aren't limited to yellow or white; several healthful brands and flavors, such as brown rice and black bean, flax seed, or blue corn and sesame, are available on the snack aisle of larger markets, so check out some of the more interesting new varieties.

# French Country Tuna Burgers, Green Bean Salad, and *Poutine*

My love of salade niçoise inspired this French country herbed tuna burger and green bean salad. My love of *poutine*—French Canada's gravy-smothered fries, a national treasure—inspired my version here. *Bon appétit!*

1 bag **frozen crinkle-cut** or waffle fries

5 tablespoons **EVOO** (extra-virgin olive oil), plus some for liberal drizzling

1 tablespoon **butter**

6 slices **Canadian bacon**, chopped

1 **red onion**, ¼ chopped, the rest thinly sliced

2 **garlic cloves**, chopped

2 tablespoons all-purpose **flour**

½ bottle **Molson or other Canadian beer**

¾ cup **chicken stock**

**Salt** and **black pepper**

4 **tuna steaks**, 6 to 8 ounces each, cut into large chunks

2 fresh **rosemary sprigs**, leaves stripped and finely chopped

4 fresh **thyme sprigs**, leaves stripped and chopped

Zest and juice of 1 **lemon**

1 pound **green beans**, trimmed

¾ cup pitted **Niçoise olives**

3 tablespoons drained **capers**

1 (2-ounce) tin **flat anchovy fillets**, drained

2 ripe **tomatoes**, cut into wedges

2 **hard-boiled eggs** (can be found at the salad bar counter), chopped

4 large **crusty rolls**, split in half

8 leaves of **leaf lettuce**

1 cup shredded **mozzarella** cheese

Preheat the oven to 450°F. Place the fries on a baking sheet and bake according to the package directions, about 18 minutes.

Heat a small saucepot over medium-high heat with 1 tablespoon of the EVOO and the tablespoon of butter. Add the Canadian bacon, the chopped red onion, and the garlic. Cook for 5 minutes, until softened. Add the flour, cook for a minute, stirring constantly, then whisk in the beer and the stock. Season with salt and pepper and cook over low heat until thickened, about 2 minutes. Keep warm.

Place an inch of water in a skillet and bring to a boil.

Place the tuna in a food processor and coarsely chop, then transfer to a bowl. Add the herbs and half of the lemon zest, season with salt and pepper, and combine. Form 4 large patties and reserve them on a plate in the refrigerator until ready to cook.

Salt the boiling water, and add the green beans. Cook for 5 minutes, or until just tender, then rinse the beans under cold, running water to stop the cooking. Drain and reserve.

Wash the food processor bowl and return it to the base. Place the olives, capers, anchovies, the remaining lemon zest, and a drizzle of EVOO in the processor and process into a smooth paste.

Combine the green beans with the tomatoes and the thinly sliced onion. Dress the salad with 2 tablespoons of the EVOO, the lemon juice, salt, and pepper. Top with the chopped hard-boiled eggs.

Heat the remaining EVOO in a nonstick skillet over medium-high heat. Cook the tuna burgers for 3 minutes on each side for rare, or 6 minutes on each side to cook through completely. Spread the black olive paste on the rolls and top each burger with leaf lettuce. Serve the green bean salad alongside.

Divide the fries among 4 small bowls. Top with mozzarella and pour the bacon gravy on top.

# Swordfish Burgers

The catch of the day is a big ol' swordfish burger! This is a great way to get the kids into eating some nice, healthful fish. Who knows, even a stubborn adult might be convinced by this baby; it's that good.

1½ to 2 pounds **swordfish steaks**
1 **orange**
   A handful of fresh **flat-leaf parsley**, finely chopped
3 to 4 **garlic cloves**, grated or minced
2 to 3 **scallions**, white and green parts finely chopped
   **Salt** and **black pepper**
¼ cup **EVOO** (extra-virgin olive oil), 4 times around the pan
4 **jarred roasted red peppers**
4 **kaiser rolls** or other crusty rolls
   Leaves from 1 heart of **romaine**
½ **red onion**, thinly sliced
1 bag fancy **olive oil–flavor potato chips**

Trim any dark flesh near the bloodline of the swordfish steaks and cut away the skin. Cut the fish into chunks and pat dry. Place the fish chunks in a food processor and pulse on and off to grind coarse.

Place the ground fish and the zest of the orange in a mixing bowl (reserve the orange). Add the parsley, garlic, scallions, and salt and pepper and mix to combine. Form the mixture into 4 large 1-inch-thick patties.

Heat the EVOO in a large skillet over medium-high heat. Cook the burgers for 10 to 12 minutes, turning once.

While the burgers cook, wash out the processor bowl and return it to the base. Add the red peppers and process until they are pureed. With a sharp knife, cut off any remaining skin and pith from the orange, then slice it into thin disks and reserve.

To assemble, split the rolls and set a swordfish burger on each bun bottom. Top the burgers with sliced oranges, romaine leaves, and red onions. Smear the bun tops with a generous slather of roasted red pepper puree and set in place. Serve with a few chips.

# New England Chicken Patty Sammies

Another flavorful chicken burger.

1 package **ground chicken** (average weight 1⅓ pounds)
**Salt** and **black pepper**
1 teaspoon **poultry seasoning**
4 tablespoons **EVOO** (extra-virgin olive oil), plus some for drizzling
1 small **red onion**, thinly sliced
1 **Granny Smith apple**, quartered, cored, and thinly sliced
4 sandwich-size **English muffins**, split and toasted
8 slices **sharp aged Cheddar cheese**
4 tablespoons **honey mustard**
1½ cups **watercress** (a small bunch), chopped
1 sack of **specialty chips**, your choice

Preheat the broiler.

In a bowl, mix the chicken with salt and black pepper to taste and the poultry seasoning. Form 4 thin patties. Preheat one large and one medium-size skillet over medium-high heat. Add about 2 tablespoons of the EVOO, twice around the pan, to each skillet. Place the chicken patties in the large skillet and cook for 5 minutes on each side.

Meanwhile, add the onions and apples to the second skillet, season with salt and pepper, and cook until tender, 6 to 7 minutes.

Place a chicken patty on each English muffin bottom and top with some of the apples and onions and 2 slices of cheese. Slide them under the broiler for a minute or two to melt the cheese. Spread each muffin top with a tablespoon of honey mustard. Top the chicken patties with a handful of watercress, set the muffin tops in place, and serve with a few chips.

# Calzone Rolls with Salami, Tomato, and Basil

My hubby loves these. Try swapping spinach for the salami if you want to make a healthier calzone-in-a-kaiser.

4   large, crusty **kaiser rolls**
1½  cups **ricotta cheese**
    **Salt** and **black pepper**
¼   pound **salami**, chopped
¼   cup grated **Parmigiano-Reggiano** cheese, a handful
8   slices **fresh mozzarella** cheese
8   slices ripe **tomato**
8   fresh **basil leaves**, torn or sliced

Heat the oven to 325°F.

Split the kaiser rolls, making the bottom half a little bigger than the top. Scoop a little of the white soft insides out of the bottoms.

Season the ricotta with a little salt and pepper, then stir in the salami and grated cheese. Fill the rolls with the ricotta mixture, then cover the ricotta with 2 slices each of mozzarella and tomato and 2 basil leaves.

Replace the roll tops and place the filled sammies on a baking sheet. Bake for 10 to 12 minutes or until heated through. Cut in half and serve.

# Italian Barbecue Sliced Steak Sammies

Serve with a green salad.

- 1 tablespoon **EVOO** (extra-virgin olive oil), plus some for drizzling
- 1 large **red onion**, chopped
- ¼ cup **dark brown sugar**
- ¼ cup aged **balsamic vinegar** (eyeball it)
- 2 tablespoons **Worcestershire sauce** (eyeball it)
- 1 (15-ounce) can **tomato sauce**
  **Salt** and **black pepper**
- 6 tablespoons (¾ stick) **butter**, melted
- 4 **garlic cloves**, finely chopped
- 1 large loaf of **crusty Italian bread**, split and cut into 4 sections
- 4 (12-ounce) **strip steaks**
- 8 slices **Provolone**, from the deli counter

Preheat the oven to 375°F. Preheat a grill pan or outdoor grill to high.

Heat a small saucepot over medium-high heat with the tablespoon of EVOO. Add the onions and cook until tender, 7 to 8 minutes, then add the brown sugar, vinegar, and Worcestershire. Stir to combine, then stir in the tomato sauce. Reduce the heat, season with salt and lots of pepper, and simmer for 15 minutes.

Combine the butter and garlic and brush the cut surfaces of the bread. Toast in the oven until golden, 15 minutes.

Drizzle the steaks with a little EVOO, season with salt and pepper, and grill for 8 to 10 minutes for medium. Transfer the meat to a cutting board and let it rest for 5 minutes.

Switch the broiler on. Slice the steaks and layer a steak onto each quarter loaf of bread. Top with ½ cup of sauce and 2 slices of Provolone. Broil until the cheese browns, about 1 minute.

# Eggplant Subs à la Norma

Pasta à la Norma is a favorite of mine—even sans pasta!

2 medium to large **eggplants**
½ to ⅔ cup **EVOO** (extra-virgin olive oil)
  **Salt** and **black pepper**
4 **crusty sub rolls**, split
8 **plum tomatoes**, lightly seeded and chopped
1 cup **fresh basil leaves**, 20 leaves, thinly sliced or torn into small bits
2 **garlic cloves**
½ pound **ricotta salata cheese**, crumbled

Preheat the broiler. Prepare an outdoor grill or heat a grill pan over medium-high heat.

Trim off the ends of the eggplants, then square off the eggplant by removing most of the skin in 4 long slices. Work lengthwise, turning the eggplant a quarter turn each time you remove a section of skin; this will leave you a large rectangle shape to work with. Cut the eggplants lengthwise into ½-inch-thick eggplant "steaks." Brush the eggplant steaks on both sides with EVOO, then season with salt and pepper. Grill the eggplant steaks for 6 to 8 minutes total, or until tender. Allow to cool for 5 minutes, then cut the steaks into thirds.

Toast the sub rolls under the broiler until golden, about 3 minutes.

Place the tomatoes and basil in a bowl. Grate the garlic into the bowl using a Microplane or the small side of a box grater. Season the tomatoes with lots of salt and pepper. You should have a few tablespoons of EVOO left in the bowl from the preparation of the eggplant; pour some over the tomatoes, then toss to combine.

Layer the eggplant onto the toasted rolls with lots of raw tomato sauce. Top with the cheese and open wide! Yum-o!

**tidbit**
Use the grilled eggplant and tomato sub filling to top small toast rounds for a fun any-night appetizer or a party snack. Chop the eggplant as small as the tomatoes for this use.

SAMMIE NIGHT

# Turkey Meatball Heroes with Tomato and Red Onion Salad

This hero is faster than a speeding bullet and fills bellies in a single round!

1 (10-ounce) box **frozen spinach**, defrosted in the microwave for 3 or 4 minutes on high

2 pounds **ground turkey breast**

1 small **onion**, grated or finely chopped

4 **garlic cloves**, grated or finely chopped

1 **egg**

½ cup **bread crumbs**, a couple of generous handfuls

½ cup grated **Parmigiano-Reggiano** cheese

2⅓ cups **milk**

**Salt** and **black pepper**

7 tablespoons **EVOO** (extra-virgin olive oil)

3 tablespoons **butter**

2 rounded tablespoons all-purpose **flour**

1 cup **chicken stock**

¼ teaspoon freshly grated **nutmeg** (eyeball it)

5 medium **plum tomatoes**, halved lengthwise, lightly seeded, and thinly sliced

1 small **red onion**, peeled, halved lengthwise, and thinly sliced

½ cup fresh **flat-leaf parsley** leaves, a couple of handfuls

4 **crusty hero rolls**

1 (10-ounce) sack shredded **Provolone** cheese, 2 cups

Preheat the oven to 425°F. Wring the spinach dry in a clean kitchen towel.

Place the turkey in a bowl and make a well in the center. Into the well, add the grated onion and garlic, egg, bread crumbs, Parmigiano, about ⅓ cup of the milk, the spinach, salt, and pepper. Form into 16 large balls and arrange on a nonstick baking sheet. Drizzle the meatballs with about 4 tablespoons of the EVOO, and roast for 12 to 15 minutes, or until cooked through.

While the meatballs are in the oven, heat the butter in a small saucepot over medium heat. When melted, whisk in the flour and cook for 1 minute, then whisk in the remaining 2 cups of milk and the chicken stock. Bring to a boil, then reduce the heat and simmer until thickened, a minute or two. Season the sauce with salt, pepper, and nutmeg, and turn the heat down to low.

In a salad bowl, toss the tomatoes and red onions with the parsley, the remaining 3 tablespoons of EVOO, and lots of salt and pepper.

Split the hero rolls in half lengthwise and scoop out a little bit of the soft bread so there is more room for the meatballs and sauce. Transfer to a baking sheet and toast in the oven cut side up, until golden brown.

Place 4 meatballs on each toasted roll and top with some of the white sauce and the Provolone cheese. Place back in the oven or under the broiler to melt the cheese. Serve the tomato and onion salad alongside.

## tidbit

To lightly seed a plum tomato, cut it in half lengthwise. Squeeze it gently, then use your finger or a spoon to sweep out the seeds. Don't worry about getting every last one.

# Rustic Overstuffed Pizz-O

This huge pizza has a thick folded crusty rim that makes it look like a giant O!

### Arugula Pesto

- 1 (10-ounce) bag **arugula**
- 1 **garlic clove**
- ½ cup **walnut pieces**, toasted
- ½ cup grated **Parmigiano-Reggiano** cheese
- 1 teaspoon **lemon zest**
- ½ cup **EVOO** (extra-virgin olive oil)
- **Salt** and **black pepper**

### Pizza

- 1 tablespoon **EVOO** (extra-virgin olive oil), plus some for drizzling
- ½ pound bulk **sweet Italian sausage**
- ½ pound bulk **hot Italian sausage**
- 2 **portobello mushrooms**, chopped into chunky pieces
- 2 **roasted red peppers**, chopped
- 2 cups **ricotta cheese**, at room temperature for easy spreading
- 2 teaspoons **lemon zest**
- 1 tablespoon fresh **thyme leaves**, 4 to 5 sprigs, finely chopped
- ½ cup grated **Parmigiano-Reggiano** cheese
- Freshly ground **black pepper**
- **Cornmeal**, for the pan
- 2 pounds **fresh pizza dough**, from your favorite pizza joint or market
- 8 slices **prosciutto di Parma**
- 2 cups grated **scamorza or smoked mozzarella**

Preheat oven to 425°F.

**To make the pesto:** Combine the arugula, garlic, walnuts, cheese, lemon zest, EVOO, salt, and pepper in a food processor. Grind into a thick paste.

**To make the pizza:** Heat a skillet with the tablespoon of EVOO, once around the pan, over medium-high heat. When the pan is hot, add both the sweet and hot sausage, breaking it up into little pieces with the back of a wooden spoon. Cook for 7 to 8 minutes or until the sausage is cooked through. Add the mushrooms. Once the mushrooms have wilted and turned deep brown in color, 5 to 7 minutes, stir in the roasted red peppers. Remove from the heat.

In a bowl stir together the ricotta, lemon zest, thyme, ¼ cup of the Parmigiano, and lots of pepper.

To assemble the pizza, sprinkle a large round pizza pan with cornmeal. This will keep your pizza from sticking when it is baking and will help it slide off the pan when it is done. Roll out the pizza dough in a huge circle 3 or 4 inches bigger in diameter than your pan. Don't worry if it isn't perfect; it should look rustic. Roll it up and around the rolling pin and transfer it to the pizza pan. It will hang off the sides a couple of inches all around. Spread the pesto across the center of the dough, using the back of a spoon to get it everywhere. (If you have more than you need, you can always serve the extra later in the week over your favorite pasta or even freeze it. Yum-o!) Top the pesto with the prosciutto, then spread the ricotta mixture over it and sprinkle with some Parmigiano. Add the reserved sausage mixture to the center, leaving about a 2-inch border around the pie. Top the sausage with the scamorza or smoked mozzarella and fold the edge over until it meets the sausage. Keep the pizza round by pleating the edge as you work your way around the pie. Brush the crust with some EVOO for a beautiful golden brown color.

Bake until the cheese is bubbly and the crust is deep golden brown, 25 to 30 minutes.

Remove from the oven, let stand for 5 to 10 minutes, then slice and enjoy! Delish!

# Sausage, Pepper, and Onion Stromboli

For this recipe I'm sending a shout-out to my friend Rob, who gave me the big idea of Frankenstuffers: sauerkraut and mustard–wrapped dogs. Also, to Michelle, who said "Could you do that with sausage?" Yes, you can, and here is the proof!

This recipe makes eight sausage rolls. I fill up on one, but John can easily eat two. Serve with a green salad alongside. Yum-o!

8 links of **hot or sweet Italian sausage**

3 tablespoons **vegetable oil or EVOO** (extra-virgin olive oil), plus some to brush the stromboli

4 **garlic cloves**, chopped

2 **cubanelle peppers**, seeded, quartered lengthwise, and thinly sliced

2 jarred **roasted red peppers**, quartered and thinly sliced

2 tablespoons **hot sliced pepper rings**, chopped, plus a splash of their juice

3 tablespoons **tomato paste**
**Salt** and **black pepper**

1 tube **refrigerated pizza dough** from the dairy aisle

2 cups shredded **Provolone cheese**

2 tablespoons **sesame seeds**

¼ cup grated **Parmigiano-Reggiano** cheese, a handful

2 tablespoons finely chopped fresh **rosemary**, a couple of sprigs

Preheat the oven to 400°F.

Pierce the sausages in a few places with the tines of a fork. Place the sausages in a skillet; add about an inch of water and a tablespoon of the oil to the pan. Place the pan over high heat and bring the water to a boil, then reduce the heat to medium. The water will cook away after 15 minutes, then the casings will crisp up in the oil that was floating on the water. Remove the sausages and set aside until cool enough to handle.

While the sausages cool, add the remaining 2 tablespoons of oil to the skillet along with the garlic and cubanelle pepper slices. Cook the peppers for 3 to 4 minutes to soften, then add the roasted peppers and hot pepper rings and a splash of the pickling juice to loosen the brown bits. Add the tomato paste and distribute it around the pan, then stir in ½ cup water and season with salt and pepper. Turn off the heat.

Roll the pizza dough out into a big rectangle. Cut the dough in half lengthwise with a small knife, then cut each strip into four equal pieces so that you end up with 8 small rectangular pieces of dough. Across the center of each rectangle place a couple of spoonfuls of saucy peppers, and sprinkle a handful of Provolone on top. Set the sausage diagonally across the dough and wrap and roll the pizza dough around the sausage like a blanket. Set the seam side down on a nonstick baking sheet. The sausage should be peeking out from each end.

In a small bowl combine the sesame seeds, grated Parmigiano, and rosemary. Lightly brush the stromboli with some oil and sprinkle the tops with the cheese mixture. Bake the stromboli for 15 to 18 minutes, until golden.

# Carbonara Deep-Dish Pasta-Crusted Pan Pizza

Pasta carbonara is fantastic, but it must be eaten right when it is made. By turning it into a cross between a frittata and a pizza it can hang out for a much longer period, making it a more forgiving dish. Served with either a fruit salad or green salad, it is perfect for B, B, L, D— breakfast, brunch, lunch, or dinner!

**Salt**

2 (9-ounce) packages **fresh linguine**

3 tablespoons **EVOO** (extra-virgin olive oil), 3 times around the pan

¼ pound **pancetta**, cut as thick as bacon, chopped

3 to 4 **garlic cloves**, grated or chopped

½ to 1 teaspoon **red pepper flakes**, depending on how spicy you like it

½ cup grated **Parmigiano-Reggiano** cheese, a couple of handfuls

4 large **eggs**

½ cup **cream**

**Black pepper**

2 cups **ricotta cheese**

A handful of fresh **flat-leaf parsley**, finely chopped

1 cup shredded **Provolone** or mozzarella cheese

Preheat the oven to 425°F.

Bring a large pot of water to a boil. When it boils, salt it generously, add the pasta, and cook for 3 minutes.

While the pasta water heats, heat the EVOO in a large ovenproof skillet over medium-high heat. Add the pancetta and brown, 3 to 4 minutes. Add the garlic and red pepper flakes, and cook for a minute more, stirring once or twice.

Drain the pasta and add it to the skillet, tossing to coat the pasta with the garlic oil. Add the Parmigiano and toss again. Beat the eggs with the cream and salt and pepper and pour over the pasta. Reduce the heat to medium and cook the eggs for 1 minute or until they begin to set, then pat the pasta into an even layer to make the "pizza pie" crust. Transfer the skillet to the oven and bake for 5 minutes.

Mix together the ricotta and parsley. Remove the pasta pie from the oven and smooth the ricotta over the top. Sprinkle with the Provolone or mozzarella and return to the oven. Bake for 10 minutes more, or until the cheese is melted and golden at the edges. Let the pie sit a couple minutes to settle the ricotta, then cut into wedges and serve directly from the skillet.

# Spanish Ham and Cheese Quesadillas

Say "cheese" to a picture-postcard-perfect Spanish supper.

4 large **flour tortillas**
**Olive oil cooking spray**
¼ cup **Spanish olives** with pimiento, chopped
8 **marinated mushrooms**, drained and sliced
A handful of fresh **flat-leaf parsley**, chopped
8 slices **Serrano ham** or prosciutto
½ pound **Fontina** cheese, thinly sliced
1 small **shallot**, grated
3 tablespoons **sherry vinegar**
⅓ cup **EVOO** (extra-virgin olive oil)
2 hearts of **romaine lettuce**, chopped
¼ **seedless cucumber**, thinly sliced
4 roasted **Spanish piquillo peppers** or 2 roasted red peppers, chopped
¼ cup **sliced toasted almonds**, plain or flavored
**Salt** and **black pepper**

Preheat the oven to 250°F. Place a foil-lined baking sheet in the middle of the oven. Preheat a skillet over medium to medium-high heat. Spray a tortilla lightly on both sides with cooking spray and place in the hot skillet. Heat the tortilla until it starts to blister, about 1 minute, then flip it and top half of the tortilla's surface with one quarter of the olives, mushrooms, and parsley. Top with 2 slices each of the ham and Fontina. Fold the tortilla over the filling and cook for another minute on each side to melt the cheese and crisp. Transfer to the warm oven and repeat with the remaining tortillas and filling.

Combine the shallot with the vinegar and whisk in the EVOO. Combine the romaine, cucumbers, peppers, and almonds in a salad bowl and toss with the dressing. Season with salt and pepper to taste. Cut the quesadillas into quarters and serve with the salad.

# Tomatillo and Chicken Tostadas

Figure-friendly Tex-Mex in 15 minutes—who wouldn't love that?

- 3 tablespoons **EVOO** (extra-virgin olive oil)
- 1 medium **zucchini**, quartered lengthwise and chopped
- 4 **scallions**, green and white parts, chopped
- 1 **store-bought rotisserie chicken**, skin removed, meat shredded
- 1 teaspoon **ground cumin**
- 1 cup good-quality **store-bought tomatillo salsa**
  **Salt** and **black pepper**
  Juice of 1 **lime**
- 8 (6-inch) **flour tortillas**
- 1 cup shredded **Pepper Jack cheese**
- 1 cup shredded **white Cheddar cheese**
- 2 to 3 tablespoons chopped fresh **cilantro**

Preheat the oven to 425°F.

Heat a skillet over medium-high heat with 2 tablespoons of the EVOO, twice around the pan. When it's hot, add the zucchini and sauté until golden brown, about 5 minutes. Add the scallions and shredded chicken, and sprinkle with the cumin. Add the tomatillo salsa and heat through. Season with salt and pepper to taste. Squeeze the lime juice over the chicken and remove from the heat.

While the chicken is cooking, place the tortillas on 2 baking sheets in a single layer. Brush lightly with EVOO and bake until crispy, about 6 minutes. Remove from the oven but don't turn off the oven.

Top each crisped tortilla with some of the chicken, followed by a pile of the shredded cheeses. Return the tostadas to the oven to melt the cheese. Garnish with chopped cilantro. Yum-o!

# Poquito and Grande: Taquitos and Burritos

Here's a fun Mexican supper that'll please 'em all, big *and* small!

### Taquitos

- 2 cups shredded **rotisserie chicken**
- 1 teaspoon **ground cumin**
- ½ teaspoon **dried oregano**
  **Salt** and **black pepper**
- 1 (4-ounce) can chopped **green chilies**
  A few leaves of fresh **cilantro** or **flat-leaf parsley**, finely chopped
  **Vegetable or canola oil**, for frying
- 12 (6-inch) **corn tortillas**

### Dipping sauce

- 1 tablespoon **EVOO** (extra-virgin olive oil)
- 1 **red onion**, chopped
- 2 **garlic cloves**, grated or finely chopped
- 1 teaspoon **sugar**
- 1 tablespoon **chili powder**, a palmful
- 1½ teaspoons **ground cumin**, ½ palmful
  A pinch of **ground cinnamon**
  **Salt** and **black pepper**
- 1 (28-ounce) can crushed **fire-roasted tomatoes**

### Burritos

- 3 tablespoons **EVOO** (extra-virgin olive oil)
- 1½ pounds **ground pork**
- 1 small **zucchini**, grated
- 2 **garlic cloves**, grated or finely chopped
- 2 to 3 tablespoons medium to hot **chipotle in adobo**, mashed into a paste
  **Salt**
- 1 large (19-ounce) can **black beans**

**Black pepper**

8 (8-inch) **flour tortillas**

2 cups shredded **Chihuahua**, Monterey Jack, or Cheddar cheese

½ head of **iceberg lettuce**, or 1 heart of romaine, shredded

Preheat the oven to 425°F.

**To make the taquitos:** Season the shredded chicken with the cumin, oregano, salt, and pepper in a mixing bowl. Stir in the chilies and cilantro or parsley. Pour about 1 inch of oil into a skillet and heat over medium heat until warm, not hot. Dip the tortillas in the warm oil to soften. Roll a couple of forkfuls of chicken up in each tortilla and place them in a baking dish seam side down. Bake for 12 minutes.

**To make the dipping sauce:** Heat a saucepot over medium heat and add the EVOO, red onion, and garlic; cook for 5 minutes to soften. Season with the sugar, chili powder, cumin, cinnamon, salt, and pepper and stir in the fire-roasted tomatoes. Reduce the heat to low and simmer.

**To make the burritos:** Heat a large skillet over medium-high heat with 2 tablespoons of the EVOO. Add the pork, cook it for 2 minutes to brown, then add the zucchini, garlic, chipotle in adobo, and salt. Cook for 7 to 8 minutes longer.

Heat the last tablespoon of EVOO in a small nonstick skillet. Add the black beans and mash with a fork. Season the beans with salt and pepper and fry until crisp at the edges, 3 to 4 minutes.

Soften the flour tortillas in a microwave or in the hot oven. On each tortilla pile a little refried black beans, cheese, pork, and lettuce. Tuck in the sides, then wrap and roll the tortilla.

Arrange 3 taquitos and 2 burritos on each serving plate; pass the dipping sauce at the table.

two

# Hot Pots

## Stoups, Choups, Chilis, and Stews

**If I had to pick one** chapter where those extra 30 minutes can really come in handy sometimes, it would be this one. Soups, stoups, and "choups" (a chowder that's like a soup, or is it the other way around?) are my favorite in my 30-minute bag of tricks because they taste as if they've been simmering half the day and they are all-in-one pot meals that everybody loves. For those times making a quick soup is all about combining a few great ingredients with some broth or other liquid and letting the ingredients simmer together just long enough to blend the flavors, I rely on these 15-minute or 30-minute gems. But if I have a little more time I like to make a really big pot of something with really big flavors—chilis and stews that just get more delicious the longer they cook, and that taste even better the next day. So however much time you've got, you can serve up a hot bowl of something delicious.

# Tuna and Tomato Bread Stoup

Italian comfort food in a steaming bowl. I make this when I feel a cold coming on.

2 tablespoons **EVOO** (extra-virgin olive oil), twice around the pan
1 medium **onion**, quartered and thinly sliced
4 **garlic cloves**, chopped
½ teaspoon **red pepper flakes**
1 fresh or dried **bay leaf**
2 (6-ounce) cans **Italian tuna in EVOO**, lightly drained
2 cups **chicken stock**
2 cups **tomato sauce**
1 (28-ounce) can **diced tomatoes**, undrained
**Salt** and **black pepper**
½ loaf medium-size **semolina bread**, coarsely chopped or torn, about 3 cups
A handful of fresh **flat-leaf parsley**, chopped
Grated **Parmigiano-Reggiano** cheese

Heat the EVOO in a medium pot or deep skillet over medium-high heat. Add the onions and cook for 2 to 3 minutes, then add the garlic, red pepper flakes, and bay leaf. Cook for 2 minutes more, then add the tuna, breaking it up with a fork. Add the chicken stock, tomato sauce, and the diced tomatoes and their juice. Bring to a boil and reduce the heat a bit so the stoup simmers. Season with salt and pepper and simmer for 5 to 6 minutes, then stir in the bread and remove from the heat. Use a wooden spoon to break up the bread pieces so they can soften and thicken the stoup. Discard the bay leaf. Serve the thick, delicious stoup in shallow bowls topped with parsley and grated cheese.

# Pea and Parsley Soup with Canadian Bacon

Serve this soup either hot or cold topped with crisp bits of Canadian bacon to mix in; it's awesome either way.

3 tablespoons **EVOO** (extra-virgin olive oil)
2 **shallots**, chopped
1 (16-ounce) bag frozen **green peas**
5 cups **chicken stock**
  **Salt** and **black pepper**
8 slices **Canadian bacon**, cut in ¼-inch dice
½ cup **flat-leaf parsley** leaves

Heat 2 tablespoons of the EVOO, twice around the pan, in a medium soup pot. Add the shallots and sauté for 3 to 4 minutes. Add the peas and, if you are serving the soup cold, sauté the peas over medium heat for a minute or two, just to take the chill off. For hot soup, add 1 cup of the stock and heat the peas through, 5 minutes. Season with salt and pepper.

While the peas are heating, add the remaining tablespoon of EVOO to a small nonstick skillet and add the Canadian bacon. Toss over medium-high heat for 3 or 4 minutes to crisp it up.

Transfer the peas to a food processor with the parsley and puree, adding some of the stock to the cold peas as needed to make a smooth puree. Puree until smooth. Return to the pot, stir in the remaining stock and serve as is or reheat for 2 to 3 minutes.

Sprinkle the hot or cold soup with the crispy bacon pieces on top.

# Stuffed Pepper Stoup

The man who owns my local oil company makes a great stuffed pepper soup, but it takes too long for me to make it for myself. Here's my sped-up stoup version. Mr. Waterhouse's is tops, but this is a close second—if you don't know Mr. Waterhouse.

- 2 tablespoons **EVOO** (extra-virgin olive oil), twice around the pan
- 1½ pounds **ground sirloin**
  **Salt** and **black pepper**
- ½ teaspoon **ground allspice** (eyeball it)
- 4 **garlic cloves**, chopped
- 1 large **onion**, cut into bite-size dice
- 3 green **bell peppers**, seeded and cut into bite-size dice
- 1 **bay leaf**
- 1 quart (4 cups) **chicken stock**
- 1 (28-ounce) can **crushed tomatoes**
- 1 cup **orzo pasta**
- 12 to 15 fresh **basil leaves**, shredded or torn
  Grated **Parmigiano-Reggiano**, to pass at the table

Heat a medium soup pot over medium-high heat with the EVOO. When the oil is hot, add the beef and season with salt, pepper, and the allspice. Cook the meat for 5 minutes or until browned, then add the garlic, onions, peppers, and bay leaf. Cook for 7 to 8 minutes, until tender. Stir in the stock and tomatoes and bring to a boil. When the soup is bubbling, add the pasta and cook al dente, 7 to 8 minutes. Turn off the heat and fold in the basil. Discard the bay leaf. Serve in shallow bowls topped with some grated cheese.

# Harvest Creamy Corn "Choup"

Somewhere between chowder and soup, this is a tasty vegetable mixture that you eat with crackers on top!

2 tablespoons **EVOO** (extra-virgin olive oil), twice around the pan

4 **bacon slices**, chopped

1 **onion**, chopped

4 to 5 large ears of **corn**, cut off the cob, or 1 (10-ounce) box frozen corn

1 medium or 2 small **zucchini**, chopped

1 pound small **potatoes**, chopped

½ red **bell pepper**, seeded and chopped

1 **bay leaf**

5 to 6 fresh **thyme sprigs**

1 teaspoon **paprika**

**Salt** and **black pepper**

3 tablespoons all-purpose **flour**

1 quart (4 cups) **chicken stock**

1 cup **milk**

1 cup **heavy cream**

½ cup fresh **flat-leaf parsley**, a couple of generous handfuls, chopped

A few dashes of **hot sauce**, to taste

**Oyster crackers** or white Cheddar popcorn, to pass at the table

Heat the EVOO in a medium soup pot over medium-high heat. Add the bacon to the hot oil and cook until crisp at the edges, 2 to 3 minutes. Add the onions, corn, zucchini, potatoes, and bell pepper as you get them chopped. Add the bay leaf, thyme sprigs, paprika, and salt and pepper to taste. Cook for 7 to 8 minutes, until the veggies begin to soften. Sprinkle the flour around the pot, and stir and cook for 1 minute, then stir in the stock and bring it up to a bubble. When it thickens up a bit, stir in the milk, cream, and parsley and simmer for 5 minutes. Turn off the heat and discard the bay leaf. Season the choup with salt, pepper, and hot sauce to taste and serve with crackers or popcorn to float on top.

# Hoppin' John Stoup with Rice

My John hops with joy when I make this updated version of a southern comfort standard.

     3   tablespoons **EVOO** (extra-virgin olive oil)
 1½   cups **rice**
 6¾   cups **chicken stock**
     1   package (4 links) **andouille sausage**, casings removed, diced
     5   to 6 **celery ribs** from the heart with leafy tops, chopped
     2   green **bell peppers**, seeded and chopped
     1   large **onion**, chopped
     1   fresh or dried **bay leaf**
     1   **sweet potato**, peeled and diced
   ¼   cup **hot sauce**, or to taste
     1   pound frozen **black-eyed peas**
     1   (28-ounce) can **stewed tomatoes**

Heat 1 tablespoon of the EVOO in a medium-size saucepot over high heat. Add the rice and stir to coat in the oil. Add 2¾ cups of the chicken stock and bring to a boil, then reduce the heat, cover, and cook until the rice is tender, 18 minutes.

Once the rice is cooking, place a large soup pot over medium-high heat with the remaining 2 tablespoons of EVOO. Add the andouille and cook until brown and crispy, 4 to 5 minutes. Stir in the celery, bell peppers, onions, bay leaf, sweet potatoes, and hot sauce and cook for about 5 minutes, stirring every now and then, until the onions start to get tender. Add the black-eyed peas, stewed tomatoes, and the remaining 4 cups of chicken stock. Bring to a bubble, then lower the heat to medium and simmer for 10 minutes or until the sweet potatoes are tender. Discard the bay leaf.

To serve, place a large scoop of rice in each soup bowl and add enough hoppin' John to almost cover the rice; give it a stir.

# Curried Vegetable Stoup

This one was written for the most dashing vegetarian I know, Rupert Everett. It's comforting and filling and will satisfy meat eaters *and* meat free-ers, warming them inside and out. It's also an affordable hearty menu if you're cooking to stretch a buck.

2  medium **eggplants**

3  tablespoons **EVOO** (extra-virgin olive oil), 3 times around the pan

1  small head of **cauliflower**, cored and cut into florets

3  to 4 **Yukon Gold potatoes**, peeled and diced into 1-inch chunks

1  large **red bell pepper**, chopped

1  large **onion**, chopped

3  **garlic cloves**, chopped

   **Salt** and **black pepper**

1  quart (4 cups) **vegetable or chicken stock**

3  tablespoons **mild curry paste**, more if desired

1  cup **mango chutney**

1  (15-ounce) can **chickpeas**

1  (28-ounce) can diced **fire-roasted tomatoes**

1  pound triple-washed **spinach**, stemmed and coarsely chopped

1  bag of pita chips or **toasted pita wedges**

Peel half of the skin off the eggplants and dice into bite-size pieces. (I leave half the skin on for texture.)

Place a large pot over medium to medium-high heat with the EVOO. Add the eggplant and cook, stirring, for 3 to 4 minutes while you chop the rest of the vegetables. Add the cauliflower and potatoes and cook for 5 minutes. Add the red bell pepper, onions, garlic, salt, and pepper, adding a little more oil if the mixture seems dry. Continue to cook the vegetables for 7 to 8 minutes more. Add 3 cups of the stock and bring up to a simmer.

While the stoup is coming up to a simmer, combine the remaining 1 cup of stock with the curry paste and mango chutney in a food processor or blender and puree until smooth.

Add the curry mixture to the pot along with the chickpeas and tomatoes. Season with some salt and pepper, bring the mixture up to a bubble, and simmer for 10 to 15 minutes. Fold the spinach in to wilt. Turn off the heat.

To serve, ladle up a good amount of the stoup into serving bowls and top with some pita chips.

## tidbit

To make your own pita chips, cut pitas into 8 to 10 wedges (you can separate them into individual layers before you cut them if you prefer thinner, crisper chips). Spray the wedges with olive oil cooking spray and bake at 375° to 400°F for 8 to 10 minutes, or until crisp.

# Panzanella Stoup

I love bread salad, so I thought, what would happen if you heated it up? The result is a thick stoup somewhere between *pappa al pomodoro* and *ribollita*. Maybe this will become a new classic!

- 3 tablespoons **EVOO** (extra-virgin olive oil), plus some to pass at the table
- 3 green or yellow **bell peppers**, seeded and diced into bite-size chunks
- 1 softball-size **onion**, chopped
- 4 **garlic cloves**, grated or finely chopped
- ¼ cup good-quality **balsamic vinegar** (eyeball it)
- 1 quart (4 cups) **chicken stock**
- 1 (28-ounce) can **crushed tomatoes**
- 4 cups torn or chopped **stale crusty bread**, about ½ loaf
  **Salt** and **black pepper**
- 1 cup fresh **basil leaves**, about 20, torn
  Shredded **Parmigiano-Reggiano** or Romano cheese, to pass at the table

Place a soup pot over medium-high heat with 3 tablespoons of EVOO, 3 times around the pan. Add the bell peppers, onions, and garlic: as you chop them, drop them into the pot. Cook the veggies for 10 minutes, then stir in the balsamic vinegar. Cook it down for 1 minute, then add the chicken stock and crushed tomatoes. Bring to a boil and add the bread. Reduce the heat to a simmer. Within 5 minutes the bread will bloat; stir to break it up, then simmer for another 5 minutes to really thicken the stoup. Season the stoup with salt and pepper to taste. Fold in the basil. The stoup is done when a spoon stands upright in the pot. Ladle the stoup into bowls and top with a drizzle of EVOO and some shredded cheese.

# Spicy Lentil Stoup

Lentils bring good luck to the eater, especially on New Year's Day: they symbolize coins and promise a prosperous year. Eat and earn! Serve with crusty rolls.

2 tablespoons **EVOO** (extra-virgin olive oil), twice around the pan
2 **anchovy fillets**
¼ pound **pancetta**, diced
1 teaspoon **red pepper flakes**
1 **onion**, chopped
3 to 4 **garlic cloves**, grated or chopped
2 **carrots**, peeled and grated or finely chopped
1 large **starchy potato**, such as russet, peeled and cut in small dice
2 teaspoons **smoked sweet paprika** or ground cumin
½ teaspoon **ground allspice**
1 fresh or dried **bay leaf**
2 to 3 fresh **rosemary sprigs**
**Salt** and **black pepper**
1½ cups **lentils**
2 quarts (8 cups) **chicken stock**
1 (14-ounce) can diced **fire-roasted tomatoes**
1 bunch of **kale** or dinosaur kale, stemmed and coarsely chopped

Heat the EVOO in a heavy-bottomed pot over medium to medium-high heat. Add the anchovies and stir until they melt into the oil, then add the pancetta and red pepper flakes and cook until the pancetta is crisp, 3 to 4 minutes. Add the onions, garlic, carrots, and potatoes and season them with the smoked paprika or cumin, allspice, bay leaf, rosemary, and salt and pepper. Cook for 7 to 8 minutes to soften the veggies, then add the lentils, stock, and tomatoes and bring to a boil. Reduce the heat to a simmer and add the greens, stirring them into the stoup as they wilt. Cook the stoup for 25 minutes or until the lentils are tender. Discard the bay leaf and serve.

# Oven-Roasted Cioppino

*Ciao* down on a warming bowl of fish and savory broth with craggy hunks of bread for mopping up every drop of goodness. It's Italian comfort food from the sea!

- 4 **celery ribs**, sliced on a long angle
- 1 large **fennel bulb**, cored and thinly sliced, ¼ cup fennel fronds reserved
- 2 medium **onions**, thinly sliced
- 4 large **garlic cloves**, chopped
- 1 teaspoon **red pepper flakes**
- 1 cup fresh **flat-leaf parsley** leaves
  **Salt** and **black pepper**
- ½ cup **EVOO** (extra-virgin olive oil)
- 1 cup **dry white wine**
- 1 cup **seafood stock** or chicken stock
- 1 (28-ounce) can **crushed tomatoes**
- 2 pounds **fresh cod**, cut into 2-inch chunks
- 12 **jumbo sea scallops**
- 12 **jumbo shrimp**, peeled or not, as you prefer
- 1 loaf **crusty bread**
  Zest of 1 **orange**

Preheat the oven to 425°F.

In a large roaster or casserole combine the celery, fennel, onions, garlic, red pepper flakes, and a couple of handfuls of the parsley. Dress the vegetables with salt and pepper and about ¼ cup of the EVOO. Add the wine, stock, and crushed tomatoes.

Season the seafood with salt and pepper; nestle the fish, scallops, and shrimp among the vegetables; and pour the remaining ¼ cup of EVOO over the top. Roast uncovered until the cod is cooked through, 40 to 45 minutes. At the midway point, ladle some of the liquids over the seafood to keep the top moist.

Cut or tear the bread into large chunks. Place them on a baking sheet and toast in the oven until lightly charred, 8 minutes or so.

While the bread is toasting, chop the remaining parsley together with the orange zest and reserved fennel fronds to create a gremolata garnish.

Serve the cioppino in large bowls topped with the gremolata, with the charred bread chunks for dunking.

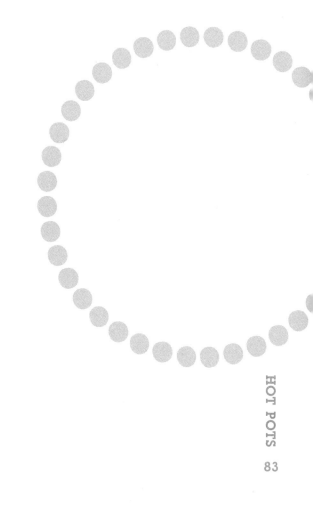

# Sardinian-Style Fish Chowder

Heavy cream makes this smooth and rich—yum-o!

¼ cup **EVOO** (extra-virgin olive oil; eyeball it)

1 teaspoon **fennel seeds**

1 medium to large **onion**, chopped

2 **russet potatoes**, peeled and diced

1 **bay leaf**

1 **carrot**, shredded

1 medium **zucchini**, shredded

**Salt** and **black pepper**

½ cup **dry white wine**

2 cups **chicken stock**

1 (15-ounce) can **crushed tomatoes**

½ teaspoon **ground turmeric**

¼ teaspoon **saffron threads** or an envelope of saffron powder

2 pounds **cod, halibut, or haddock**, cut into large cubes

1 cup **heavy cream**

**Crusty bread**, for mopping

Heat the oil in a deep skillet or stew pot over medium to medium-high heat. Add the fennel seeds and toast them for a minute, then add the onions, potatoes, and bay leaf and cook for 5 to 6 minutes. Add the carrot and zucchini, season with salt and pepper, and cook for a few minutes more. Stir in the wine and let it evaporate almost completely, about 1 minute. Add the stock, tomatoes, turmeric, and saffron and bring the liquids to a bubble. Season the fish with salt and pepper, then add it to the soup and poach gently for 10 to 12 minutes. Add the cream, stir gently to combine, and return the soup to a bubble. Simmer for a few final minutes, then adjust the salt and pepper. Discard the bay leaf and ladle the soup and fish into shallow bowls. Pass crusty bread at the table for mopping.

# Chicken Parm Soup

I ladle this soup over big cheesy toasts so they get soft and I can spoon them up with the soup.

- 3 to 4 tablespoons **EVOO** (extra-virgin olive oil), plus more for drizzling
- 1 pound **chicken tenderloins** or cutlets, chopped into bite-size pieces
  **Salt** and **black pepper**
- 4 **garlic cloves**, 3 chopped and 1 halved
- 1 large **red onion**, very thinly sliced
  **Red pepper flakes**, to taste
- 1 (28-ounce) can **crushed tomatoes**
- 1 quart (4 cups) **chicken stock**
- 4 thick slices **Italian semolina bread**
- 1 cup grated **Parmigiano-Reggiano** cheese
- 1 cup fresh **basil**, about 20 leaves, shredded or torn

Preheat the broiler.

Heat the EVOO in a soup pot over medium-high heat. Add the chicken, season with salt and pepper to taste, and cook until lightly browned, 3 to 4 minutes. Add the chopped garlic, the onions, and red pepper flakes, and cook to soften the onions, 5 to 6 minutes. Stir in the tomatoes and stock and cook until heated through.

While the soup cooks, char the bread on both sides under the broiler. Rub with the garlic halves and drizzle with EVOO, then mound with handfuls of Parmigiano cheese and return to the broiler to melt the cheese, a minute more.

Turn off the heat and stir in the basil. Place the large toasts at the bottom of shallow soup bowls and ladle on the soup or ladle in the soup and float the toasts on top to keep them crunchy— your choice.

# Chicken or Shrimp Fajita-Tortilla Soup

Make any night into Cinco de Mayo in less than 15 minutes with this easy, versatile soup!

- 2 tablespoons **EVOO** (extra-virgin olive oil), twice around the pan
- 1½ pounds **chicken tenders or** 1½ pounds **peeled, deveined shrimp**, tails removed
- 1 tablespoon **ground coriander**, a palmful
- 2 tablespoons **fresh thyme leaves** (5 to 6 sprigs, stripped), chopped
  **Salt** and **black pepper**
- 1 large **onion**, quartered and thinly sliced
- 1 large **bell pepper**, seeded, quartered, and thinly sliced
- 1 **jalapeño**, seeded and thinly sliced
- 1 (28-ounce) can diced **fire-roasted tomatoes**
- 1 quart (4 cups) **chicken stock**
- 1 bag **white corn tortilla chips**
- 1 cup shredded **Pepper Jack** or sharp white Cheddar cheese, plus more to pass at the table
- 1 ripe **avocado**
  Juice of 1 **lime**
- 4 **scallions**, chopped
  A handful of fresh **cilantro** or flat-leaf parsley, chopped

In a large skillet heat the EVOO over medium-high to high heat. Add chicken or shrimp, season with the coriander, thyme, salt, and pepper, and cook for 3 to 4 minutes. If using shrimp, remove them from the pan and set aside to keep them from overcooking. Add the onions, bell pepper, and jalapeño to the pan, season with more salt and pepper, and cook for 6 to 7 minutes, stirring frequently. The veggies should be charred at the edges but still a bit crispy. Add the tomatoes and stock and heat through. (If you have removed the shrimp, return them to the soup just before dishing it up to reheat briefly.)

While the soup is working, lightly crush some tortilla chips and divide among 4 bowls; you'll need a couple of handfuls per bowl. Top the chips with $\frac{1}{4}$ cup of the cheese per serving. Peel and dice the avocado and toss it with the lime juice.

To serve, ladle the soup over the chips and cheese, and garnish each serving with avocado, scallions, and cilantro or parsley. Pass some extra cheese for those who want it.

## tidbit

Shrimp cook more quickly than the chicken tender pieces, so be sure not to let them overcook if using.

# Double Dumpling Chicken Stoup

Mini meatballs are cooked in the stoup, as dumplings. Then, gnocchi—potato dumplings—are added, doubling the dumpling factor.

2 tablespoons **EVOO** (extra-virgin olive oil), twice around the pan

4 **celery ribs** from the heart, chopped

2 medium **onions**, chopped

1½ to 2 cups store-bought shredded **carrots**

1 fresh or dried **bay leaf**

**Salt** and **black pepper**

6 cups **chicken stock**

1 pound **ground chicken**

2 **garlic cloves**, finely chopped or grated

A little freshly **grated nutmeg**, about ¼ teaspoon

1 **egg**

½ cup **Italian seasoned bread crumbs**, a couple of handfuls

½ cup grated **Parmigiano-Reggiano cheese**, a couple of handfuls

1 package fresh **gnocchi**, from the refrigerated aisle

1 cup **frozen peas**

A handful of fresh **flat-leaf parsley**, finely chopped

**Crusty bread**, for mopping

Heat the EVOO in a soup pot over medium to medium-high heat. Add the celery, onions, carrots, and bay leaf; season with salt and pepper; and cook for 5 minutes. Add the stock, cover, and bring to a gentle boil.

While the stock heats, place the chicken in a bowl and season with salt and pepper. Add the garlic, nutmeg, egg, bread crumbs, and cheese. Combine the chicken mixture with your hands, then roll into walnut-size meatballs and add to the soup. Cook for 3 to 4 minutes, then add the gnocchi to the pot and cook for 5 minutes longer, or until they float to the surface. Add the peas and parsley, and cook for 2 minutes longer. Turn the heat off under the stoup and allow it to stand on the stovetop for 5 minutes to cool and thicken up a bit. Discard the bay leaf, ladle into bowls, and serve with crusty bread.

# Winter White Chicken Stew

Getting slow-cooked, subtle flavors from a simple and quick-cooking dish is a great trick to have up your sleeve. Here's a hearty example that tastes as if it simmered for hours.

3 tablespoons **EVOO** (extra-virgin olive oil), 3 times around the pan
1 cup all-purpose **flour**
  **Salt** and **black pepper**
2½ pounds boneless, skinless **chicken breasts and thighs** cut into large chunks
2 fresh or dried **bay leaves**
3 **garlic cloves**, chopped
2 **onions**, cut into bite-size dice
1 large **fennel bulb**, cored and cut into bite-size dice, plus a few tablespoons of chopped fronds
3 large **Yukon Gold potatoes**, peeled and cut into 1-inch chunks
1 cup **dry white wine**
1 quart (4 cups) **chicken stock**
1 cup **green Sicilian olives**, pitted and coarsely chopped
¼ cup **pine nuts**
½ cup fresh **flat-leaf parsley** leaves
  Zest and juice of 1 **lemon**
1 loaf **crusty bread**

Heat the EVOO in a large pot over medium-high heat. Place the flour on a plate, season the chicken pieces liberally with salt and pepper, then transfer the chicken to the flour. Toss to coat the pieces and shake off any excess flour. Transfer the chicken to the hot pot and brown for about 5 minutes, giving it a stir every now and then. Add the bay leaves, garlic, onions, fennel, half of the fennel fronds, and the potatoes and continue to cook for about 10 minutes, or until the onions are tender. Add the white wine and cook for 1 minute while scraping the bottom of the pan. Add the chicken stock and bring up to a bubble, then reduce the heat and simmer for 20 minutes. Add the olives for the last 5 minutes of cooking.

While the stew is simmering, prepare the gremolata garnish. Place the pine nuts in a dry skillet over medium heat and cook, tossing frequently, until toasted, just a couple of minutes. Place the parsley, lemon zest, and toasted pine nuts in a pile on a cutting board and run a knife through the pile until it is finely chopped. Mix in the remaining fennel fronds.

To serve, squeeze the juice of the lemon over the stew and combine. Discard the bay leaves. Ladle the stew into shallow bowls and sprinkle with some of the gremolata. Serve with crusty bread for mopping.

# Hunter's Chicken Stoup with Whole-Wheat Pasta

So hearty and so healthy, this one is delicious proof that not all comfort food is bad for you. Yum-o!

**Salt**
1 pound **whole-wheat gemelli** or penne
6 tablespoons **EVOO** (extra-virgin olive oil)
4 (¼-inch-thick) slices **pancetta**, chopped
2 pounds boneless, skinless **chicken thighs** cut into large bite-size pieces
**Black pepper**
6 **portobello mushroom caps** cut into bite-size dice
1 large **onion**, chopped
1 **carrot**, peeled and grated
1 fresh or dried **bay leaf**
1 teaspoon **red pepper flakes**
4 **garlic cloves**, grated or finely chopped
4 fresh **rosemary sprigs**, finely chopped
1 cup **dry red wine**
2 cups **chicken stock**
1 (28-ounce) can **crushed fire-roasted tomatoes**
2 tablespoons **butter**, cut into pieces
1 cup grated or shredded **Parmigiano-Reggiano** cheese

Bring a large pot of water to a boil. Salt it liberally, add the pasta, and cook al dente.

While the water heats and the pasta cooks, make the stoup. Heat a deep skillet over medium-high heat with 3 tablespoons of the EVOO, 3 times around the pan. Add the pancetta and cook for a couple of minutes to crisp it up, then remove it to a plate. Add the chicken and season with salt and pepper. Brown the chicken for 10 minutes then transfer it to the plate with the pancetta. Add the remaining 3 tablespoons of EVOO and heat. When it's hot, add the mushrooms and soften them up for 3 to 4 minutes. Stir in the onions, carrot, bay leaf, red pepper flakes, garlic, and rosemary, and season with salt and pepper. Cook until the mushrooms are dark and the onions are tender, another 6 to 8 minutes. Add the wine and deglaze the pan, stirring up any bits from the bottom, then stir in the stock and tomatoes. Slide the chicken and pancetta back into the pan. Discard the bay leaf.

Just before the pasta is done, add 2 ladles of the starchy pasta cooking water to the skillet with the chicken. Drain the pasta and return it to the hot pot. Add the butter, a couple ladles of the stoup, and the cheese. Toss to combine.

Serve shallow bowls of pasta and top with ladles of the chicken and mushroom stoup to be mixed together.

# Italian Chicken Chili with Pancetta Crouton Toppers

Potlucks are often held on weekends, when we can all slow down a bit, a perfect time to make a pot of this chili. Even though it is a 60-minute meal, I promise this takes no more work than a 30-minute meal; it just takes its own sweet time. This will serve 6 to 8.

½ cup **EVOO** (extra-virgin olive oil)
3 pounds **ground chicken**
**Salt** and **black pepper**
2 large **onions**, chopped
3 **carrots**, peeled and grated
1 fresh or dried **bay leaf**
4 jarred **roasted red peppers**
⅓ cup aged **balsamic vinegar**
4 to 5 sprigs of **fresh thyme**
2 teaspoons **smoked sweet paprika**, ⅔ palmful
2 tablespoons **chili powder**, 2 palmfuls
¼ teaspoon **ground allspice** (eyeball it)
1 quart (4 cups) **chicken stock**
⅓ pound **pancetta**, sliced ⅛ inch thick, chopped into fine dice
3 tablespoons **butter**, cut into pieces
1 medium-size loaf, about 1 pound, **crusty bread**, cut into 1-inch squares
6 large **garlic cloves**, crushed
1 cup freshly grated **Pecorino Romano** cheese
3 tablespoons finely chopped fresh **rosemary**, 4 to 5 sprigs

In a large, heavy-bottomed pot, heat ¼ cup of the EVOO over medium-high heat. Add the ground chicken, season with salt and pepper, and cook until lightly browned, 7 to 8 minutes. Add the onions, carrots, and bay leaf, then cook until the veggies get tender, 10 to 12 minutes more.

While the vegetables cook, place the roasted peppers in a food processor and grind until they make a smooth sauce. Stir the balsamic vinegar into the pot with the vegetables and deglaze the pan, scraping up the brown bits, then stir in the pureed peppers. Throw in the thyme sprigs; season with the smoked paprika, chili powder, and allspice; and adjust the salt and pepper. Add the chicken stock and mix well. Bring the mixture to a bubble, then reduce the heat to a simmer and cook for 20 minutes. Discard the bay leaf and thyme sprigs.

While the chili cooks, preheat the oven to 350°F.

Heat the remaining $\frac{1}{4}$ cup of EVOO in a small skillet over medium-high heat. Add the pancetta and brown it, about 5 minutes. Remove with a slotted spoon to a paper-towel-lined plate. Add the butter to the cooking oil, turn off the heat, and let the butter melt into the EVOO.

Place the bread and garlic in a large mixing bowl. Pour the butter and EVOO evenly over the bread. Sprinkle the pancetta, cheese, rosemary, and lots of pepper over the bread cubes and toss to coat and combine. Spread the croutons out on a rimmed baking sheet and bake until evenly golden, tossing things up a bit every now and again, 15 to 18 minutes. Cool.

Serve the chili in mugs and top with the pancetta croutons. Pass me a cold Peroni!

# Mu Shu Stoup

My favorite Chinese take-out menu item is mu shu, a stir-fried shredded cabbage dish that is eaten wrapped in soft pancakes. This healthy cabbage stoup tastes a lot like my favorite take-out, and dropping a few pot stickers into each bowl gives a wink and a nudge to the whole pancake thing.

¼ cup **vegetable oil**
1 pound medium **shrimp**, peeled and deveined, or 1 pound **chicken cutlets**, thinly sliced, or 1 pound thin-cut **pork loin chops**, thinly sliced
½ pound **shiitake mushrooms**, stemmed and sliced
1 cup shredded **carrots**
4 **garlic cloves**, chopped
1 small head of **Savoy cabbage**, cored and shredded
1 (13-ounce) package **pot stickers** from the frozen-food aisle
6 **scallions**, whites and greens cut into 1-inch pieces on an angle
⅓ cup **tamari** (aged soy sauce; eyeball it)
   **Black pepper**
2 quarts (8 cups) **chicken stock**
2 **eggs**, beaten

In a soup pot heat 2 tablespoons of the vegetable oil over medium-high to high heat. Add your protein of choice and stir-fry: cook shrimp until just pink, 2 to 3 minutes; chicken or pork until lightly browned, 4 to 5 minutes. Add the mushrooms, carrots, and garlic, and cook for 2 minutes, then add the cabbage and cook until it is wilted, 5 minutes.

While the cabbage cooks, heat the remaining 2 tablespoons of vegetable oil in a skillet and arrange the pot stickers in it. Add ⅔ cup of water and turn the heat to medium-high. Cook for 8 minutes to evaporate the water, then let the pot stickers brown for another minute.

While the pot stickers cook, add the scallions, tamari, and black pepper to the soup pot and stir to combine. Add the stock and bring to a boil. Reduce the heat to a simmer, stir in the beaten eggs, and cook, stirring, until they are set and mixed throughout the stoup.

Place a few pot stickers in the bottom of each soup bowl and top with the hot Mu Shu Stoup. Yum-o!

# Spicy Sausage, Chicken, and Bean Pot

This one-pot meal is a wink and a nudge to cassoulet—in 30 minutes.

2 tablespoons **EVOO** (extra-virgin olive oil), twice around the pan
¾ pound bulk **hot Italian sausage**
¾ pound **andouille sausage**, cut on an angle into 1-inch lengths
1½ pounds boneless, skinless **chicken thighs**, cut into large chunks
**Salt** and **black pepper**
1 large **onion**, quartered and thinly sliced
2 **carrots**, peeled and shredded
3 to 4 **celery ribs** from the heart, thinly sliced
1 fresh or dried **bay leaf**
2 (15-ounce) cans **white beans** (cannellini)
Leaves from 5 to 6 fresh **sage sprigs**, thinly sliced
1 cup **dry white wine**
2 cups **chicken stock**
½ baguette or loaf of **Italian bread**
3 tablespoons **butter**, melted
A handful of fresh **flat-leaf parsley**, chopped
3 to 4 fresh **thyme sprigs**, chopped

Heat the EVOO in a Dutch oven over medium-high heat. Add the Italian sausage, crumble into large pieces with a wooden spoon, and cook until it begins to brown, 2 to 3 minutes. Add the andouille and cook until crisp at the edges, 2 to 3 minutes. Remove the browned sausages to a paper-towel-lined plate and add the chicken to the skillet, seasoning it with salt and pepper. Lightly brown the chicken for a couple of minutes on each side, then add the veggies, bay leaf, and more salt and pepper. Cook for 7 to 8 minutes more to soften the veggies. Add the sausages back to the pan with the beans and sage. Pour in the wine and stir to deglaze the pan, then stir in the stock.

Turn the broiler on and set the rack in the middle of the oven.

Coarsely chop the bread in a food processor to make large crumbs. Remove the blade and drizzle with the melted butter. Add the parsley, thyme, and salt and pepper and stir to combine. Cover the sausage and chicken with the seasoned bread crumbs and place in the oven to brown for 2 to 3 minutes. Serve directly from the pot. Keep an eye out for that bay leaf!

# Roasted Poblano and Sliced Steak Chili

My hubby and I were heatin' up our kitchen one night when we came up with this one together. It's serious enough to entertain with.

 3 large **poblano peppers**
 2 pounds **sirloin shell steak**
 3 tablespoons **EVOO** (extra-virgin olive oil), 3 times around the pan
   **Salt** and **black pepper**
 1 large **red onion**, chopped
 4 to 5 **garlic cloves**, chopped
 1 teaspoon **smoked sweet paprika**, ⅓ palmful
 1½ teaspoons **ground cumin**, ½ palmful
 1½ teaspoons **ground coriander**, ½ palmful
 1 tablespoon **chili powder**, a palmful
 1 bottle **dark Mexican beer**, such as Negra Modelo
 1 (28-ounce) can diced **fire-roasted tomatoes**
   Zest and juice of 1 **lime**
   Black bean or blue **corn tortilla chips**, lightly crushed, for garnish

Preheat the broiler to high and place the poblanos on a broiler pan or baking sheet. Char and blacken the skins all over under the hot broiler, 15 to 16 minutes. Leave the oven door cracked to prevent steam from wafting out when you open the door. Set the poblanos in a bowl and cover the bowl with plastic wrap. Let stand for 10 to 15 minutes. When the peppers have cooled, peel off the skins, discard the seeds, and cut the peppers into large bite-size pieces.

Trim the steak and cut it into thin bite-size strips about 1½ inches long and ¼ inch thick. Heat the EVOO in a stew pot over high heat. When it ripples add the beef and sear on all sides, seasoning it with salt and pepper. Add the onions and garlic and reduce the heat to medium-high. Cook the onions for 5 minutes, then stir in the smoked paprika, cumin, coriander, and chili powder, distributing the spices well. Deglaze the pan with the beer, scraping up the browned bits, and cook for a minute to reduce. Add the tomatoes and lime zest, then stir in the poblano peppers. Reduce the heat to low and simmer the chili for 15 to 20 minutes. Squeeze the lime juice over the chili and turn off the heat. Serve in shallow bowls garnished with a few crushed tortilla chips.

three

# Using Your Noodle

Pasta, Noodle Bowls,
Couscous, and Baked Pastas

(continued)

## Pasta is my favorite comfort food and the perfect

blank canvas for any cook. In this book I present more 30-minute pastas, of course, but the first collection of 15- and 60-minute pastas, too. Pasta is so versatile—if all you have is 15 minutes, try the 15-minute paella with couscous; thanks to the ready-in-5-minute couscous, paella can now be ready in 15 minutes. And the pasta shells with pancetta, peas, and shrimp? You couldn't get served in any bistro quicker than this. If you have time to prepare some hearty family fare, try the Crab-Stuffed Shells or Sausage, Mushroom, and Polenta Lasagna, which you'll find in the 60-minute meals. And if you wanna feel even better about choosing pasta, look for healthy whole-wheat pasta recipes; you'll get more whole grains into your meals and *that's* really using your noodle.

# Cheesy Pasta Presto

This one's a crowd-pleaser that's equally pleasing for one.
I could eat the whole pot, easy!

**Salt**
1 pound **short-cut pasta**, such as penne
2 tablespoons **EVOO** (extra-virgin olive oil), twice around the pan
5 ¼-inch-thick slices **pancetta**, finely diced
1 small **onion**, chopped
4 large **garlic cloves**, grated or finely chopped
**Black pepper**
1 teaspoon **red pepper flakes**
1 **lemon**
1 **orange**
½ to ¾ cup **chicken stock** (eyeball it)
1 cup fresh **basil**, about 20 leaves
4 cups **arugula** leaves, 2 small bunches or 1 prewashed bag or container
1 cup **whole-milk ricotta cheese**
1 cup grated **Parmigiano-Reggiano**, plus more for passing at the table

Place a large pot of water over high heat and bring to a boil. Salt the water liberally, add the pasta, and cook al dente. Heads up: right before draining, remove and reserve about 1 cup of the pasta cooking liquid.

Once the water is almost ready for the pasta, place a large skillet over medium-high heat. Add the EVOO and pancetta and cook until crispy, 3 to 4 minutes. Add the onions and garlic, and season with salt, pepper, and the red pepper flakes. Zest the lemon and orange directly into the pan, then squeeze the juice from both into the pan. Add the chicken stock and bring it up to a bubble, then turn off the heat. Coarsely chop the basil and arugula. Drain the pasta and add it and the reserved cooking liquid to the skillet. Stir in the ricotta, Parmigiano, basil, and arugula. Transfer to serving dishes.

# Scotch Salmon with Farfalle

For years my mom served this dish at caterings to raves. It's a great simple supper and weekend brunch dish.

**Salt**
1 pound **farfalle** (bow-tie pasta)
2 tablespoons **EVOO** (extra-virgin olive oil), twice around the pan
1 tablespoon **butter**
2 large **shallots**, chopped
2 tablespoons all-purpose **flour**
1/4 cup **Scotch** whiskey
2 cups **chicken stock**
**Black pepper**
1/2 cup **heavy cream**
1/4 cup prepared **sun-dried tomato pesto** (available in jars on the Italian specialty foods aisle)
1 cup frozen **petite peas**
1/2 pound thinly sliced **smoked salmon**, preferably Scottish, cut into strips
A generous handful of fresh **flat-leaf parsley**, finely chopped

Bring a large pot of water to a boil for the pasta. When it boils, salt it liberally, add the farfalle, and cook until al dente. Drain, reserving 1/2 cup of the starchy pasta water.

While the pasta cooks, in a large deep skillet, heat the EVOO and butter over medium to medium-high heat. When hot, add the shallots and cook for 3 to 4 minutes, then add the flour and cook for a minute more. Whisk in the whiskey, then the chicken stock, and season with salt and pepper. Cook the sauce for 2 to 3 minutes to thicken a bit, then stir in the cream and bring to a bubble. Stir in the sun-dried tomato pesto, peas, salmon, and parsley, stir for 1 minute to blend the flavors, then remove from the heat. If the sauce is very thick, add a bit of the reserved pasta water to loosen it up. Gently toss the drained pasta with the salmon sauce and serve immediately.

# Spring Pea-sto with Whole-Wheat Penne

If you like this dish, check out Pasta Shells with Pancetta, Peas, and Shrimp on page 116 the next time you're in the mood for a pasta night. It's also a 15-minute meal!

**Salt**
1 pound **whole-wheat penne pasta**
1 (10-ounce) package **frozen peas**, defrosted
¼ cup **pine nuts**, lightly toasted in a dry skillet
1 cup fresh **basil**, lightly packed, about 20 leaves
6 to 8 fresh **tarragon sprigs**, leaves stripped
1 **garlic clove**, cracked away from its skin
1 teaspoon grated **lemon zest**
½ cup grated **Parmigiano-Reggiano**, a couple of handfuls, plus more to pass at the table
½ cup **EVOO** (extra-virgin olive oil; eyeball it)
**Black pepper**

Bring a large pot of water to a boil, then season the water with salt and cook the penne al dente. Heads up: you will need to reserve a ladle or two of the starchy cooking water, ½ to ¾ cup, before draining the pasta.

Place half of the peas in the bottom of a serving dish. Place the rest of the peas in a food processor with the pine nuts, basil, tarragon, garlic, lemon zest, cheese, and olive oil. Add a little salt and pepper, then process into a coarse paste. Adjust the seasonings.

Pour the reserved pasta water over the peas in the serving bowl, then add the pesto. Pour the hot, drained pasta over the peas and pesto and toss vigorously to coat and combine. Adjust the seasoning and serve, passing extra cheese at the table.

# Pancetta, Bay, and Onion Sauce with Whole-Wheat Pasta

This is as rich and satisfying as it is healthful, so have two bowls. You'll be very happy.

**Salt**
1 pound **whole-wheat gemelli** or penne pasta
3 tablespoons **EVOO** (extra-virgin olive oil), 3 times around the pan
⅓-pound chunk of **pancetta**, chopped into small dice
2 medium **onions**, chopped
3 fresh or dried **bay leaves**
4 **garlic cloves**, grated or finely chopped
1 (28-ounce) can Italian **San Marzano tomatoes** (I think the imports are worth it for this particular sauce.)
1½ cups **chicken stock**
**Black pepper**
½ cup grated **Pecorino Romano** or other sheep's-milk cheese

Place a large pot of water over high heat to boil. Salt the boiling water liberally and cook the pasta al dente—leave a good bite to it.

While the pasta water is coming to a boil, heat a large, deep skillet over medium-high heat with the EVOO. Add the pancetta and cook for 3 to 4 minutes until crisp, then add the onions, bay leaves, and garlic. Cook the onions until very soft and tender, 7 to 8 minutes. Add the tomatoes to the pan and break them into pieces with a wooden spoon. Add the stock and season with lots of pepper and a little salt. Let the sauce reduce while the pasta finishes cooking.

Drain the pasta and toss with the sauce for 1 minute. Remove the bay leaves and serve the pasta with lots of grated cheese.

USING YOUR NOODLE

# Moussaka Pasta Toss and Spanakopita Salad

I made this up for Melina Kanakaredes, a girlfriend of Greek heritage who is both gorgeous and a total foodie. She gave it two thumbs up; I say it's a Greco-great!

**Salt**

1 pound **penne rigate**

5 tablespoons **EVOO** (extra-virgin olive oil)

1 pound **ground lamb**

4 **garlic cloves**, chopped

1 large **onion**, chopped

½ teaspoon **ground allspice**

2 pinches of **ground cinnamon** (eyeball it)

1 teaspoon **ground cumin**, ⅓ palmful

1 teaspoon **dried oregano**

**Black pepper**

1 small **eggplant**

2 tablespoons **butter**

2 tablespoons all-purpose **flour**

2 to 2½ cups **milk**

¼ teaspoon freshly grated **nutmeg** (eyeball it)

1 pound **spinach**, stems removed, coarsely chopped

1 small **red onion**, thinly sliced

1 cup **feta cheese crumbles**

¼ cup **fresh dill**, chopped

Juice of 1 **lemon**

½ cup fresh **flat-leaf parsley**, about 2 handfuls, chopped

½ cup grated **Parmigiano-Reggiano**

Bring a large pot of water to a boil, salt it, and add the pasta. Cook until the pasta is just al dente. Heads up: you will need to reserve a ladle of the starchy cooking water just before the pasta is drained.

Preheat a large, deep skillet over medium heat with 2 tablespoons of the EVOO, twice around the pan. Add the lamb and cook until browned, breaking it up into small pieces with the back of a wooden spoon, 3 to 4 minutes. Add the garlic and chopped onions; season with allspice, cinnamon, cumin, oregano, salt, and pepper. Cook for another couple of minutes while you chop the eggplant.

Peel off about half of the eggplant's skin. I leave a little skin on for texture and flavor. Chop the eggplant into a very small dice and add it to the lamb. Cook, stirring often, until it becomes soft, 8 to 10 minutes more.

Melt the butter in a saucepot over medium heat. Whisk in the flour and cook for 1 minute, then whisk in the milk. Bring this mixture up to a bubble and cook until smooth and thick, about 5 minutes. Season with salt, pepper, and nutmeg.

While the pasta cooks, mix together the spinach, red onions, feta cheese, and dill in a large salad bowl. Dress the salad with the lemon juice and about 3 tablespoons EVOO. Season the salad with black pepper. The feta cheese is very salty and the salad might not need any extra salt.

Stir the thickened white sauce into the meat, then add a bit of the starchy pasta cooking water to loosen up the mixture. Add the pasta to the pan and toss for a minute to coat with the sauce. Serve in shallow bowls and top liberally with parsley and grated cheese. Serve the salad along with the pasta.

# Cold Chicken Satay Noodles

Make this on hot nights and chill out!

**Salt**
1 pound **whole-wheat spaghetti**
¼ to ⅓ cup smooth or chunky **peanut butter** (eyeball it)
2 tablespoons **honey**
¼ cup **warm water** (eyeball it)
¼ cup **tamari** (aged soy sauce; eyeball it)
1 **garlic clove**, grated with a Microplane or box grater
Juice of 2 **limes**
1 tablespoon **hot sauce** (eyeball it)
3 tablespoons **vegetable, peanut, or sunflower oil** (eyeball it)
A handful of shredded **carrots**
4 **scallions**, thinly sliced on an angle
½ sack (5 ounces) triple-washed **spinach**, stemmed and thinly sliced
¼ cup **chopped peanuts**
2 tablespoons chopped fresh **cilantro** or flat-leaf parsley
2 cups cooked, shredded **chicken meat**, from a store-bought rotisserie chicken

Bring a large pot of water to a boil. Salt the water liberally, then add the pasta and cook al dente. Drain, then run the cooked pasta under cold water to cool. Drain well and reserve.

While the pasta water is coming to a boil, heat the peanut butter briefly in the microwave to soften, about 30 seconds. Whisk the softened peanut butter with the honey and warm water in a large bowl. Whisk in the tamari, garlic, lime juice, and hot sauce. Add the oil in a steady stream, whisking constantly. Add the drained noodles to the dressing and toss until the sauce coats the noodles evenly. Add the vegetables and chopped nuts, and toss to distribute the ingredients. Serve the noodles in shallow bowls and top each serving with cilantro or parsley and ½ cup of the shredded chicken.

# Gnocchi with Spinach and Gorgonzola

Comfort in under 15 minutes. You'll be full and asleep in less than 30!

2 (10-ounce) boxes **frozen chopped spinach**
**Salt**
2 (14- to 16-ounce) packages **fresh gnocchi**
½ cup chopped **walnuts**
¼ cup **EVOO** (extra-virgin olive oil), 4 times around the pan
3 to 4 **garlic cloves**, grated or finely chopped
**Black pepper**
1 cup **chicken stock**
8 ounces **Gorgonzola cheese**, crumbled

To defrost the spinach, place it on a plate and microwave on high for 5 minutes. Wring it dry in a clean kitchen towel and set aside.

Bring a large pot of water to a boil for the gnocchi and season it liberally with salt. Cut open the gnocchi packages and set aside.

Place the walnuts in a small skillet and toss over medium-low heat for 3 to 4 minutes until toasted and fragrant.

In a deep skillet, heat the EVOO over medium heat. Add the garlic to the warm oil, then add the spinach, separating the clumps as you add it to the garlic oil. Season the spinach with salt and pepper, add the stock, and bring to a bubble over medium heat. Add the Gorgonzola to the spinach and stir until it melts.

While the spinach heats, cook the gnocchi in the boiling water for 2 to 3 minutes, or until they float to the surface. Drain, then add to the spinach and toss for 1 minute to coat, then adjust the seasonings. Serve the gnocchi topped with the toasted walnuts.

USING YOUR NOODLE

# Tuna Pasta Puttanesca

Here's a new way to enjoy an old fave! By substituting tuna for the traditional anchovies, you up the protein, too.

**Salt**
1 pound **penne pasta**
3 tablespoons **EVOO** (extra-virgin olive oil), 3 times around the pan
6 large **garlic cloves**, finely chopped
½ to 1 teaspoon **red pepper flakes**, depending on how spicy you like it
2 (5.5- to 6-ounce) cans **Italian tuna** in oil or water, drained well
A generous handful of **black olives** such as Gaeta, pitted and chopped
3 tablespoons **capers**, drained
⅓ cup **white vermouth** or ½ cup dry white wine (eyeball it)
1 (28-ounce) can **diced plum tomatoes**
A generous handful of fresh **flat-leaf parsley**, chopped
2 teaspoons grated **lemon zest**
**Black pepper**
**Crusty bread**

Place a large pot of water over high heat and bring to a boil. Salt the water, add the pasta, and cook al dente. Reserve a couple of ladles of the cooking water (about ⅔ cup) before draining.

Meanwhile, in a large skillet heat the EVOO over medium heat. Add the garlic and red pepper flakes, cook for a minute or two, then add the tuna and break it up with a wooden spoon. Add the olives and capers, cook for a minute or two more, then stir in the vermouth. Cook down for a minute, then stir in the tomatoes and their juices. Add the parsley, lemon zest, and black pepper and simmer the sauce for a couple minutes more.

Add the reserved pasta cooking water to the sauce. Add the pasta to the skillet and toss to coat. Serve with some nice crusty bread.

# Paella in Quince

Thanks to my friend John McCally, who suggested I make a paella with couscous rather than rice: HUGE!

- ¼ cup **EVOO** (extra-virgin olive oil), 4 times around the pan
- ½ pound precooked **chorizo**, casings removed, cut into bite-size dice
- ¾ pound **chicken breast cutlets** or tenderloins, cut into bite-size dice
- 1 medium **onion**, chopped
- 4 **garlic cloves**, finely chopped or grated
- ½ teaspoon **red pepper flakes**
- 1 fresh or dried **bay leaf**
- 4 to 5 fresh **thyme sprigs**
- 1 pound medium **shrimp**, peeled and deveined
  **Salt** and **black pepper**
- 2½ cups **chicken stock**
- 1 teaspoon **turmeric** (eyeball it in your palm)
- 1 envelope **saffron powder** or a pinch of threads
- 2 cups **couscous**
- 1 cup frozen **green peas**
- 1 **lemon**, zested and cut into wedges
- 2 **piquillo peppers** or 1 roasted red pepper, chopped
  A generous handful of fresh **flat-leaf parsley**, chopped
  **Hot sauce**, to pass at the table

Heat the EVOO in a deep skillet over medium-high to high heat. Add the chorizo and render some of its fat, 1 to 2 minutes, then add the chicken and brown, 2 to 3 minutes. Add the onions, garlic, red pepper flakes, bay leaf, thyme, and shrimp; season with salt and pepper; and cook for 3 to 4 minutes more. Add the stock, turmeric, and saffron, bring to a boil, and stir in the couscous, peas, lemon zest, and piquillo peppers. Cover and turn off the heat. Let stand for 5 minutes, then fluff with a fork. Remove the bay leaf and thyme stems. Top each serving of paella with some chopped parsley, hot sauce, and juice from the lemon wedges.

USING YOUR NOODLE

115

# Pasta Shells with Pancetta, Peas, and Shrimp

This one will be a fast family favorite!

**Salt**
1  pound medium **pasta shells**
2  tablespoons **EVOO** (extra-virgin olive oil)
⅓  pound **pancetta**, sliced ⅛ inch thick
1  medium **onion**, chopped
3  to 4 **garlic cloves**, grated or finely chopped
1  pound medium **shrimp**, peeled and deveined
**Black pepper**
1  (16-ounce) bag **frozen peas**, defrosted for 2 minutes in the microwave
Zest and juice of 1 **lemon**
A generous handful of fresh **flat-leaf parsley**
1  to 1½ cups **chicken stock** (eyeball it)

Bring a large pot of water to a boil. Salt it liberally, then drop in the shells. Undercook the pasta a bit; it should be slightly al dente, about 8 minutes.

While the pasta cooks, heat a deep skillet over medium-high heat. Add the EVOO, twice around the pan, and when the oil ripples, add the pancetta. Brown and crisp the pancetta for 3 to 4 minutes, then add the onions and garlic and cook for 2 to 3 minutes more. Add the shrimp, season with salt and pepper, and cook for 3 minutes, just until they become firm and pink.

Place two thirds of the peas in a food processor along with the lemon zest and juice, parsley, and chicken stock. Puree until smooth. Add the pureed peas and remaining whole peas to the cooked shrimp and stir until just heated through, a minute or two. Toss the cooked and drained pasta shells with the peas and shrimp for a minute to absorb the flavor and liquids.

# Mac and Cheese Lorraine

Real men may not eat quiche, but they'll eat this!

**Salt**
1 pound **gemelli pasta** or other short cut pasta
½ pound **bacon**, chopped
1 tablespoon **EVOO** (extra-virgin olive oil), once around the pan
2 **onions**, quartered and thinly sliced
½ cup **dry white wine**
2 tablespoons **butter**
2 tablespoons all-purpose **flour**
1 cup **chicken stock**
1 cup **whole milk**
**Black pepper**
2 cups shredded **Gruyère**
A little freshly grated **nutmeg**, to taste
1 rounded tablespoon **Dijon mustard**

Bring a large pot of water to a boil. Salt the water liberally, add the pasta, and cook al dente. Drain.

Cook the bacon in the EVOO in a deep skillet over medium-high heat. When crisp, 5 to 6 minutes, remove to a paper-towel-lined plate with a slotted spoon and drain off all but 2 to 3 tablespoons of the fat. Add the onions and cook for 10 minutes, or until they are beginning to caramelize. Add the wine and cook for another minute.

While the onions cook, melt the butter in a saucepan over medium heat. Whisk in the flour. Cook for 1 minute, then whisk in the stock and milk and bring to a bubble. Cook for a few minutes to thicken, then season with salt and pepper. Stir in the cheese, then add the nutmeg, mustard, and salt and pepper.

Toss the pasta with the onions, then stir in the cheese sauce. Top each serving with some of the crispy bacon.

# Sorta-Soba Bowls

I love Tokyo Lamen, a Japanese noodle shop in New York City that delivers. When they're closed or when I am upstate, I make this dish instead, and I get it even quicker!

**Salt**
1 pound **whole-wheat spaghetti**
2 tablespoons **vegetable oil**, plus some for the pasta and some for drizzling
1 large **onion**, thinly sliced
2 large **garlic cloves**, chopped
1 cup shredded **carrots**
1 medium **zucchini**, halved and sliced into half moons ½ inch thick
16 to 20 **shiitake mushrooms**, stemmed and thinly sliced
1 head of **bok choy**, cored and coarsely chopped
2 quarts (8 cups) **chicken or vegetable stock**
1 cup fresh **bean sprouts**
2 tablespoons **toasted sesame seeds**
1 tablespoon **ground coriander**
1 tablespoon **chili powder**
½ teaspoon **cayenne pepper**
 **Tamari** (aged soy sauce)

Place a large pot of water over high heat and bring to a boil. Liberally salt the water, add the pasta, and cook al dente. Drain and toss with a little bit of vegetable oil.

While the pasta water is coming to a boil, place a large soup pot over medium-high heat and add the 2 tablespoons of vegetable oil, twice around the pan. Add the onion, garlic, carrots, and zucchini and cook until the onions and zucchini start to get tender, 4 to 5 minutes. Add the mushrooms and bok choy and cook for another

2 to 3 minutes. Add the stock, bring up to a bubble, and simmer for 5 minutes. Add the bean sprouts and remove from the heat.

In a small bowl, combine the toasted sesame seeds, ground coriander, chili powder, and cayenne pepper and reserve for garnishing the soup.

To serve, use a pair of tongs to twist a portion of the whole-wheat noodles into a nest and transfer to a soup bowl. Douse the noodles with some tamari and sprinkle with the sesame-spice mixture. Ladle the vegetables and broth over the noodles and serve with chopsticks and large soupspoons for slurping.

# Creamy Mushroom Orzo with Sweet Salad

**Salt**

1 pound **orzo**

2 cups **chicken stock** (eyeball it)

1 ounce **dried porcini mushrooms**

3 tablespoons plus ¼ cup **EVOO** (extra-virgin olive oil)

3 **portobello mushrooms**, stems removed, gills scraped out with a spoon, caps sliced

1 pound **cremini mushrooms**, brushed clean with a damp cloth

5 to 6 fresh **thyme sprigs**

2 to 3 fresh **rosemary sprigs**

3 large **garlic cloves**, chopped or grated

1 small **onion**, chopped

**Black pepper**

¼ cup **pine nuts**

3 tablespoons **honey** (eyeball it)

Juice of 2 **lemons**

1 **fennel bulb**, halved, cored, and thinly sliced

¾ cup **white wine** (eyeball it)

½ cup **heavy cream** (eyeball it)

½ cup fresh **flat-leaf parsley** leaves, a couple of handfuls, coarsely chopped

1 cup grated **Parmigiano-Reggiano** cheese

2 cups **arugula**

2 **hearts of romaine**, chopped

Bring a large pot of water to a boil over high heat. Salt the water, add the orzo, and cook until just slightly shy of al dente.

Place the chicken stock in a small saucepot. Add the dried mushrooms and bring up to a simmer. Turn off the heat and set aside to let the mushrooms plump.

Heat a large skillet over medium-high heat with the 3 tablespoons of EVOO, 3 times around the pan. Add the fresh mushrooms, spread them out in an even layer, and add the thyme and rosemary sprigs. Cook for 5 to 6 minutes, then stir in the garlic, onions, and some salt and pepper. Continue to cook for 8 to 10 minutes to soften the onions.

Place the pine nuts in a small skillet and toast over medium heat until they are golden, 2 to 3 minutes. Remove them from the heat and reserve.

In the bottom of a salad bowl combine the honey with the lemon juice and some salt and pepper. Whisk in the 1/4 cup of EVOO, adding it in a slow, steady steam. Add the fennel to the bowl and toss to combine.

Remove the dried mushrooms from the chicken stock using a slotted spoon; add the mushrooms to the skillet with the fresh mushrooms. Add the white wine and heavy cream to the skillet, then carefully pour in the chicken stock you used to steep the dried mushrooms, making sure that any sand or grit is left in the bottom of the pot and doesn't make its way into the skillet. Bring the liquids up to a bubble and simmer until there is only about 1 cup of liquid left in the skillet, a couple of minutes. Remove the thyme and rosemary stems.

Add the drained orzo to the skillet with the mushrooms, toss to combine, and continue to cook for about 1 minute. Add the parsley and the Parmigiano, and stir to combine.

Divide the creamy mushroom orzo among 4 shallow serving bowls. Add the arugula, romaine, and pine nuts to the dressed fennel; toss to combine and coat the greens in the dressing. Serve the salad alongside the creamy mushroom orzo.

# Cavatelli with Homemade Sausage, Eggplant, and Saffron Cream

This is a tasty postcard meal: it is my version of a delicious lunch I shared with my husband at a small café in Montalcino when we were in Italy celebrating our first anniversary.

**Salt**
1 pound **cavatelli pasta**
¼ teaspoon **saffron threads** or an envelope of saffron powder
1 **teaspoon** turmeric
1½ cups **chicken stock**
¼ cup **EVOO** (extra-virgin olive oil)
1 pound **ground pork**
1½ teaspoons **fennel seeds**, ½ palmful
3 to 4 **garlic cloves**, finely chopped
¼ teaspoon **red pepper flakes**
Freshly ground **black pepper**
1 **eggplant**, half of the skin peeled off, then chopped into a small dice
2 tablespoons **fresh thyme**, 5 to 6 sprigs, chopped
½ cup **dry white wine**
½ cup **heavy cream**
½ cup freshly grated **Parmigiano-Reggiano** or Pecorino Romano cheese, plus extra to pass at the table

Bring a large pot of water to a boil. Salt it, add the pasta, and cook until al dente (5 to 7 minutes for frozen or about 14 minutes for dried). Drain.

Add the saffron to a saucepan with the turmeric and the stock. Steep over low heat.

While the pasta is working, in a large, deep skillet, heat 2 table-spoons of the EVOO, twice around the pan, over medium-high heat. Add the pork, breaking it into small bits with a wooden spoon; sprinkle in the fennel seeds and cook until browned, 3 to 4 minutes. Add the garlic and the red pepper flakes, and season with salt and black pepper.

Push the meat to the side of the pan and add the remaining 2 table-spoons oil and the eggplant to the center of the pan; season with salt, pepper, and thyme. Cook the eggplant until just tender, 5 to 6 minutes. Combine with the meat. Deglaze the pan with the wine and cook for 1 minute. Add the saffron stock and combine. Stir in the cream and reduce the heat to low; gently cook for 5 minutes more. Turn off the heat and toss with the pasta and about ½ cup cheese. Pass extra cheese at the table.

## tidbit
When I peel an eggplant I leave on half the skin— I like the color and texture it gives the dish.

# Oh, Baby! Pasta with Shrimp, Grape Tomatoes, and Baby Arugula

Tasty things come in tiny shapes. Go little and get big flavor in this pasta dish.

**Salt**
1 pound baby **penne** with ridges or small shells
2 pints **grape tomatoes**
5 tablespoons **EVOO** (extra-virgin olive oil)
**Black pepper**
5 to 6 **garlic cloves**, chopped
24 small-medium **shrimp**, peeled and deveined
6 **scallions**, green and white parts chopped
Zest and juice of 1 **lemon**
1 cup fresh **basil**, 20 leaves, sliced into thin ribbons
4 cups (about 6 ounces) **baby arugula**, coarsely chopped

Preheat the oven to 400°F.

Bring a large pot of water to a boil for the pasta. Add a generous amount of salt and the pasta. Cook until al dente. Drain the pasta, reserving about 1 cup of starchy pasta cooking water.

While the water comes to a boil, place the tomatoes on a rimmed baking sheet, drizzle with 2 tablespoons of the EVOO, and season with salt and pepper. Roast the tomatoes in the hot oven for 20 minutes.

When the tomatoes have about 8 minutes of cooking time left, heat a large skillet over medium to medium-high heat with 3 table-spoons of the EVOO, 3 times around the pan. Add the garlic; cook just until fragrant, about 30 seconds; then add the shrimp. Cook the shrimp until firm and pink, 5 to 6 minutes, then add the scallions and cook for another minute. Add the drained pasta to the pan with the shrimp along with the reserved pasta water. Season with salt and pepper and 2 teaspoons of the zest and the juice of the lemon. Remove the tomatoes from the oven and mash right on the baking sheet with a potato masher. Add the tomatoes, basil, and arugula to the skillet and toss to combine.

Serve the pasta in shallow bowls.

# Florentine Mac and Cheese and Roast Chicken Sausage Meatballs

Mac and cheese and meatballs aren't just for the kiddies; this version is all dressed up and ready to go!

    Salt
1   pound **cavatappi** (hollow, corkscrew-shaped pasta)
1½  pounds **ground chicken**
    **Black pepper**
2   to 3 fresh **rosemary sprigs**, stripped and finely chopped
2   teaspoons **fennel seeds**
3   **garlic cloves**, grated
1   teaspoon **red pepper flakes**
1   cup **ricotta cheese**
1½  cups grated **Parmigiano-Reggiano** cheese
1   **egg**
½   to ¾ cup **bread crumbs**
3   tablespoons **EVOO** (extra-virgin olive oil)
3   tablespoons **butter**
2   tablespoons all-purpose **flour**
1   cup **chicken stock**
1   cup whole **milk**
⅛   teaspoon grated **nutmeg** (eyeball it)
2   (10-ounce) boxes chopped **frozen spinach**, defrosted (see Tidbit)

Preheat the oven to 450°F.

Place a large pot of water on to boil. When it comes to a boil, salt it, add the pasta, and cook al dente.

While the water is coming to a boil, in a large mixing bowl combine the chicken, salt and pepper, rosemary, fennel seeds, garlic, red pepper flakes, ricotta cheese, $\frac{1}{2}$ cup grated Parmigiano, the egg, and the bread crumbs. If the mixture is too wet, add another handful of bread crumbs. Form 8 large balls, 3 to 4 inches in diameter. Coat the balls in a couple tablespoons of the EVOO and lightly grease a rimmed baking sheet with another tablespoon of the EVOO. Arrange the balls on the sheet and roast for 17 to 18 minutes, or until the juices run clear.

While the meatballs roast, melt the butter in a medium saucepot over medium heat. Whisk in the flour, cook for 1 minute, then whisk in the stock and milk. Season with salt, pepper, and nutmeg and cook for 5 to 6 minutes to thicken. Stir in the remaining cup of grated Parmigiano and reduce the heat to the lowest setting.

Add the spinach to the white sauce, separating the clumps as you go. Mix thoroughly.

Drain the pasta and place in a large bowl. Pour the spinach sauce over the pasta and toss to combine. Adjust the seasonings.

Serve the Florentine Mac and Cheese topped with 2 meatballs per serving.

## tidbit

To defrost frozen spinach, place it in a microwave for 8 to 10 minutes on the "defrost" setting; place the boxes in a shallow dish to catch any runoff. Wring the defrosted spinach completely dry in a clean kitchen towel.

# Mac 'n' Cheese 'n' Burgers

Two basics come together and become one classic
sammie. Why didn't I think of this sooner?

**Salt**
1 pound **cavatappi** (hollow corkscrew pasta) or penne
1 tablespoon **EVOO** (extra-virgin olive oil), once around the pan
1 pound **ground sirloin**
3 to 4 tablespoons grated **onion** and juice
2 teaspoons **Worcestershire sauce** (eyeball it)
**Black pepper**
4 tablespoons (½ stick) **butter**, cut into pieces
3 tablespoons all-purpose **flour**
1 cup **chicken stock**
2 cups **whole milk**
1 tablespoon **Dijon mustard**
2 cups shredded **Cheddar cheese**
¼ cup chopped **dill pickles**, for garnish (optional)
2 **plum tomatoes**, seeded and diced (optional)

Bring a pot of water to a boil. Salt liberally, add the pasta, and cook
al dente.

While the pasta works, heat a nonstick skillet with the EVOO over
medium-high heat. Add the beef and cook until brown, breaking it
up with a wooden spoon into bite-size pieces. Add the grated
onion and juice, Worcestershire, and salt and pepper to the skillet
and combine.

While the meat browns, heat a saucepot over medium to medium-
high heat. Add the butter and, when it melts, whisk in the flour.
Cook it for a minute, then whisk in the stock and milk and season
with salt and pepper. Bring the sauce to a bubble, then cook for a

few minutes to thicken it up. Stir in the mustard, then add the cheese a few handfuls at a time, stirring in a figure-eight motion as it melts into the sauce. Adjust the salt and pepper.

Drain the pasta, then return it to the hot pasta pot along with the beef and cheese sauce. Stir to combine the mac 'n' cheese 'n' burger, adjust the seasoning, and serve in shallow bowls garnished with chopped pickles and tomatoes, if you like.

## tidbit
You'll need about ½ a small onion to get 3 to 4 tablespoons grated, but start with a whole onion to spare your fingertips; save the rest for another use. To save time and cleanup, grate directly into the bowl.

# Chicken Riggies and 'Scarole with Soul

In western New York State the Italian American community has a specialty, chicken riggies. It is made in many versions but they all have in common chicken and rigatoni tossed with sweet and hot peppers and tomato sauce. Here's my chicken riggies. It's my mom's and my hubby's new favorite meal. Spicy escarole makes a perfect partner to this dish.

**Salt**

1 pound **rigatoni**

¾ pound boneless, skinless **chicken thighs**

¾ pound **chicken tenders**

**Black pepper**

6 tablespoons **EVOO** (extra-virgin olive oil)

1 large **onion**, chopped

7 to 8 **garlic cloves**, grated or finely chopped

2 large or 3 small **cubanelle peppers**, seeded and chopped

3 jarred **roasted red peppers**, chopped

6 jarred **hot cherry peppers** (look in the Italian foods aisle)

1 (28-ounce) can **crushed tomatoes**

⅓ to ½ cup **heavy cream** (eyeball it)

⅓ pound thick-cut **capocollo hot ham**, chopped

2 heads of **escarole**, coarsely chopped

1 cup **chicken stock**

4 slices **crusty bread**

½ cup fresh **basil**, about 10 leaves, thinly sliced or shredded

Grated **Romano** or Parmigiano-Reggiano cheese, to pass at the table

Bring a pot of water to a boil for the "riggies." Salt the water, add the pasta, and cook al dente. Heads up: you will need to reserve a cup of the cooking water just before you drain the pasta.

Trim the chicken thighs of any skin or fat and chop the chicken into bite-size pieces. Season the chicken with salt and pepper.

Heat 3 tablespoons of the EVOO in a large, high-sided skillet over medium-high to high heat. Add the chicken to the hot pan and cook until browned all over, 7 to 8 minutes. Remove the chicken to a plate. Add the onions, about half of the garlic, and the cubanelle peppers to the skillet, then season with salt and pepper and cook for 6 to 7 minutes to soften. Add the roasted red peppers. Cut the tops off the hot peppers and scoop out the seeds with a teaspoon, then chop the hot peppers and add them to the skillet. Stir in the tomatoes, then add the chicken back to the sauce. Bring the sauce to a bubble and stir in about 1 cup of the reserved starchy cooking water from the pasta. Add the cream, twice around the pan; reduce the heat to the lowest setting; and simmer the sauce for a couple of minutes. Add the drained pasta and toss to combine.

While the chicken and peppers are cooking, heat the remaining 3 tablespoons of EVOO in a large skillet over medium-high heat. Add the chopped ham and cook for 2 minutes, then add the remaining garlic and reduce the heat a bit. Add the greens and turn them over in the pan to wilt them down, about 2 minutes. Season the greens with salt and pepper, add the stock, and simmer for 5 to 6 minutes. Place a slice of bread in each of 4 bowls and ladle the greens and broth over the bread.

Top the pasta with the shredded basil. Pass the cheese to sprinkle on both the pasta and the greens.

# Green-with-Envy Orecchiette and Red Wine–Braised Sausages

*Orecchiette* means "little ears," and the ears will be burning over this recipe, which is tasty and super good for you. The friends and family you make it for will be green with envy because you're able to make something so delicious!

      2   pounds **hot or sweet Italian sausages**, 8 short links or 4 large
      2   cups **dry red wine**
    ½   cup **EVOO** (extra-virgin olive oil)
          **Salt**
      1   pound **orecchiette pasta**
    ½   cup chopped **hazelnuts**
      1   package or bunch of fresh **chives**, coarsely chopped
      2   **garlic cloves**, cracked away from their skins
    12   fresh **tarragon stems**, leaves stripped from the stems
          **Black pepper**
    ½   cup grated **Parmigiano-Reggiano** cheese, plus more to pass at the table
      1   bunch of **green Swiss chard**, stems removed and coarsely chopped
          A little freshly grated **nutmeg**

Place the sausages in a skillet and add the wine and 1 tablespoon of the EVOO, once around the pan. Place the pan over medium-high heat and let the wine reduce and evaporate, 15 to 18 minutes. By this point, the sausage casings will have crisped up and the wine and oil will glaze the casings.

Bring a large pot of water to a boil. Salt the water, add the pasta, and cook al dente. Heads up: you will need to set aside 1½ cups, a couple of ladlefuls, of the starchy cooking water just before you drain the orecchiette.

Toast the hazelnuts in a small skillet over medium-low heat for 5 minutes. Remove from the skillet and cool for a few minutes.

Place the chives, 1 garlic clove, tarragon, salt and pepper, and nuts in a food processor and turn it on. Stream in about 5 tablespoons of the EVOO and process to make a smooth but thick sauce. Transfer the sauce to a bowl and stir in the cheese. The herby green color stays brighter if you stir rather than process the cheese into the sauce.

Heat the remaining 2 tablespoons of EVOO in a large skillet over medium-high to high heat. Add the remaining crushed garlic clove and cook until lightly browned, 2 to 3 minutes. Add the chard and season with salt, pepper, and nutmeg to taste. Sear the greens, tossing them as they wilt down, for 3 or 4 minutes.

Add the reserved pasta cooking water to the pesto in the bowl, then add the pasta and greens. Toss to combine thoroughly and coat the pasta with the green sauce.

Serve 2 braised sausages per person with lots of green ears alongside.

# Can't Beet That! Drunken Spaghetti

Spaghetti? Boiled in wine? You betcha! I wish I could say that I thought of this tasty idea first, but this is a beet-sweet take on a Tuscan classic.

**tidbit**
To keep your hands from getting stained when you handle raw beets, rub your palms with vegetable oil first.

2 (750-ml) bottles **red wine** or 1 large (1.5-liter) bottle—don't spend a fortune, $10 to $15 a bottle, tops
**Salt**
1 pound **spaghetti**
1 large **red beet**
3 tablespoons **EVOO** (extra-virgin olive oil), 3 times around the pan
4 **garlic cloves**, grated or finely chopped
1 large **shallot**, chopped or thinly sliced
**Black pepper**
1 bunch of **red Swiss chard**, stemmed and coarsely chopped
A little freshly grated **nutmeg**, ⅛ teaspoon or to taste
1 cup **chicken stock**
2 tablespoons **butter**
⅓ pound **ricotta salata cheese**, crumbled or grated

Pour the wine into a pasta pot and add enough water to reach the level you would otherwise fill the pot to for pasta. Bring to a boil over high heat, salt the water generously, and drop in the pasta. Cook al dente. Heads up: you will need to set aside about 1 cup of the starchy cooking liquid before draining.

While the liquids come to a boil, peel the beet. Place a box grater in a shallow bowl and grate the beet into the bowl. Heat the EVOO in a large deep skillet over medium heat. Add the garlic and shallots to the pan, cook for a minute, then add the grated beets and season with salt and pepper. Raise the heat to medium-high. Cook the beets for 7 to 8 minutes, then add the greens to the pan, turning them to wilt evenly. Season them with nutmeg, salt, and pepper.

Stir the chicken stock into the skillet and simmer for 5 minutes, then add the reserved cup of pasta-cooking liquid. Stir to combine and add the butter, swirling and stirring to melt it. Turn off the heat, add the drained spaghetti, and toss for 1 minute. Adjust the salt and pepper. Serve in shallow bowls with lots of crumbled ricotta salata on top.

## tidbit

To stem chard, hold each leaf upside down. Make a loose fist with your other hand and grab the leaf at the base of the stem, placing 2 fingers on either side of the stem. Pull down in a quick motion and strip the greens away from the stem. Easy!

# Meatballs in Meat Sauce with Rigatoni

Meat, meet meat! This one's never met a hunger it couldn't beat!

¼ cup **EVOO** (extra-virgin olive oil; eyeball it)

1½ pounds **ground beef, pork, and veal mix**

4 **garlic cloves**, grated or finely chopped

1 **carrot**, peeled and grated

1 **onion**, grated or finely chopped

·1 **bay leaf**

  **Salt** and **black pepper**

2 cups **chicken stock**

1 (14-ounce) can **crushed tomatoes**

1 (28-ounce) can San Marzano **whole plum tomatoes**

½ cup **walnut pieces**

½ cup fresh **flat-leaf parsley**, a couple of handfuls, coarsely chopped

2 slices of torn **white bread** or ½ cup bread crumbs

⅓ cup **whole milk**

1 **egg**

  A couple pinches of **ground allspice**

1 cup grated **Romano cheese**

1 pound **rigatoni**

2 tablespoons **butter**, cut into small pieces

Heat the EVOO in a saucepot or deep skillet over medium to medium-high heat. Add about ½ pound of the meat and break it up into very small pieces. Lightly brown the meat for a couple of minutes, then add half of the garlic and the carrot, onions, and bay leaf to the pan. Season the meat and veggies with salt and pepper and cook until the veggies are tender, 5 to 6 minutes. Stir in the stock and crushed tomatoes. Drain the whole plum tomatoes, then crush them with a wooden spoon and add to the sauce. Reduce the heat to low.

While the vegetables cook down, bring a pot of water to a boil over high heat. Toast the walnuts in a dry skillet over medium heat until fragrant and light golden brown, about 4 minutes. Let them cool for a minute or two, then crush them or chop fine in a food processor.

Place the remaining pound of meat in a bowl and add the parsley, bread, milk, egg, salt, pepper, allspice, a handful of the Romano, and the walnuts. Roll the meat into 16 balls, $1\frac{1}{2}$ to 2 inches around, then drop them into the sauce to simmer. Once the last ball has been added to the sauce, cook the meatballs 10 to 12 minutes longer to make sure they are all cooked through.

About 8 minutes before the meatballs are done, salt the pasta water and add the rigatoni; cook al dente. Drain the pasta, then return it to the hot pot along with the butter, the remaining Romano cheese, and a few ladles of the pasta sauce. Stir to melt the butter and coat the rigatoni with cheese and sauce. Transfer to a large serving platter and top with the remaining sauce and the meatballs, or serve the meatballs and sauce right from the pot.

# Dinner at The Ivy, East

Though my husband tries a new entrée each time we visit, when I dine at The Ivy restaurant in Los Angeles I am a creature of habit. I order the stuffed artichoke appetizer followed by the mushroom tagliatelle. Here is my at-home, East Coast version.

### Tomato Salad Stuffed Artichokes

Juice of 2 **lemons**

4 **globe artichokes**

2 pints **cherry tomatoes**

½ **red onion**, finely chopped

¼ cup fresh **flat-leaf parsley**, finely chopped

1 cup fresh **basil**, 20 leaves, thinly sliced into ribbons

4 tablespoons **EVOO** (extra-virgin olive oil)

**Salt** and **black pepper**

Fill a large pot with water and the lemon juice. Throw the juiced lemons into the pot and bring to a boil.

Cut the top quarter and stems off the artichokes. Using kitchen scissors, trim the spiked tips off the lower leaves. Place the artichokes in the boiling water and set a clean kitchen towel directly on top to keep the artichokes submerged. Cook until tender, 20 to 25 minutes. Remove the artichokes from the water and set upside down on a towel to drain and cool. Gently pry open the artichokes, using your fingers to pull out the palest of the leaves around the choke until you have exposed the fuzzy center. Using a spoon, carefully scoop out the choke from the center of the artichoke and discard.

In a mixing bowl, thoroughly combine the cherry tomatoes, red onion, parsley, basil, EVOO, salt, and pepper. Distribute the salad mixture evenly among the 4 artichokes, filling the cavity and letting some spill over onto the plate. Let stand, or chill while you prepare the pasta.

## Mushroom Tagliatelle

2 cups **chicken stock**

1 ounce **dried porcini mushrooms**

3 tablespoons **EVOO** (extra-virgin olive oil), 3 times around the pan

2 **shallots**, finely chopped

4 **garlic cloves**, finely chopped

½ pound **shiitake mushrooms**, stems removed, thinly sliced

½ pound **cremini mushrooms**, wiped with a damp towel and thinly sliced

**Salt** and **black pepper**

3 tablespoons **butter**

2 tablespoons all-purpose **flour**

1 cup **dry white wine**

2 (9-ounce) packages **fresh linguine** (from the refrigerated case)

¼ cup fresh **flat-leaf parsley**, finely chopped

1 cup grated **Parmigiano-Reggiano** cheese

Place the stock and dried mushrooms in a small pot and bring to a simmer. Let the mushrooms steep for 5 minutes or so.

Bring a large pot of water to a boil for the pasta.

Heat a large skillet over medium to medium-high heat with the EVOO. Add the shallots and garlic and cook for a minute, then add the shiitake and cremini mushrooms and continue to cook until they brown, 7 to 8 minutes. Season with salt and pepper.

Move the mushrooms to the side in the pan and add the butter to the center. Once the butter is melted, add the flour and cook together for a minute, then whisk in the wine. Carefully remove the porcinis from the stock with a slotted spoon; then whisk all but the last few spoonfuls of the stock into the sauce. Coarsely chop the porcinis and add to the sauce. Reduce the heat to a simmer.

Salt the pasta water and add the linguine. Cook for 2 to 3 minutes, al dente. Using tongs, transfer the linguine to the sauce and toss in the parsley and cheese. Adjust the salt and pepper.

# Wild About Mushrooms Sauce with Whole-Wheat Pasta, Arugula, and Hazelnuts

How many opportunities in life do you get to go wild and nutty at the same time?

**Salt**

1 pound **whole-wheat gemelli** or penne pasta

1 ounce **dried porcini mushrooms**

3 cups **chicken or vegetable stock**

¼ cup **EVOO** (extra-virgin olive oil), 4 times around the pan

8 **portobello mushroom caps**, wiped clean and sliced

½ pound **shiitake mushrooms**, stems removed and thinly sliced

4 **garlic cloves**, finely chopped

2 large **shallots**, thinly sliced

5 to 6 fresh **thyme sprigs**

¼ teaspoon **ground allspice** (eyeball it)

Coarse **black pepper**

2 cups **arugula leaves**, shredded

**Pecorino Romano** or other sheep's-milk cheese, for shaving or grating liberally

½ cup chopped **hazelnuts**, toasted

Luxurious option for really earthy mushroom freaks: **truffle oil**, for drizzling

Bring a large pot of water to a boil. Salt the boiling water and cook the pasta al dente.

While the pasta water is coming to a boil, place the porcini mushrooms in a small pot with the stock and bring to a simmer. Turn the heat to low and simmer for 5 to 10 minutes, until the mushrooms are tender.

In a deep skillet heat the EVOO over medium-high heat. Add the portobellos, shiitakes, garlic, shallots, thyme, allspice, and pepper. Cook for 10 to 12 minutes, stirring occasionally, until the mushrooms are dark and tender. Transfer half the mushrooms to a food processor. Draw off a cup of the porcini-flavored stock and add to the processor. Finely chop the mushrooms into a thick puree and add back to the skillet. Use a slotted spoon to lift the porcinis out of the remaining stock; chop and add to the skillet. Ladle in the remaining stock but do not add the last few spoonfuls at the bottom of the pot, as any grit in the dried mushrooms will have settled there. Season the sauce with salt to taste. Remove the thyme stems.

Drain the pasta when it still has a nice bite to it and add it to the mushroom sauce. Cook together for a minute so the pasta can absorb the mushroom flavor. Add the arugula and toss together just until it is wilted. Adjust the seasonings. Top bowlfuls of pasta with cheese and nuts, and with a drizzle of truffle oil if you want to experience true 'shroom madness!

# Creamy Spaghetti and Beans

Risotto meets pasta e fagioli in this Tuscan classic.

5 to 6 cups **chicken stock**
2 tablespoons **EVOO** (extra-virgin olive oil), twice around the pan
2 tablespoons **butter**
¼ pound **pancetta**, chopped into a small dice
4 **garlic cloves**, chopped
1 pound **spaghetti**
1 medium **onion**, chopped
2 **carrots**, peeled and cut into small dice
1 fresh or dried **bay leaf**
5 to 6 fresh **thyme sprigs**
 **Salt** and **black pepper**
1 cup **dry white wine** (eyeball it)
1 (15-ounce) can **Roman beans** or small white beans
1 cup grated **Parmigiano-Reggiano** cheese
 A generous handful of fresh **flat-leaf parsley**, finely chopped

In a saucepot, heat the stock to a boil, then reduce to a simmer.

Heat the EVOO and the butter in a very large, deep skillet over medium to medium-high heat. Add the pancetta and cook for 2 or 3 minutes to crisp. Add the garlic, then the spaghetti, and toast the noodles lightly, 2 minutes. Add the onions, carrots, bay leaf, and thyme and season with salt and pepper. Cook the veggies to soften a bit, 5 minutes or so. Add the wine and allow it to be completely absorbed. Add the beans, then add a few ladles of stock and stir the pasta. Keep adding stock a few ladles at a time, allowing the liquid to be mostly absorbed before adding more, as if you were preparing a risotto. When the spaghetti is cooked al dente, 12 to 15 minutes, stir in the cheese. Adjust the salt and pepper. Turn off the heat and stir for another minute. Remove the bay leaf and thyme stems. Serve in shallow bowls garnished with parsley.

# Citrus Spaghetti with Shredded Radicchio

Brighten up a winter day or get in the spirit of summer with the light, tangy flavors of this simple supper.

**Salt**
1 pound **spaghetti**
¼ cup **EVOO** (extra-virgin olive oil), 4 times around the pan
2 large **garlic cloves**, grated or finely chopped
2 **shallots**, thinly sliced
2 **carrots**, grated
1 medium **zucchini**, sliced into matchsticks or grated
**Black pepper**
Zest and juice of 1 **orange**
Zest and juice of 1 **lemon**
2 tablespoons **butter**, cut into small pieces
2 tablespoons chopped **fresh thyme leaves**, from 4 to 5 stems
A handful of fresh **flat-leaf parsley**, finely chopped
A handful of fresh **mint leaves**, finely chopped
1 small head of **radicchio**, cored and shredded

Bring a large pot of water to a rolling boil and salt it liberally. Drop in the spaghetti and cook al dente.

While the water comes to a boil and the pasta cooks, heat the oil in a large skillet over medium heat. When the oil is hot, add the garlic, shallots, carrots, and zucchini. Season the vegetables with salt and pepper and cook for 10 minutes, stirring often. Add the zest and juice of the orange and lemon, combine, and heat through. Add the butter and swirl the pan to melt it into the sauce, then turn off the heat. Drain the spaghetti and add it to the skillet along with the chopped herbs. Toss the spaghetti for 1 minute to incorporate the veggies and let the pasta absorb the sauce. Serve the pasta in shallow bowls with shredded radicchio on top as a spicy garnish.

USING YOUR NOODLE

143

# Broccoli Rabe and Salami Pasta

We call this one "Rabes and Salames" around the house. Enjoy!

**Salt**
2 bunches of **broccoli rabe**, trimmed and coarsely chopped
1 pound **rigatoni with ridges**
¼ cup **EVOO** (extra-virgin olive oil), 4 times around the pan
4 **garlic cloves**, grated or finely chopped
½ teaspoon **red pepper flakes**
1½ cups **ricotta cheese**
½ cup grated **Parmigiano-Reggiano** cheese, plus some to pass at the table
⅓ pound **salami**—Genoa, sopressata, hot or sweet, or a mix—chopped
**Black pepper**

Bring 2 inches of water to a boil in a deep skillet for the broccoli rabe and bring a large pot of water to a boil for the pasta. Salt the water liberally.

Simmer the broccoli rabe for 10 to 12 minutes, then drain. Return the skillet to medium heat and add the EVOO. Add the garlic and red pepper flakes to the oil and cook gently for a couple of minutes, then add the broccoli rabe and cook for 5 minutes longer, turning and stirring to coat in the oil.

While the broccoli rabe cooks, drop the rigatoni in the boiling water to cook al dente. Just before draining, reserve 1 cup of the starchy pasta cooking liquid.

Combine the ricotta, Parm, and salami in a pasta bowl. Season with black pepper, then stir in the reserved pasta water. Add the broccoli rabe and pasta and toss for 2 minutes to coat the pasta.

# Whole-Wheat Pasta Arrabbiata with Fire-Roasted Tomatoes and Arugula

Whole-wheat pasta is so good for you that I've been taking every opportunity to get it into my recipes. And if you're gonna get healthy, why not start by clearing out your sinuses? The fiery flavors going on here go great with that rich whole-wheat texture.

**Salt**
1 pound whole-wheat **penne** or gemelli pasta
¼ cup **EVOO** (extra-virgin olive oil), 4 times around the pan
4 **garlic cloves**, grated
1 teaspoon **red pepper flakes**
1 small **red onion**, finely chopped
1 tablespoon **aged balsamic vinegar**
1 (28-ounce) can diced **fire-roasted tomatoes**
**Black pepper**
1 cup grated **Pecorino Romano** cheese
4 cups **arugula**, coarsely chopped

Bring a large pot of water to a boil. Salt the water liberally, add the pasta, and cook al dente. Just before draining the pasta, reserve about ½ cup of the starchy cooking water.

In a deep skillet, heat the EVOO over medium heat. Add the garlic, red pepper flakes, and onions and cook for 5 to 6 minutes. Stir in the vinegar, then the tomatoes, and season with salt and pepper. Simmer for 10 minutes over low heat.

Drain the pasta and transfer to a serving bowl. Add the reserved pasta water, the arrabbiata sauce, and the cheese and toss for 1 minute. Add the arugula and toss until it wilts, then serve.

USING YOUR NOODLE

145

# Un-beet-lievable Pasta, Tomato, and Rocket Lettuce Salad

Call Ripley's! Believe it or not, this creamy, golden sweet pasta is to die for! (But you'll want to live on to eat it again!)

8 to 10 **baby golden beets**, greens removed

6 tablespoons **EVOO** (extra-virgin olive oil), plus more for drizzling
   **Salt**

1 pound **rigatoni with ridges** or gemelli pasta

2 large **shallots**, finely chopped

2 large **garlic cloves**, grated or finely chopped

1 (10-ounce) box **frozen petite peas**
   **Black pepper**

1½ cups **ricotta cheese**
   Zest and juice of 1 **lemon**
   A handful of fresh **flat-leaf parsley**, finely chopped

½ cup grated **Parmigiano-Reggiano** cheese, plus some to pass at the table

4 cups washed **arugula** or baby arugula

4 small ripe **plum tomatoes**, chopped

Heat the oven to 375°F. Coat the beets in a drizzle of EVOO and place in a roasting pan. Cover the pan with foil and place in the oven. Roast the beets for 30 minutes, then remove from the oven and let them cool for 15 minutes or until cool enough to handle.

Just before the beets come out of the oven, bring a large pot of water to a boil for the pasta. Salt the water liberally, add the pasta, and cook al dente. Heads up: you will need to reserve 1 cup of the starchy cooking water before you drain the pasta.

While the beets cool, heat 3 tablespoons of the EVOO in a skillet over medium heat. Add the shallots and garlic and sauté for a few minutes until they start to soften, then add the peas. Gently cook until heated through, 3 or 4 minutes, then season the peas with salt and pepper.

Peel the beets and add them to a food processor with the ricotta cheese. Process for 1 minute or until combined into a smooth and golden mixture. Transfer the ricotta to a large pasta bowl and season it with about 2 teaspoons of the lemon zest, salt, pepper, the parsley, and the ½ cup grated Parmigiano. Add the reserved starchy cooking water, the hot pasta, and the peas and shallots. Combine and toss the pasta for a minute to absorb the flavors. Serve immediately.

Toss the arugula with the tomatoes, lemon juice to taste, the remaining 3 tablespoons of EVOO, and salt and pepper. Pass at the table.

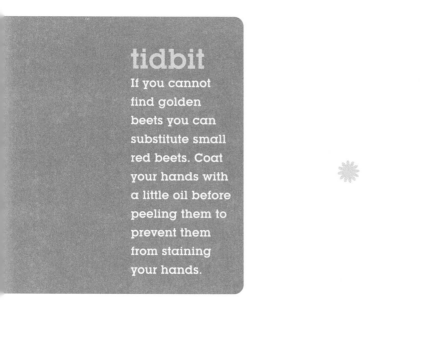

## tidbit
If you cannot find golden beets you can substitute small red beets. Coat your hands with a little oil before peeling them to prevent them from staining your hands.

# Sausage, Mushroom, and Polenta Lasagna

This sausage-y, shroomy lasagna stacks up to any traditional, high-maintenance lasagna in half the time—and
with half the layers.

2 tablespoons **butter**, softened

1 tablespoon **EVOO** (extra-virgin olive oil), once around the pan

1 pound bulk **hot Italian sausage**

6 **portobello mushrooms**, stemmed and cut into large chunks

2 medium or 1 large **red onion**, chopped

4 **garlic cloves**, grated or chopped

**Salt** and **black pepper**

3 cups **chicken stock**

1 cup **whole milk**

1½ cups **quick-cooking polenta**

1 cup shredded **Provolone cheese**

½ cup shredded **Asiago cheese**

1 cup **ricotta cheese**

¼ cup aged **balsamic vinegar**

1 (15-ounce) can **crushed tomatoes**

½ cup fresh **flat-leaf parsley** leaves, a couple of handfuls, coarsely
chopped

1 cup fresh **basil**, 20 leaves, torn or coarsely chopped

Preheat the oven to 400°F. Butter a 3-quart baking dish.

Heat the EVOO in a large skillet over medium-high heat. Once it is
hot, add the sausage and break it up into very small bits with the
back of a spoon as it cooks and browns, about 5 minutes. Add the
mushrooms and cook, stirring every now and then until they begin
to brown, 5 to 6 minutes. Add the onions, garlic, and some salt and

pepper, and continue to cook until the onions start to get tender, 7 to 8 minutes.

While the onions are cooking, bring 2 cups of the chicken stock and the milk to a boil in a large saucepot over medium heat for the polenta. Pour the polenta into the stock and milk, whisking constantly. Cook, still whisking, for about 3 minutes or until really thick. Remove from the heat and add half of the shredded Provolone and Asiago cheese and all of the ricotta cheese, combining thoroughly. Keep warm.

Once the onions and mushrooms are tender, add the balsamic vinegar and stir to deglaze the pan. Cook for 1 minute to reduce a bit, then stir in the remaining cup of chicken stock and the crushed tomatoes and bring up to a simmer.

Pour about two thirds of the polenta into the bottom of the prepared baking dish, spreading it out to cover the entire bottom of the dish. Top the polenta with the sausage and mushroom mixture. Dot the rest of the polenta on top in 12 large dollops. Sprinkle with the remaining Provolone and Asiago cheese. Bake for 20 minutes.

Cut the lasagna into 12 squares and serve 2 per person with room for seconds, scattering lots of parsley and basil across each portion.

# Spinach Spag-zagna with Tomato and Cucumber Salad

Warning! You may drift off into a carb coma after this stick-to-your-ribs supper. No operating heavy machinery!

**Salt**

1 pound **bucatini** (fat, hollow spaghetti)

3 tablespoons plus ¼ cup **EVOO** (extra-virgin olive oil)

2 large **onions**, sliced

4 **garlic cloves**, sliced or grated

4 tablespoons (½ stick) **butter**

4 tablespoons all-purpose **flour**

2 cups **chicken stock** (eyeball it)

2 cups **whole milk** (eyeball it)

**Black pepper**

½ teaspoon freshly grated **nutmeg** (eyeball it)

1 **lemon**, zested and halved

1 cup grated **Parmigiano-Reggiano**, a few generous handfuls

½ cup **dry white wine** (eyeball it)

2 (10-ounce) boxes **frozen chopped spinach**, defrosted (see page 127)

3 cups **whole-milk ricotta**

½ cup fresh **flat-leaf parsley** leaves, coarsely chopped

1 cup fresh **basil**, 20 leaves, coarsely chopped

1 **egg**, lightly beaten

2 cups **shredded mozzarella** cheese

2 tablespoons **Dijon or spicy brown mustard** (eyeball it)

1 tablespoon **Worcestershire sauce**

1 pint **cherry tomatoes**, halved

½ **seedless cucumber**, thinly sliced

2 **hearts of romaine lettuce**, chopped

Bring a large pot of water to a boil over high heat for the pasta. When it boils, salt the water, add the pasta, and cook al dente.

While the pasta water is heating, place a large skillet over medium-high heat with 3 tablespoons of the EVOO, 3 times around the pan. Add the onions and garlic and cook until caramelized, 15 to 20 minutes, stirring every now and then.

Once you have the onions going, make a white sauce. Melt the butter in a medium saucepot over medium heat. Add the flour and cook for 1 minute. Whisking constantly, pour in the chicken stock, then whisk in the milk. Season with some salt, pepper, the nutmeg, and 2 teaspoons of the lemon zest. Bring up to a simmer and cook for 5 minutes. Once the sauce is thick, remove it from the heat and stir in the grated Parmigiano-Reggiano. Reserve the sauce.

When the onions are caramelized, add the white wine and chopped spinach and season with salt and pepper. Cook for about 1 minute and then remove from the heat.

In a bowl, combine the ricotta, parsley, basil, salt, pepper, and egg.

Preheat the oven to 400°F.

Drain the pasta and return it to the pot in which it was cooked. Add three quarters of the white sauce and 1 cup of the shredded mozzarella and stir to combine. Transfer half of the pasta mixture to a medium casserole or baking dish. Spread the spinach and onion mixture over the pasta and then top that with the ricotta mixture. Finish with the remaining pasta and cheese sauce. Pour the reserved white sauce over the pasta and sprinkle with the remaining cup of mozzarella cheese. Transfer to the oven and bake for 15 minutes or until the top is nice and brown.

While the pasta bakes, squeeze the lemon juice into a salad bowl and whisk in the mustard, Worcestershire, salt, and pepper. Whisk in the ¼ cup of EVOO, pouring it in a slow, steady stream. Add the tomatoes, cucumber, and romaine and toss to coat in the dressing.

Remove the lasagna from the oven and serve alongside the salad.

# Lasagna Casserole

Who says you can't please everybody?! This one'll feed the masses and taste even better the next day! Serve this with a simple green salad.

**Salt**
1 pound **campagnelle** (curly pasta; I like Barilla brand)
3 tablespoons **EVOO** (extra-virgin olive oil), 3 times around the pan
1 pound **ground beef, pork, and veal mix**
1 **carrot**, peeled and grated
1 **onion**, finely chopped
4 **garlic cloves**, grated
**Black pepper**
1 (28-ounce) can **Italian plum tomatoes**
1 cup **chicken stock**
½ cup fresh **basil leaves**, shredded or torn
A handful of fresh **flat-leaf parsley**, coarsely chopped
2 cups **ricotta cheese**
½ cup grated **Parmigiano-Reggiano** cheese, a couple of handfuls

Bring a pot of water to a boil. When it boils, salt the water liberally, add the pasta, and cook just shy of al dente, 6 to 7 minutes; there should still be a good bite left to it.

While the pasta water comes to a boil, heat the EVOO in a skillet over medium-high heat. Add the ground meat and break it up into small bits; brown it lightly, 3 to 4 minutes. Add the carrots, onions, and garlic; season with salt and pepper; and cook for 5 to 6 minutes to soften. Add the tomatoes to the pan and use a wooden spoon to crush them up. Add the stock. Simmer for 15 minutes, then fold in the basil and parsley.

Preheat the oven to 400°F.

Drain the pasta and place in a large bowl. Add the sauce and ricotta cheese and mix well, then transfer to a casserole dish and top with the Parmigiano cheese. Bake for 15 minutes to get the top a bit crusty. Serve with a green salad that you can prepare while the pasta is in the oven.

# Crab-Stuffed Shells

Pearls aren't the only treasure to come out of a shell. This is one to save for special occasions. Be sure to use the best crabmeat you can afford.

**Salt**

16 large **pasta shells**

5 tablespoons **EVOO** (extra-virgin olive oil)

2 **shallots**, chopped

3 to 4 **garlic cloves**, finely chopped

1 teaspoon **red pepper flakes**

1 fresh or dried **bay leaf**

3 to 4 fresh **thyme sprigs**

¼ cup **dry sherry** (eyeball it)

1 cup **chicken stock**

1 (28-ounce) can **crushed tomatoes**

**Black pepper**

10 to 12 ounces **lump crabmeat**, picked over to remove any stray shells or cartilage

2 cups **ricotta** cheese

½ cup **Parmigiano-Reggiano** cheese, a couple of handfuls

1 teaspoon **orange zest**

1 teaspoon **lemon zest**

A handful of fresh **flat-leaf parsley**, finely chopped

2 tablespoons **butter**

½ cup **sliced almonds**, a couple of handfuls

1 heart of **romaine lettuce**

½ head of **escarole**

Juice of 1 **lemon**, to pass at the table

Preheat the oven to 400°F.

Bring a large pot of water to a boil. Salt the water and add the pasta shells. Cook for a minute less than the package directions suggest; you want them just shy of al dente. Drain and rinse under cool running water until cool enough to handle. Drain on a kitchen towel.

While the pasta is cooking, heat 3 tablespoons of the EVOO, 3 times around the pan, in a deep skillet over medium heat. Add the shallots and garlic and cook for 3 to 4 minutes, then stir in the red pepper flakes, bay leaf, and thyme. Add the sherry to the pan, stir to combine, then add the stock and tomatoes. Reduce the heat to a simmer and season with salt and pepper. Discard the bay leaf.

In a mixing bowl, gently stir together the crabmeat, ricotta, Parmigiano, citrus zest, parsley, and salt and pepper. Pour a thin layer of the sauce into the bottom of a baking dish. Fill the shells with the crabmeat mixture and arrange the stuffed shells as you work in the baking dish. Pour the remaining sauce down over the shells. Bake to heat the cheese through, 18 to 20 minutes.

While the shells bake, melt the butter in a small skillet over medium-low heat. Add the almonds and toast until golden, 3 to 4 minutes or until fragrant.

Tear the romaine and escarole into bite-size pieces and combine in a salad bowl. Dress with the lemon juice, the remaining 2 tablespoons of EVOO, and salt and pepper.

Remove the shells from the oven and scatter the almonds across the top. Serve 4 shells per person with a little salad alongside.

four

# The Salad Bar

Entrée Salads and
Veggie Mains

# There's no chance of anyone confusing me with a vegetarian,

so you know if the recipes in this chapter—whether a main-course salad or a true vegetarian entrée—keep me happy, they're gonna do the trick for you and your carnivorous friends and family, too. I've re-imagined some of my tried-and-true take-out standbys, like a turkey club and a BLT, as salads, making them a little bit lighter but every bit as satisfying. There are great stuffed vegetable meals that make impressive and hearty entrées whether you're cooking for vegetarian friends or you wanna break from meat.

# Italian Surf 'n' Turf Salad

You'll go to this one again and again. It's good in any season but is an especially welcome summer supper for a hot night.

½ pound **bresaola** (air-dried beef, available at larger delis or in packages on the deli aisle near the prosciutto)

2 **portobello mushroom caps**, gills scraped out with a spoon, thinly sliced

5 to 6 cups **arugula**

2 **celery ribs**, thinly sliced

¼ **red onion**, thinly sliced

Juice of 1 **lemon**

**Salt** and **black pepper**

5 tablespoons **EVOO** (extra-virgin olive oil)

16 **scallops**, muscles removed

Cover a serving platter or 4 individual serving plates with the bresaola slices. Set aside.

In a large mixing bowl, combine the sliced portobellos, arugula, celery, onions, lemon juice, salt, pepper, and 3 tablespoons of the EVOO. Toss to coat and mound on top of the beef.

Heat a large, heavy stainless-steel skillet over medium-high to high heat. Pat the scallops very dry, then drizzle with the remaining 2 tablespoons of EVOO. Let the pan get screaming hot, then add the scallops and cook for 2 to 3 minutes on each side until nicely golden and caramelized. Season the scallops liberally with salt and pepper, arrange them atop the salad (or individual salads), and serve.

THE SALAD BAR

# Green Caponata with Sweet, Creamy Polenta

¼ cup **EVOO** (extra-virgin olive oil), 4 times around the pan

2 **cubanelle peppers**, seeded, quartered lengthwise, and sliced 1 inch thick

1 large **onion**, chopped in 1-inch dice

4 to 6 **celery ribs** from the heart with leafy tops, sliced 1 inch thick

2 small to medium **eggplants**, peeled and cut into 1-inch dice

4 large **garlic cloves**, grated or chopped

**Salt** and **black pepper**

A generous handful of **golden raisins**

¾ cup green **Sicilian pitted olives**, chopped

¼ cup white **balsamic vinegar**

1½ cups **chicken stock**

1½ cups **milk**

1 cup **quick-cooking polenta**

3 tablespoons **honey**

3 tablespoons **butter**

½ cup grated **Parmigiano-Reggiano** cheese, a couple of generous handfuls

½ cup slivered **almonds**

½ cup **flat-leaf parsley**, chopped

1 cup, about 20 leaves, fresh **basil**, chopped

Heat the EVOO in a large, high-sided skillet over medium-high heat. Add the vegetables to the pot as you chop them—peppers, onions, celery, eggplant, and then garlic. Toss to coat the veggies in the oil and season them with salt and pepper. Stir in the raisins and olives and cook until tender, 15 to 20 minutes. Add the balsamic vinegar, stir to combine, and reduce the heat to low.

Meanwhile, bring the stock and milk to a boil. Pour in the polenta and whisk until the polenta masses and thickens, 2 minutes. Stir in honey and butter and stir until the butter melts. Add the grated cheese and salt and pepper to taste and remove from heat. Toast the nuts in a small skillet for a couple of minutes over medium heat until lightly golden and fragrant.

Pile a few large spoonfuls of polenta into shallow dinner bowls and make a well in the center. Fill the well with caponata. Top with lots of nuts, parsley, and basil and serve.

# Caesar-ish Salad and Fried Ravioli

Yet another version of the world's most famous salad!

**Salt**

1 pound **fresh large ravioli** in any flavor that appeals to you, such as seafood, chicken and prosciutto, wild mushroom, or plain cheese

½ cup **EVOO** (extra-virgin olive oil)

1 cup **cornmeal**

1 cup grated **Parmigiano-Reggiano**, or more to taste

Lots of **black pepper**

Zest and juice of **1 lemon**

1 large **garlic clove**, grated or finely chopped

1 tablespoon **Dijon mustard**

1 teaspoon **anchovy paste**

1 teaspoon **hot sauce**, such as Tabasco

1 tablespoon **Worcestershire sauce** (eyeball it)

3 hearts of **romaine lettuce**, chopped

Bring a large pot of water to a boil for the ravioli. Salt the water and cook the pasta until they float to the surface; drain well.

Heat about ¼ cup of the EVOO in a large nonstick skillet with deep sides over medium to medium-high heat. Combine the cornmeal with ½ cup of the Parmigiano-Reggiano and lots of pepper on a plate. Working in batches, coat the drained ravioli with the cornmeal and cheese mixture, shaking off the excess. Fry the ravioli in the hot EVOO until golden, 2 minutes on each side, then transfer to a paper-towel-lined plate to drain. Season them with salt. While the pasta cooks, whisk together the lemon zest and juice, garlic, mustard, anchovy paste, hot sauce, and Worcestershire in a bowl. Stream in the remaining ¼ cup of EVOO, whisking constantly. Toss the romaine with the dressing, then season with pepper and the remaining Parmigiano and toss again. Divide the salad among 4 large bowls and top with crispy ravioli.

# Italian Turkey Club Salad

Take a panzanella bread salad, mix in some turkey cutlet bites, and you've got one satisfying bowlful.

5 tablespoons **EVOO** (extra-virgin olive oil)
4 **turkey cutlets**
  **Salt** and **black pepper**
2 fresh **rosemary sprigs**, finely chopped
¼ pound **pancetta**, chopped
1 large **red onion**, chopped
1 **cubanelle pepper**, seeded and chopped
2 jarred **roasted red peppers**, chopped into bite-size dice
¼ cup good-quality **balsamic vinegar** (eyeball it)
4 **plum tomatoes**, coarsely chopped
2 cups coarsely chopped **arugula**
1 cup fresh **basil**, about 20 leaves, chopped or torn
4 cups cubed **semolina bread**
1 **lemon**, cut into wedges
  **Parmigiano-Reggiano**, for shaving

Heat 2 tablespoons of the EVOO in a nonstick skillet over medium-high heat. Season the cutlets with salt, pepper, and the rosemary. Cook until golden on both sides, 10 to 12 minutes in all.

While the turkey cooks, heat a high-sided skillet with the remaining 3 tablespoons of EVOO. Add the pancetta and sauté for a couple of minutes to crisp. Add the onions and cubanelle pepper and cook for 3 to 4 minutes. Add the roasted red peppers and heat for 1 minute. Add the balsamic vinegar and deglaze the pan, scraping up the bits on the bottom of the pan. Add the tomatoes, greens, and bread to the pan, then turn off the heat and let stand for 2 to 3 minutes so the bread can soak up the juices. Chop the turkey into bite-size pieces and mix into the bread salad. Serve with lemon wedges alongside to squeeze over the salad. Garnish with cheese shavings.

THE SALAD BAR

# Lamb Patties on Fattoush Salad

Fattoush is as fun to make as it is to say. *Fattoush!!* Add these tasty lamb patties and you've got a hearty, healthful dish that just might become a family favorite.

- 3 **pita breads**, torn into pieces
- 1½ pounds **ground lamb**
- 1 cup **full-fat plain yogurt**, preferably Greek-style yogurt
- ¾ cup fresh **flat-leaf parsley leaves**, three handfuls, chopped
- 2 **garlic cloves**, grated with a Microplane or the small side of a box grater
- 1 tablespoon **ground cumin**, a palmful
- 1 teaspoon **dried oregano**, ⅓ palmful
- 1½ teaspoons **sweet paprika**, ½ palmful
- 1 tablespoon **grill seasoning**, such as McCormick's Montreal Steak Seasoning
  Pinch of **ground cinnamon**
- 3 tablespoons **EVOO** (extra-virgin olive oil), plus more for drizzling
- ½ seedless **European cucumber**, cut into bite-size dice
- 1 green **bell pepper**, seeded and cut into bite-size dice
- 4 **celery ribs** with leafy tops, chopped
- ½ large **red onion**, chopped
- 3 ripe **tomatoes**, lightly seeded and diced
- ½ pound **feta cheese**, crumbled
- ½ cup pitted **kalamata olives**, coarsely chopped
- 6 jarred **pepperoncini peppers**, chopped
  Juice of 2 **lemons**
  **Salt** and **black pepper**

Preheat the oven to 375°F.

Arrange the torn-up pieces of pita bread on a baking sheet. Toast in the oven until crispy, 6 to 7 minutes.

While the pitas are toasting up, start the burgers. Use your hands to combine the ground lamb in a mixing bowl with the yogurt, ¼ cup of the chopped parsley, the garlic, cumin, oregano, paprika, grill seasoning, and cinnamon. Score the meat into 4 equal portions with the side of your hand, then form the mixture into 4 patties about 1 inch thick. Preheat a large nonstick skillet with a liberal drizzle of EVOO until the oil ripples. Add the patties and cook for 5 minutes on each side.

While the burgers cook, combine the remaining ½ cup of chopped parsley, the cucumber, bell pepper, celery, red onion, tomatoes, feta, olives, and pepperoncini peppers in a bowl for the salad. Squeeze the lemons over the mixture, pour the 3 tablespoons of EVOO over all, season with salt and pepper, and toss to coat. Add the toasted torn pita and toss again. Let the salad stand while the burgers finish cooking. Taste to adjust the seasonings.

Top mounds of the fattoush salad with the lamb patties and serve.

# BLT: Beef, Leek, and Tomato Salad

Here's another BLT remix with a combo that is just as satisfying as the original!

4 small **strip steaks**, 1 to 1½ inches thick
⅓ cup **EVOO** (extra-virgin olive oil), plus more for drizzling
   **Salt** and **black pepper**
8 **bacon slices**, chopped
2 large or 4 small **leeks**, trimmed of rough tops and roots
1 tablespoon **Worcestershire sauce**
3 tablespoons **red wine vinegar**
2 tablespoons **Dijon mustard**
2 hearts of **romaine lettuce**, shredded
2 big **beefsteak tomatoes**

Set the steaks out at room temp to take the chill off. Heat a grill pan or grill to medium-high. Drizzle the steaks with EVOO and season on both sides with salt and pepper.

Grill the steaks for 10 to 12 minutes total for pink centers, turning twice. Let the meat rest for 5 minutes before slicing.

While the meat cooks, brown the bacon in a drizzle of EVOO in a medium to large skillet over medium-high heat.

Chop the leeks, then soak them in a large bowl of water or separate the chopped leeks by running under water. Dry the leeks in a kitchen towel.

Place the cooked bacon on paper towels to drain and cool. Pour off and discard all but about a tablespoon of the bacon drippings, then add the leeks and cook until they have wilted down, 3 to 4 minutes. Season the cooked leeks with salt and pepper.

Transfer the cooled bacon to a food processor; make sure it has cooled or your dressing will separate. Add the Worcestershire, vinegar, mustard, and some pepper. Combine and, with the processor running, stream in the ⅓ cup EVOO.

Arrange a bed of shredded romaine and thickly sliced tomatoes on each dinner plate. Slice the meat against the grain and arrange the slices on top of the sliced tomatoes. Scatter the leeks over the sliced steak and pour the bacon dressing on the top.

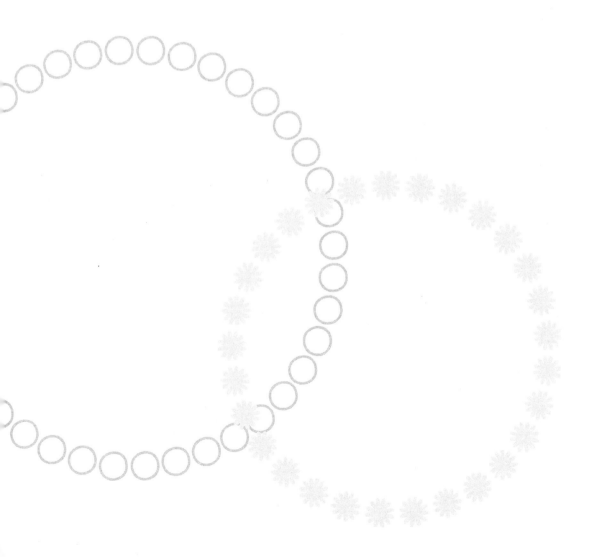

# Grilled Eggplant Roll-ups with Hot Ham

What's purple and pink and grilled all over? You got it— and you're gonna love it, too.

- 1 large or 2 medium firm **eggplants**; you will need 8 eggplant steaks, ¼ to ½ inch thick, as your yield
- ½ cup **EVOO** (extra-virgin olive oil)
  **Salt** and **black pepper**
- 2 cups **ricotta cheese**
- ½ cup grated **Pecorino Romano** cheese, a couple of handfuls
- ¼ cup fresh **flat-leaf parsley**, a generous handful, chopped
- 1 small **onion**, grated or finely chopped
- 3 to 4 **garlic cloves**, finely chopped or grated
- 1 fresh or dried **bay leaf**
- 1 (28-ounce) can **crushed fire-roasted tomatoes**
- 2 pinches of **ground cinnamon**
- 8 slices **capocollo** hot Italian ham
- 8 thin slices **smoked mozzarella**, from a 1-pound ball

Preheat the oven to 375°F.

Heat a large grill pan or grill to medium-high. Trim a long strip of skin off one side of the eggplant so it doesn't roll around on your cutting board. Trim a slice of skin off the first side, then cut the eggplant lengthwise into eight ¼- to ½-inch-thick slices. Pour the EVOO into a dish and use it to brush the eggplant slices; season with salt and pepper. Grill the eggplant slices for 3 minutes on each side, or until tender and seared with grill marks. (You may need to do this in 2 batches.)

While the eggplant is working, stir the ricotta together with the Pecorino Romano and parsley. In a small saucepot over medium to medium-high heat, heat 2 tablespoons of the oil left over from brushing the eggplant. Add the onions, garlic, and bay leaf and season with salt and lots of pepper. Cook for 5 minutes to soften, then add the tomatoes and cinnamon. Simmer for 5 minutes more.

Top each eggplant steak with a slice of ham. Place ¼ cup of the ricotta mixture on one end of each steak and wrap and roll the eggplant. Set the rolls into a small casserole seam side down and top each with a spoonful of tomato sauce and a slice of smoked mozzarella. Bake for 20 minutes, until the ricotta is set and the mozzarella is melted, golden, and bubbly on top. Pass the extra sauce at the table.

# Charred Chili Relleno
# with Green Rice

I am lucky in a thousand ways, but I got even luckier when the best Mexican in NYC opened practically right outside my door! Mexicana Mama serves roasted rellenos; I thought they all had to be battered, fried, and fattening, no? NO! Sadly, the restaurant closes once a week for an entire day and night, so, on Mondays, I make this dish at home. This dish is so health-conscious, you might want to double the recipe, because you can have guilt-free seconds!

4 cups **chicken or vegetable stock**

1 **bay leaf**

2 cups **white rice**

4 large **poblano peppers**

4 to 5 ears of corn or 3 cups frozen **corn kernels**

3 tablespoons **canola or vegetable oil**

1 **red onion**, chopped

1 **jalapeño**, seeded and chopped

4 **garlic cloves**, chopped

1 (28-ounce) can **diced fire-roasted tomatoes**, drained well

1½ teaspoons **ground cumin**, ½ palmful

1 teaspoon **dried oregano** (eyeball it in your palm)
   **Salt** and **black pepper**

½ cup **cilantro leaves**

1 (10-ounce) sack **baby spinach**

4 **scallions**, coarsely chopped
   Zest and juice of 1 **lime**

1 cup shredded **Chihuahua** or Monterey Jack cheese

Preheat the broiler or a grill pan to high.

In a saucepot heat about 3½ cups of the stock with the bay leaf to boiling. Add the rice, then cover the pot, reduce the heat to low, and simmer for 18 minutes or until tender. Discard the bay leaf.

While the rice cooks, place the poblanos under the broiler or on the hot grill and char evenly all over, about 15 minutes.

While the peppers and rice are working, scrape the corn off the cob. To do this efficiently, invert a small bowl and place it in the bottom of a large bowl. Stand the cobs on the inverted bowl and use a sharp knife to slice off the kernels; they will collect in the large bowl. If you are using frozen corn, pop it in the microwave to take the chill off: a couple of minutes on the defrost setting will do it. Drain and dry the defrosted corn by spreading it out on a clean kitchen towel.

Heat 2 tablespoons of the oil in a skillet over high heat. When the oil ripples add the corn, onions, and jalapeño and toss until the vegetables char at the edges and the onions are tender, 4 to 5 minutes. Reduce the heat to medium-high and add the garlic, tomatoes, cumin, oregano, and salt and pepper. Cook for another minute or two, then remove from the heat.

Place the cilantro, spinach, scallions, lime zest, the remaining ½ cup of stock, and the remaining tablespoon of oil in a food processor and puree into a coarse green paste.

Sprinkle the lime juice over the corn mixture.

Split the charred peppers open but not in half with a small sharp knife, then scoop out the seeds with a small spoon. Place the peppers in a shallow baking dish and stuff each pepper with lots of the corn mixture, mounding it out of the peppers. Top each with ¼ cup cheese. Place the stuffed peppers back under the broiler to melt and char the cheese until bubbly and browned, a minute or two.

Stir the green paste into the hot rice and serve with the peppers.

# Sicilian Roasted Stuffed Eggplants

Make them an eggplant they can't refuse. I'm serious; an eggplant has no business packing this much flavor.

2 medium-size **eggplants**
¼ cup **EVOO** (extra-virgin olive oil; eyeball it)
1 medium **onion**, chopped
4 **garlic cloves**, finely chopped
2 **celery ribs**, chopped
1 **cubanelle pepper**, seeded and chopped
1 jarred **roasted red pepper**, chopped
**Salt** and **black pepper**
A handful of **pine nuts**, lightly toasted
2 tablespoons drained **capers**
A handful of **green Sicilian olives**, coarsely chopped
1 (28-ounce) can San Marzano whole **plum tomatoes** or diced tomatoes, drained (Reserve a few tablespoons of the juices.)
1 cup fresh **basil leaves**, about 20, torn or chopped
1 pound fresh **mozzarella** or smoked mozzarella
**Crusty bread**, for passing at the table

Heat the oven to 400°F.

Prick the skin of the eggplants with a fork, place them on a rack in the upper half of the oven, and roast for 20 minutes. Remove the eggplants and set aside for 10 minutes or until cool enough to handle.

Heat the EVOO in a skillet over medium-high heat. Add the onions, garlic, celery, and cubanelle pepper. While they cook, cut up the eggplants. Split the eggplants in half lengthwise and cut away most of the flesh, leaving just a little attached to the skins to hold their shapes. Arrange the eggplant shells on a rimmed baking sheet. Coarsely chop the flesh and add to the skillet with the veggies. Add the roasted red pepper and season the vegetables with salt and pepper. Cook for 5 minutes, then add the nuts, capers, and olives.

Add the whole tomatoes to the veggies along with a few spoonfuls of the juices to just moisten the veggies, using a spoon to break up the tomatoes (skip this step if using diced tomatoes). Add the basil and stir to wilt the leaves into the vegetables. Spoon the vegetable mixture into the eggplant halves. Top with sliced mozzarella and bake for 10 minutes to melt the cheese and set the filling. Serve one stuffed half eggplant per person with crusty bread for mopping.

# Spanish-Style Stuffed Peppers

How fun are stuffed peppers? It's like wrapping up a nice big present and giving it to yourself! What's not to like?

½ cup slivered **almonds**, a couple of handfuls

3 tablespoons **EVOO** (extra-virgin olive oil)

1 cup **long-grain white rice**

1¾ cups **chicken stock**

1 fresh or dried **bay leaf**

4 large **red bell peppers**

1⅓ pounds **all-white-meat ground chicken**
  **Salt** and **black pepper**

1 tablespoon **sweet paprika**

1 medium **onion**, finely chopped

3 **garlic cloves**, grated or finely chopped

4 jarred **piquillo peppers**, chopped, or 2 jarred roasted red peppers, chopped

¼ cup **golden raisins**, a handful, chopped

½ cup **dry sherry** (eyeball it)

1 (15-ounce) can **tomato sauce**

¼ cup fresh **flat-leaf parsley** leaves, chopped

⅓ pound **manchego cheese**, shaved or thinly sliced

Preheat the oven to 375°F.

Toast the nuts in a small pan over medium-low heat until golden, 3 to 4 minutes. Remove from the pan and reserve.

Heat 1 tablespoon of the EVOO in a saucepot with a lid over medium heat. Add the rice, stir to coat with the EVOO, and toast for 2 minutes. Add the stock and bay leaf and bring to a boil. Cover the pot, reduce the heat to low, and cook the rice for 16 minutes. The rice will be a bit tough at the center but it will continue to cook when it's baked in the pepper.

Cut the top off each bell pepper and reserve as a lid. Trim the bottoms of the peppers so they stand upright, taking care not to make holes in the bottoms of the peppers to prevent leaks. Seed the peppers and set aside.

Heat a large nonstick skillet over medium-high heat and add the remaining 2 tablespoons of EVOO. Add the chicken and season with salt, pepper, and paprika. Cook until lightly browned, about 5 minutes, breaking it up into small bits with the back of a wooden spoon as it cooks. Add the onions, garlic, piquillo peppers, and raisins. Continue to cook until the onions start to get tender, 5 to 6 minutes. Add the sherry and deglaze the pan, stirring to get any brown bits off the bottom of the skillet. Add 1½ cups tomato sauce, about three quarters of the can, and reduce the heat to low. Stir until heated through, then add the parsley, almonds, and cooked rice to the skillet. Discard the bay leaf. Stir to combine, then turn off the heat.

Thin the remaining tomato sauce with ½ cup water and pour it into an 8-inch square or round baking dish or cake pan. Set the peppers upright in the baking dish. Fill each pepper halfway with the chicken and rice mixture. Pack some manchego inside each pepper, then fill the peppers the rest of the way with the remaining chicken and rice mixture until the peppers are overflowing by an inch or so. Top with the remaining manchego and set the caps in place. Bake the peppers, uncovered, for 25 to 30 minutes. Serve 1 pepper per person.

# I'll Have the Fish

Seafood, Fish, and Shellfish Suppers

(continued)

# There's an especially big catch of 15-minute meals

in this chapter because I can't think of anything that cooks up faster than a fish fillet; you practically have to *try* to spend more than 15 minutes cooking most kinds of fish! In fact, you could probably transform a bunch of the 30-Minute Meals into 15-Minute if you substitute some simple flavored couscous for the side dish accompaniment. Either way, you'll want to keep a careful eye on your fish to prevent it from overcooking. Nothing is tastier than a crisp, moist piece of fish, and nothing is less appetizing than a dried out fillet! You'll also find lots of Fancy Fake-outs and Date Night Dinners here, because there is just something a little bit special about a beautiful plate of seared scallops or nicely charred swordfish kebabs. If you're really trying to impress, reel 'em in with the stuffed sole or individual Salmon en Croute; dishes that I guarantee will get you raves.

# Shrimp Scampi Verde

Too easy! Too good! I wrote this for Stephanie March to cook up for her hubby, the spicy Bobby Flay. It is herbaceous and ridiculously delicious. Your mate will kiss you for it again and again.

Salt
2 (12-ounce) packages **fresh linguine**
½ cup **chicken stock**
1 cup fresh **basil leaves**, loosely packed, about 20 leaves
½ cup fresh **flat-leaf parsley** leaves, packed, 3 handfuls
15 to 20 fresh **chives**, coarsely chopped
2 cups **arugula** leaves, packed (1 bunch, stemmed and cleaned)
**Black pepper**
Zest and juice of 1 **lemon**
6 tablespoons **EVOO** (extra-virgin olive oil)
1½ pounds **shrimp**, peeled and deveined
4 **garlic cloves**, finely chopped or grated with a Microplane
1 teaspoon **red pepper flakes** (eyeball it)
½ cup **dry white wine** (eyeball it)
2 tablespoons cold **butter**, cut into pieces
**Crusty bread**

Fill a pot with water for the pasta. When it boils, salt it liberally. The pasta will take only a couple of minutes to cook al dente, so add it to the water when the shrimp are about half done (watch for your cue below).

Place the stock, herbs, and arugula in the bowl of a food processor with salt and pepper to taste, lemon zest, and 2 tablespoons of the EVOO. Grind into a coarse paste.

Heat a deep skillet with the remaining ¼ cup of EVOO, 4 times around the pan, over medium-high to high heat. When the oil ripples, add the shrimp and season liberally with salt and black pepper. Toss and cook the shrimp for 3 minutes, then drop your linguine into the boiling water. Add the garlic and red pepper flakes to the shrimp and cook for 1 to 2 minutes more. Deglaze the pan with the wine, then add the green sauce from the processor to the pan. Swirl in the butter and finish the shrimp and green sauce with the lemon juice.

As soon as the pasta is al dente, use kitchen tongs to transfer it from the pot to the skillet with the shrimp and sauce. Toss to work the green sauce through the pasta and serve immediately with the crusty bread for mopping.

# Thai Shrimp Curry with Chopped Lettuce and Basil-Lime Couscous

Make Your Own Take-Out! This one is easy, flavorful, and such an eye-popper to look at, you could even entertain with it! So try it whether you're feeling exhausted or if you're feeling fabulous enough to invite a few friends over.

- 2 tablespoons **vegetable oil** (eyeball it)
- 1 pound large **shrimp**, peeled and deveined with tails removed
- 6 ounces fresh **shiitake mushrooms**, stemmed and thinly sliced
- 3 **garlic cloves**, grated or finely chopped
  1-inch piece of fresh **ginger**, peeled and grated or finely chopped
- 4 **scallions**, white and green parts chopped into 1-inch pieces
  **Salt** to taste
- 1 jarred **roasted red pepper**, chopped
- 2 tablespoons mild or hot **red curry paste**
- 1 cup "light" **unsweetened coconut milk**
- 1 cup **frozen peas**
- 1½ cups **chicken stock**
- 1 tablespoon **butter**
  Zest and juice of 1 **lime**
- 1½ cups **couscous**
- 1 cup fresh **basil leaves**, shredded
- 2 cups chopped **iceberg lettuce**, ½ small head
- ½ cup chopped **peanuts**, to pass at the table

Heat the vegetable oil in a large skillet over high heat. Add the shrimp and toss for 2 minutes, then add the mushrooms, garlic, ginger, scallions, salt, and red pepper and cook for 3 to 4 minutes more, tossing constantly. Stir in the curry paste and coconut milk, reduce the heat to low, and simmer for a few minutes. Stir in the peas and cook just long enough to heat through.

In a saucepot bring the chicken stock, butter, and lime zest to a boil. Add the couscous and stir. Turn off the heat, cover the pot, and let stand. Add the basil and lime juice to the pot and fluff with a fork.

Serve the couscous topped with a layer of chopped lettuce, then a few ladles of red curry shrimp. Garnish with the chopped peanuts.

## tidbit
**Small bags of chopped peanuts are available on the baking aisle.**

# Shrimp with Tarragon Tomato Sauce

Tarragon is a little sweeter and slightly more licorice-y in flavor than basil, but if you *love* tomato-basil sauce, try this for a change.

- 3 tablespoons **EVOO** (extra-virgin olive oil), 3 times around the pan, plus some for drizzling
- 2 **carrots**, peeled and finely chopped
- 2 **celery ribs**, finely chopped
- 3 **shallots**, thinly sliced
- 6 **white mushrooms**, chopped
- 2 pounds large **shrimp**, peeled and deveined
  **Salt** and **black pepper**
- ½ cup **dry white wine**
- 1 (15-ounce) can **tomato sauce**
- 5 to 6 fresh **tarragon sprigs**, leaves stripped and chopped
- 1 **baguette** or loaf of Italian bread, split
- 2 **garlic cloves**, peeled and cut in half

Preheat the broiler.

Heat the EVOO in a large, deep skillet over medium to medium-high heat. Add the carrots, celery, shallots, and mushrooms and sauté until tender, 7 to 8 minutes. Add the shrimp and cook until pink and almost firm, 3 to 4 minutes. Season with salt and pepper, then add the wine to the pan and deglaze, scraping up the bits from the bottom of the pan. Add the tomato sauce and tarragon and stir until heated through.

While the shrimp cook, place the bread halves under the broiler until toasted and lightly charred, a minute or two. Rub the hot bread with the garlic and drizzle with a bit of EVOO. Serve the shrimp and sauce in shallow bowls with hunks of garlicky bread.

# Scallops Bonne Femme and Spinach with Crispy Prosciutto

*Bonne femme* refers to a good wife or good woman, and every bonne femme knows how to make this classic dish. It is the prettiest 30-minute meal I have ever made. Alert my husband: I think I have finally become a bonne femme, too.

- 5 tablespoons **EVOO** (extra-virgin olive oil)
- 2 tablespoons **butter**
- 1 large **shallot**, finely chopped
- 12 **button mushrooms**, wiped clean, trimmed, and thinly sliced
- 1 tablespoon all-purpose **flour**
- ½ cup **dry white wine**
- ½ cup **chicken stock**
- 1 cup **heavy cream**
  A little freshly grated **nutmeg**, to taste
  **Salt** and **black pepper**
- 1 to 2 dashes **hot sauce**
- 4 thin slices **prosciutto**
- 20 large **sea scallops**, trimmed of any connective tissue and patted dry
- 1 cup **plain bread crumbs**
  A handful of fresh **flat-leaf parsley**, chopped
- 1 **garlic clove**, cracked from its skin
- 1 pound triple-washed **spinach**, stems removed

Place an oven rack at the center of the oven and preheat the broiler.

Heat 2 tablespoons of the EVOO and the butter in a small pot over medium heat. Add the shallots and mushrooms and cook for 5 minutes. Add the flour and cook for 1 minute, then whisk in the wine. Cook for 30 seconds to reduce a bit, then add the stock and bring to a bubble. Stir in the cream and cook just until heated through. Season the sauce with nutmeg, salt, pepper, and a couple dashes of hot sauce, then reduce the heat to low.

While the sauce is working, cover a baking sheet with foil. Arrange the prosciutto on the sheet and place it under the broiler for 2 minutes on each side to crisp it up. It will continue to crisp as it cools. Remove the baking sheet from the oven and lower the temperature to 400°F.

Heat a large, ovenproof skillet or cast-iron skillet over high heat. Season the scallops with salt and pepper and drizzle them with 1 tablespoon of the EVOO. Place the scallops in the skillet and sear for 1 to 1½ minutes on each side; they should be nicely browned. Cover them with the sauce, top with the bread crumbs and parsley, and place the skillet in the oven for 6 to 7 minutes, or until brown and bubbly.

While the scallops cook, heat the remaining 2 tablespoons of EVOO over medium heat with the garlic; cook for 1 minute and remove the garlic. Add the spinach and toss until it wilts. Season with salt and pepper.

Serve the scallops with the wilted spinach alongside and top with broken pieces of crispy prosciutto.

## tidbit

A big cast-iron skillet makes all the difference in the preparation and presentation of this dish. If you don't already own one, pick one up; they are very inexpensive and you can find them at the hardware store. Take care of it and it will literally last forever!

# Sea Bass with Herb Butter and a Frisée Salad

Fancy looking, yes, but hardly fussy. Open up your own weeknight bistro, baby!

⅓ cup **EVOO** (extra-virgin olive oil), plus some for the baking sheet

4 (6-ounce) **sea bass fillets**
   **Salt** and **black pepper**

1 stick (½ cup) **butter**

6 to 8 **fresh tarragon sprigs**, leaves stripped and chopped

1 cup **fresh basil**, about 20 leaves, cut into ribbons

8 **fresh thyme sprigs**, leaves stripped and chopped

10 **radishes**

1 large **shallot**, grated

3 tablespoons **sherry vinegar** (eyeball it)

2 heads of **frisée lettuce**, in bite-size pieces
   **Crusty bread**, to pass at the table

Preheat the broiler and set the rack 6 inches from the heating element.

Drizzle a baking sheet with a little bit of EVOO, spreading it out across the surface of the pan. Arrange the sea bass fillets (skin side down, if the fillets have skin) on the baking sheet, drizzle the fish with more EVOO—just enough to coat—then season with salt and pepper. Transfer to the broiler, leaving about 4 inches between the fish and the heating element. Broil the fish for about 6 minutes or until it is cooked through, firm and opaque.

While the fish is broiling, make the herb butter and the salad.

Place a small saucepot over low heat and add the butter. Once the butter has melted, add the chopped herbs and a few grinds of pepper.

For the salad, thinly slice the radishes, arrange them in stacks, and then thinly slice again, giving you thin sticks. Combine the shallot, vinegar, and some salt and pepper in the bottom of a salad bowl. In a slow, steady stream pour in the ⅓ cup of EVOO while whisking to combine. Add the frisée and the radish sticks and toss to combine.

To serve, arrange the cooked sea bass on 4 dinner plates and pour a bit of the herb butter over each fillet. Serve the salad alongside. Brush the crusty bread with the remaining butter.

# Cheryl's Poached Fish

My friend Cheryl gave me this recipe. She made it for her twin girls when they were children, and now that they are young ladies, I bet they make it for some handsome, lucky fellas!

2 tablespoons **butter**
2 tablespoons **EVOO** (extra-virgin olive oil)
1 large **shallot**, finely chopped
3 **garlic cloves**, finely chopped
3 tablespoons drained **capers**
2 teaspoons **Worcestershire sauce** (eyeball it)
¾ cup **dry white wine**
¾ cup **chicken or seafood stock**
4 (6- to 8-ounce) **fillets of flounder** or other white fish
**Salt** and **black pepper**
1 **lemon**, sliced
A handful of fresh **flat-leaf parsley**, chopped
**Crusty bread**, for mopping

In a large skillet melt the butter into the EVOO over medium to medium-high heat. Add the shallots and garlic and cook for 3 minutes. Add the capers, Worcestershire, and wine and allow the wine to bubble up and reduce for a minute, then stir in the stock. Pat the fish dry and season with salt and pepper on both sides. Arrange the fish in the skillet, scatter the lemon slices around the skillet, and poach the fish for 10 to 12 minutes until firm and opaque. Scatter the parsley over the fish, then transfer the fillets and sauce to shallow bowls or deep plates and serve with bread for mopping.

# Five-Spice–Sesame Sliced Tuna and Avocado

This plate is a knockout, fancy restaurant fare in minutes. It's great for entertaining and girls' night as well!

- ⅓ cup aged **balsamic vinegar** (eyeball it)
- 3 tablespoons **honey** (eyeball it)
- ¼ cup **tamari** (aged soy sauce); eyeball it
- 2 **avocados**
  Juice of ½ **lime**
- 2 tablespoons **vegetable oil** (twice around the pan)
- 4 (6-ounce) **tuna steaks**
- 2 teaspoons **Chinese five-spice powder**
  **Salt** and **black pepper**
- ½ cup toasted **sesame seeds**
- ¼ cup chopped **chives**
- ½ head **iceberg lettuce** or napa cabbage, shredded

Combine the vinegar, honey, and tamari in a small saucepan. Bring to a bubble over medium-high heat, then reduce the heat and simmer for 6 to 7 minutes, until syrupy. Remove from the heat.

Halve and peel the avocados, then slice them thick lengthwise. Squeeze a little lime juice over the slices to prevent browning.

Heat the oil in a skillet over high heat. Season the tuna with the five-spice powder, salt, and pepper and cook for 1 to 2 minutes on each side for rare, 5 to 6 minutes for well done, depending on your preference. Combine the sesame seeds and chives in a shallow bowl. Slice the tuna thick and turn each slice in the sesame seeds and chives to coat.

Scatter some lettuce on each dinner plate and top with the tuna and avocado. Drizzle with the balsamic-soy dressing.

# Poached Salmon with Cucumber-Caper Sour Cream Sauce, Green Beans, and Parsley Couscous

Perfect, easy, elegant for company, this meal can also be served at room temperature, so it's extra versatile, too.

- ⅓ **seedless cucumber**, peeled and chopped
- 3 **radishes**, trimmed and chopped
- 3 tablespoons drained **capers**
- 1 **shallot**, finely chopped
- 2 teaspoons grated **lemon zest**
- 3 tablespoons chopped **fresh dill** plus several sprigs
- 1 cup **sour cream**
  **Salt** and **black pepper**
- ¼ cup chopped fresh **flat-leaf parsley** plus several sprigs
- 2 fresh or dried **bay leaves**
- 2 cups **dry white wine**
- 4 (6-ounce) **salmon fillets**
- 1 (15-ounce) can **chicken broth**
- 2 tablespoons **butter**
- 2 cups **couscous**
- 1 pound **green beans**, trimmed (look in the produce section for pre-trimmed beans)

Combine the cucumber, radishes, capers, shallots, lemon zest, chopped dill, and sour cream in a small bowl. Mix well and season with salt and pepper to taste. Refrigerate until ready to serve.

Tie together the whole sprigs of dill and parsley with the bay leaves using kitchen twine. Place the bundle in a medium skillet with the wine. Add the fish to the pan and add enough water to bring the liquid just to the depth of the fish fillets but do not cover them. Bring to a boil, then immediately reduce the heat and simmer for 8 minutes.

In a saucepan, combine the chicken broth and butter and bring to a simmer over medium-high heat. Add the couscous and chopped parsley, turn off the heat, cover the pot, and let it stand for 5 minutes.

Bring an inch of water to a boil in a saucepot. Add the green beans and cook until tender, 5 to 6 minutes.

Serve the poached salmon with lots of sour cream sauce, green beans, and couscous alongside.

# Seared Salmon Fillets with Citrus-Dijon Spinach

I designed this menu for my healthiest friend, Mariel Hemingway, and it contains all of her favorite things in one meal. She *glows* inside and out. Eat it often and maybe you'll glow, too!

- ½ cup slivered **almonds**
- 1 **grapefruit**
- 1 **orange**
- 3 tablespoons **Dijon mustard**
- 4 tablespoons **EVOO** (extra-virgin olive oil)
- 4 (6-ounce) **salmon fillets**, skin removed
  **Salt** and **black pepper**
- ½ **red onion**, thinly sliced
- 1 pound triple-washed **spinach**, stemmed and coarsely chopped

Place the nuts in a dry small skillet. Toast over medium-low heat until fragrant, 3 to 5 minutes. Remove from the heat and reserve.

Zest the grapefruit and orange and place in a small bowl. Juice the orange into the bowl and stir in the mustard. Use a sharp knife to slice off any remaining peel and all the pith from the grapefruit and slice it.

Heat a skillet with 2 tablespoons of the EVOO, twice around the pan, over medium-high heat. Season the salmon with salt and pepper on both sides and add to the hot skillet. Cook for 3 to 4 minutes on each side, or until golden at the edges.

At the same time, heat a second skillet with the remaining 2 tablespoons of EVOO over medium to medium-high heat. Add the red onion and cook for 1 to 2 minutes just to soften. Add the spinach in large handfuls, cooking each addition just until wilted before adding another bunch to the pan. When all the spinach is wilted, season with salt and pepper and stir in the citrus mustard, tossing the spinach to coat evenly. Turn off the heat.

Layer some of the wilted greens and grapefruit slices onto each of 4 plates. Serve the salmon alongside and sprinkle all with the toasted slivered almonds.

# Individual Salmon en Croûte

A few years ago I created an individual-size beef Welling-ton that remains one of my best fake-out meals ever. It looks like it took hours to prepare and really it takes less than 30 minutes. This is the fish version.

I based this dish on a traditional Russian masterpiece called *kulebiaka*, which is made by wrapping a whole side of salmon in puff pastry with rice, sauce, eggs, mushrooms, and herbs. My way provides everyone with an individual pocket of goodness!

2   tablespoons **EVOO** (extra-virgin olive oil)
1   small **onion**, chopped
½   pound **button mushrooms** with stems, trimmed, wiped, and chopped
    **Salt** and **black pepper**
2   tablespoons chopped **fresh dill**
¼   cup fresh **flat-leaf parsley** leaves, a generous handful, chopped
    Juice of ½ **lemon**
1   tablespoon **Dijon mustard** (optional)
2   **hard-boiled eggs**, chopped (you can pick them up at the salad bar in your market)
4   (6-ounce) **salmon fillets**, skin removed
2   sheets **frozen puff pastry**, 11 x 17 inches, defrosted but still cold
1   **egg**, beaten with a splash of water
    Your choice of 1 bunch of **thin asparagus**, trimmed; 1 pound green beans, trimmed; or 1 head of broccoli, cut into florets

Preheat the oven to 425°F.

Heat 1 tablespoon of the EVOO, once around the pan, in a medium nonstick skillet over medium-high heat. Add the onions and mush-rooms, season with salt and pepper, and sauté for 6 to 7 minutes or until the mushrooms are tender and the onions softened. Transfer to a medium-size mixing bowl and stir in the dill, parsley, lemon juice, mustard, hard-boiled eggs, and salt and pepper. Combine thoroughly.

While the mushrooms cook, heat the remaining tablespoon of EVOO in a skillet over medium-high heat. Season the salmon with salt and pepper and sear for 2 minutes on each side. Remove the skillet from the heat.

Lay the puff pastry sheets out on a work surface. If the dough is more than about $\frac{1}{8}$ inch thick give it a gentle roll with a floured rolling pin. Cut each sheet in half crosswise. On each rectangle of dough, place one quarter of the mushroom mixture, then top with a salmon fillet. Lifting the corners, wrap the dough over the salmon, creating a package. Trim excess dough and seal with the egg wash using a pastry brush. Leftover dough bits can be used to decorate the tops of the packages.

Place sealed side down on a nonstick baking sheet and make a small slit in the top of each to let steam escape. Brush with a light coating of the egg wash to give it a nice sheen. Bake for 12 to 15 minutes or until golden brown.

While the salmon bakes, bring 1 inch water to a simmer, salt it, and add the vegetable of choice. Cook until tender but still bright green.

Serve the salmon packets immediately accompanied by your favorite green vegetable.

# Curry-Seasoned Cod with Cool-Spicy Yogurt Sauce

Indecisive? This meal is hot and cold, and oh so tasty, too!

- 4 tablespoons **EVOO** (extra-virgin olive oil)
- 1 small **onion**, finely chopped
- 1 **bay leaf**
- 1½ cups **chicken stock**
- 1½ cups **couscous**
- 2 **plum tomatoes**, halved and lightly seeded, diced
- 4 **cod fillets**, 6 to 8 ounces each, preferably a meaty center cut
  **Salt** and **black pepper**
- 4 teaspoons mild or hot **curry powder**
- 4 slices peeled fresh **ginger**
- 2 **garlic cloves**, cracked away from their skins
- ½ cup fresh **cilantro leaves**, 2 handfuls
- ¼ cup fresh **flat-leaf parsley** leaves, a handful
- ¼ cup fresh **mint leaves**, a handful
  Zest and juice of 2 **limes**
- 1 small **jalapeño**, seeded and coarsely chopped
- ½ cup **plain yogurt**

Heat 1 tablespoon of the EVOO, once around the pan, in a sauce-pot over medium heat. Add the onions and sauté for 5 minutes to soften. Add the bay leaf and stock and bring to a boil. Stir in the couscous and tomatoes, turn off the heat, and cover the pot. Let the couscous stand for 5 minutes.

While the onions and couscous are cooking, season the cod with salt and pepper, then dust each fish fillet with 1 teaspoon curry powder. In a large skillet, heat the remaining EVOO, 3 times around the pan, with the sliced ginger and the garlic over medium heat to infuse the oil, about 2 minutes. Remove the garlic and ginger and raise the heat to medium-high. Add the fish and cook for 3 minutes on each side, until firm and opaque.

While fish cooks, combine the herbs, lime zest and juice, and jalapeño in a food processor. Pulse on and off until finely chopped. Scrape the ground herbs and jalapeño into a small bowl and stir in the yogurt.

Fluff the couscous and remove the bay leaf. Serve the cod on a bed of couscous and top with a dollop of the spicy yogurt sauce.

# Crispy Prosciutto-Wrapped Cod and Caramelized Onion–Asparagus Salad

If you're one of those who don't eat enough fish, try this: wrap it up in ham, man. Bet you can't resist it!

- 6 tablespoons **EVOO** (extra-virgin olive oil)
- 1 large **onion**, chopped
  **Salt** and **black pepper**
- 4 slices **prosciutto di Parma**
- 4 (6- to 8-ounce) **cod fillets**
  **Salt** and **black pepper**
- 1 pound **asparagus**, trimmed and cut on an angle into bite-size pieces
- 1 tablespoon **Dijon mustard**
- 1 tablespoon fresh **thyme leaves**, chopped
- 1 **plum tomato**, seeded and finely chopped
- 1 **lemon** cut into wedges

Heat 3 tablespoons of the EVOO, 3 times around the pan, in a skillet over medium to medium-high heat. Add the onions, season with salt and pepper, and cook until caramel colored, stirring occasionally, 15 to 20 minutes.

Lay the prosciutto slices on a clean surface. Pat the cod dry and season with salt and black pepper. Place a fillet on top of each prosciutto slice and wrap the fish in the ham. Heat the remaining 3 tablespoons of oil in large nonstick skillet over medium-high heat until it ripples. Add the fish and cook for 3 to 4 minutes on each side, until the ham is crisp and the fish is firm.

While the fish cooks, pour 1 inch of water into a skillet and bring to a boil. Add salt and the asparagus and cook for 3 minutes, or until just tender. Drain.

Stir the mustard and thyme into the caramelized onions, then add the asparagus and toss to coat.

Arrange the cod and the onion-asparagus salad on dinner plates and garnish with the chopped tomato. Serve with the lemon wedges.

# Fish with Ginger-Orange-Onion Sauce

Want easy and elegant—GO FISH!

- 4 tablespoons **EVOO** (extra-virgin olive oil)
- 4 (6-ounce) **fish fillets** such as mahimahi, cod, or salmon
  **Salt** and **black pepper**
- 1 tablespoon **ground coriander**
- 1 medium-large **red onion**, quartered and very thinly sliced
- 1 large **garlic clove**, grated or finely chopped
  2-inch piece of fresh **ginger**, peeled and grated or finely chopped
- 1 teaspoon **red pepper flakes**
  Zest and juice of 1 **orange**
- 1 cup **chicken stock**
- 2 tablespoons cold **butter**
- 1 small handful of fresh **flat-leaf parsley** leaves
- 1 pound **green beans**, trimmed (look for pretrimmed raw green beans in the produce aisle)
  Crusty **whole-grain bread**, to pass at the table

Place a high-sided skillet over high heat with about 1 inch of water. Cover with a lid and bring to a boil to cook the green beans.

Place a large nonstick skillet over medium-high heat and add 2 tablespoons of the EVOO, twice around the pan. While the skillet is heating up, season the fish fillets with salt and pepper and the ground coriander. Place in the hot skillet and cook until just cooked through, about 3 to 4 minutes on each side. Remove the fish fillets to a plate and cover loosely with aluminum foil to keep warm. Add the remaining 2 tablespoons of EVOO to the skillet and add the onions, garlic, ginger, and red pepper flakes. Cook for 5 to 6 minutes to soften the onions, then add the orange zest and juice and the stock. Bring up to a bubble, then add the butter. Swirl to incorporate the butter, then stir in the parsley.

While the fish is cooking, salt the water in the skillet and drop in the green beans. Cook for 3 minutes, or until just tender, then drain and season with a little salt.

Serve the fish with lots of ginger-orange-onion sauce on top, and a few green beans and some crusty bread alongside.

# Sea Bass with Creamy Leeks and Soy Jus

From deep under the sea comes another fancy fake-out!

- 3 **leeks**, 3 to 4 inches of tough green tops and roots removed
- 3 tablespoons **EVOO** (extra-virgin olive oil)
- 4 (6-ounce) **sea bass fillets**
  **Salt** and **black pepper**
- ½ cup **cream**
- 3 tablespoons **honey** (eyeball it)
  Splash of warm **water**
- 3 tablespoons **tamari** (aged soy sauce)
- 1 teaspoon fresh **lemon juice**
  Warm sliced **baguette**, to pass at the table

Preheat the oven to 375°F.

Cut the leeks lengthwise, then slice into ¼-inch half-moons. Soak in a large bowl of cold water or wash vigorously in a colander under cold running water, separating all the layers and releasing the grit. Dry the leeks on a clean kitchen towel.

Heat 1 tablespoon of the EVOO, once around the pan, in a large skillet over medium-high heat; use a skillet you can transfer to the oven, or wrap the handle in a double layer of aluminum foil to protect it. Season the sea bass with salt and pepper. If there is skin on the fish fillets, start them skin side down. Cook on one side for 2 to 3 minutes, until crisp, then flip the fillets. Transfer the skillet to the oven for 5 minutes more or until the fillets are cooked through.

While the fish cooks, heat the remaining 2 tablespoons of EVOO in a second skillet over medium heat. Add the leeks and cook until wilted, 5 minutes, stirring often. Add the cream and simmer for 2 to 3 minutes more. Season with salt and pepper.

While the leeks cook, combine the honey, warm water, tamari, and lemon juice in a small pot. Bring to a bubble, then reduce the heat and simmer gently for 5 minutes.

Make a bed of creamy leeks on each dinner plate and top with a fish fillet. Drizzle the soy jus around the plate. Pass the warm baguette at the table.

# Halibut with Puttanesca Salsa

Top meaty halibut fillets with a spicy sauce and you've got a tasty seafood supper for eaters who like to catch *big* flavor!

4   (6-ounce) **halibut fillets**
¼   cup **EVOO** (extra-virgin olive oil), plus more for liberal drizzling
     **Salt** and **black pepper**
4   1-inch-thick slices **crusty bread**
1½ teaspoons **anchovy paste**
2   to 3 **garlic cloves**, grated
1   teaspoon **red pepper flakes**
     Juice of 1 **lemon**
3   tablespoons drained **capers**
½   cup pitted **black olives**, chopped
½   cup fresh **flat-leaf parsley** leaves, coarsely chopped
1   pint **grape tomatoes**, halved, or cherry tomatoes, quartered

Preheat a grill pan or outdoor grill to medium-high heat.

Drizzle the fish with EVOO and season with salt and pepper. Grill the fish for 3 to 4 minutes on each side until firm, cooked through, and nicely marked. While the fish grills, char the bread for 1 minute on each side.

Meanwhile, in the bottom of a medium bowl, stir together the anchovy paste, grated garlic, red pepper flakes, and lemon juice. Whisk in the ¼ cup EVOO in a slow, steady stream. Put the capers on a cutting board and run your knife through them to chop coarsely, then add to the bowl along with the olives, parsley, and tomatoes. Toss and season with black pepper, to taste.

Top each bread slice generously with the puttanesca salsa and arrange a grilled fish fillet on top.

# Tilapia Club Stacks

These BLT stacks have fewer carbs and more protein than the original, and they're too tasty!

- 8 **bacon slices**, center cut
- 2 to 2½ pounds **tilapia** (get 4 large fillets and cut across into 8 equal pieces)
  **Salt** and **black pepper**
- 1 cup **flour**
- 1 cup **cornmeal**
- 1 teaspoon **chili powder**, ⅓ palmful
- 2 teaspoons **ground coriander**, ⅔ palmful
- 2 teaspoons **dried dill** or 2 tablespoons chopped fresh dill (eyeball it)
- 5 tablespoons **EVOO** (extra-virgin olive oil)
- 1 heart of **romaine lettuce**, shredded
- 2 **plum tomatoes**, halved lengthwise then thinly sliced into half-moons
  Juice of 1 **lemon**

Preheat the oven to 375°F. Arrange the bacon on a slotted broiler pan and place on the highest oven rack. Cook until crisp, 20 to 25 minutes. Cut the bacon strips in half so you have 16 halves.

Season the fish on both sides with salt and pepper. Combine the flour, cornmeal, chili powder, coriander, and dill in a shallow dish. Coat the fish with the cornmeal mixture, pressing gently to adhere.

Heat 3 tablespoons of the EVOO, 3 times around the pan, in a large nonstick skillet over medium to medium-high heat. Add the fish and cook until deeply golden on both sides, 8 to 10 minutes total.

While the fish cooks, toss the lettuce and tomatoes with the lemon juice, the remaining 2 tablespoons of EVOO, and salt and pepper.

Layer each serving in a stack like this: a tilapia fillet, 2 crossed half-strips of bacon, a pile of salad, a second tilapia fillet, another bacon criss-cross, and a final mound of salad.

I'LL HAVE THE FISH

# Sesame-Battered Fish Tacos with Seared Cabbage and Avocado Cream

*"Baja Fresh" made fresh in your kitchen.*

1½ pounds **firm white fish**, such as mahimahi or halibut, cut in 1½-inch pieces

**Salt** and **black pepper**

2 teaspoons **ground chipotle powder**, ⅔ palmful

2 teaspoons **ground coriander**, ⅔ palmful

1 cup all-purpose **flour**

3 tablespoons **sesame seeds**

1 teaspoon **sugar**

½ teaspoon **baking powder**

1 bottle **Mexican beer**, such as Dos Equis, 1½ cups

2 tablespoons **hot sauce** (eyeball it)

**Vegetable oil** or other light oil, for frying, plus 2 tablespoons

1 small head of **Savoy cabbage**, quartered, cored, and shredded

1 **red onion**, thinly sliced

2 **limes**

2 **Hass avocados**, peeled, seeded, and chopped

1 **garlic** clove, grated or mashed with salt into a paste

½ cup **sour cream** or heavy cream

12 (6-inch) soft **flour tortillas**, wrapped in a slightly damp towel in a warm oven or microwave until heated through

Pat the fish dry and season with salt and pepper, the chipotle powder, and the coriander.

In a large bowl combine the flour, sesame seeds, sugar, baking powder, and about 1 teaspoon salt. Pour in the beer and hot sauce and stir until the mixture just forms a smooth batter.

Pour about 1 inch of oil into a large, deep skillet and heat it over medium to medium-high heat.

Pass the fish cubes through the batter using forks to help you coat the fish. Allow the batter to fall back in the bowl, then drop the fish into the hot oil. Fry the fish until deeply golden. Transfer to paper-towel-lined plates to drain.

While the fish cooks, heat about 2 tablespoons of oil in a second nonstick skillet over high heat. Add the cabbage and onions and sear the mixture, wilting the cabbage, 3 to 4 minutes. Season with salt and toss. Douse the cabbage and onions with the juice of 1 lime. Turn off the heat.

Add the avocados, garlic, and sour cream to a food processor. If you grated the garlic, add some salt to taste. If you pasted the garlic, the salt is already in your mash. Process the avocado cream into a thick sauce.

Divide the fish among 4 plates and pass the cabbage mixture and avocado cream at the table. Cut the remaining lime in wedges and add one to each plate. Use 3 warm tortillas per serving for wrapping.

# Italian Fish 'n' Chips

A fish dinner you can't refuse. If you love these you should also check out the grilled fish sammies on page 26.

- 4 white, thin-skinned **potatoes**
- 7 tablespoons **EVOO** (extra-virgin olive oil), plus some for drizzling
- 6 **garlic cloves**, cracked from their skins
- 2 tablespoons finely chopped fresh **rosemary**, 3 to 4 sprigs
  **Salt** and **black pepper**
- 4 (6- to 8-ounce) **red snapper fillets**
- ½ cup **cornmeal**
- ¼ cup all-purpose **flour**
- ½ cup grated **Parmigiano-Reggiano** cheese
  Zest and juice of 1 **lemon**
- 4 **plum tomatoes**, halved, seeded, and chopped
  A handful of fresh **flat-leaf parsley**, chopped
- 4 **scallions**, whites and greens, finely chopped

Heat the oven to 500°F.

Halve the potatoes lengthwise, then cut each half into 5 wedges. Place the potatoes on a baking sheet and drizzle with about 3 tablespoons of the EVOO. Add the crushed garlic to the potatoes and sprinkle with the rosemary; season with salt and pepper. Toss the potatoes and garlic to evenly coat in the EVOO and seasonings, then roast for 25 minutes or until tender and golden at the edges.

Once the potatoes have cooked for about 12 minutes, heat the remaining ¼ cup of EVOO in a skillet over medium-high heat. Season the fish with salt and lots of pepper.

Combine the cornmeal, flour, cheese, and the lemon zest on a plate and coat the fish evenly. Add the fish to the skillet skin side up and cook until deeply golden brown on both sides, about 8 minutes total, turning occasionally.

While the fish cooks combine the tomatoes, parsley, scallions, lemon juice, and a drizzle of EVOO in a small bowl. Season the raw sauce with salt and pepper to taste.

Serve the fish with a little raw sauce on top and with the potatoes alongside.

## tidbit
Be sure to choose thin-skinned "new" potatoes for this rather than starchier russets.

# Pan-Roasted Fish with Burst Tomato Sauce and Gnocchi with Tarragon-Chive Butter

This is a beautiful supper that tastes just as good as it looks. You might find yourself coming back to this on special occasions or when friends and family come to town!

1 pint **grape tomatoes**

3 **garlic cloves**, chopped

1 **shallot**, chopped

5 tablespoons **EVOO** (extra-virgin olive oil)
  **Salt** and **black pepper**

4 (6-ounce) **halibut** or sea bass fillets

2 (12- to 16-ounce) packages fresh **gnocchi**

4 tablespoons ($^1/_2$ stick) **butter**

6 fresh **tarragon sprigs**, leaves stripped and chopped

3 tablespoons snipped fresh **chives**

Preheat the oven to 425°F.

Place a large pot of water on the stove and bring to a boil.

Spread the tomatoes on a rimmed baking sheet. Add the garlic, shallots, 3 tablespoons of the EVOO, and salt and pepper; mix to combine; and place in the oven. The tomatoes will burst after about 10 minutes, but continue cooking them for another 10 to 12 minutes to concentrate the flavor.

About 10 minutes before you are ready to eat, season the fish with salt and pepper and heat the remaining 2 tablespoons of EVOO in an ovenproof skillet over medium-high heat. If your fish has skin, place it in the skillet skin side down. Cook for 2 minutes on each side, then transfer the skillet to the oven for 5 minutes.

Salt the boiling water and drop in the gnocchi. Cook for 2 to 3 minutes, until they rise to the surface like fluffy pillows.

Melt the butter in a skillet over low heat and stir in the herbs. Toss the cooked, drained gnocchi with the herb butter, and season with salt and pepper.

Remove the tomatoes from the oven. Mash the tomatoes with a potato masher right on the baking sheet. Top the fish with the roasted tomato sauce and serve the gnocchi alongside.

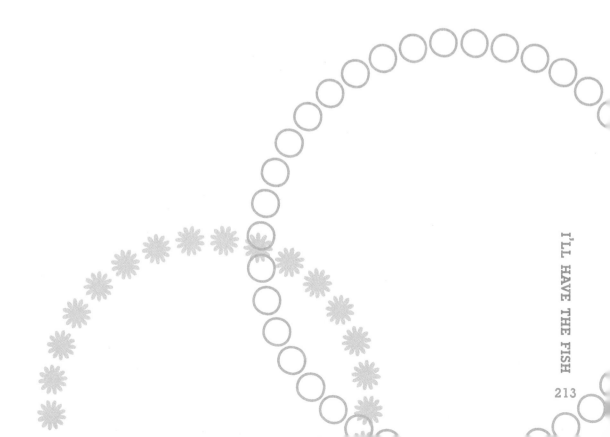

# Cuban Surf and Turf

This one's so SoBe—that's a South Beach–style sexy supper.

 3 cups **chicken stock**
 1½ cups **rice**
 3 tablespoons **ground cumin**, 3 palmfuls
 3 tablespoons **sweet paprika**, 3 palmfuls
 6 tablespoons **EVOO** (extra-virgin olive oil)
 1 teaspoon **cayenne pepper**
   Zest and juice of 2 **limes**
   Zest and juice of 1 **orange**
 2 trimmed **pork tenderloins**, cut into 20 1-inch medallions
   **Salt** and **black pepper**
 20 large **shrimp**, peeled, deveined, and butterflied
 2 tablespoons **hot sauce**
 2 tablespoons chopped fresh **cilantro**
 1 cup chopped **pineapple**
 2 **scallions**, green and white parts, chopped

Bring the stock to a boil in a saucepan with a tight-fitting lid. Stir in the rice, 1 teaspoon of the cumin, and 1 teaspoon of the paprika; return to a boil; then cover and cook over very low heat until tender, about 18 minutes.

Heat a large skillet over medium-high heat with 2 tablespoons of the EVOO, twice around the pan. In a shallow dish combine the remaining cumin and paprika, the cayenne, and the lime and orange zests. Season the pork with salt and black pepper and toss the medallions with the spice mixture to coat them. Cook the medallions in 2 batches, cooking for 2 minutes on each side. Add another 2 tablespoons of EVOO before adding the second batch to the pan. Keep the cooked pork covered with foil to keep warm.

Preheat a large nonstick skillet over medium-high heat with the remaining 2 tablespoons of EVOO. While the skillet is heating, season the shrimp with salt and pepper. Add them to the hot skillet and cook just until they are pink and cooked through, 4 to 5 minutes. Add the lime and orange juices, hot sauce, and chopped cilantro to the pan; toss to combine, then remove from the heat.

Fluff the rice with a fork, then stir in the pineapple and scallions.

Spoon a mound of rice onto each place and arrange 5 medallions beside the rice. Spoon the shrimp and a little sauce onto the medallions.

## tidbit

**Serve individual shrimp-topped pork medallions as an hors d'oeuvre at your next cocktail party, or as a great app for a sit-down supper!**

# Greek Mixed-Grill Kebabs and Pine Nut–Orzo Salad

You don't have to go out to go Greek. This one's easy, healthy, and fun.

**Salt**
½ pound **orzo pasta**
4 **garlic cloves**, grated or minced
4 fresh **oregano sprigs**, leaves stripped and finely chopped
6 fresh **rosemary sprigs**, leaves stripped and finely chopped
¼ cup **green olive tapenade**
1 teaspoon **red pepper flakes**
Zest and juice of 2 **lemons**
⅓ cup plus ¼ cup **EVOO** (extra-virgin olive oil)
1½ pounds **firm white-fleshed fish** such as halibut or swordfish, cut into 12 2-inch chunks
2 pounds boneless, skinless **chicken breast**, cut into 12 2-inch chunks
**Black pepper**
1 small **red onion**, finely chopped
½ cup fresh **flat-leaf parsley** leaves, finely chopped
1 cup **feta cheese crumbles**
¼ cup **kalamata olives**, chopped
2 **tomatoes**, diced
½ **seedless cucumber**, diced
¼ cup **pine nuts**, lightly toasted in a dry skillet for 3 to 4 minutes
8 **Greek hot peppers**

Preheat a grill pan or outdoor grill to medium-high.

Bring a large pot of water to a boil. Salt the water, add the orzo, and cook al dente.

While the pasta works, combine the garlic, oregano, rosemary, tapenade, red pepper flakes, 1 tablespoon of the lemon zest and the juice of 1 lemon with about $\frac{1}{3}$ cup EVOO in a small bowl. Place the fish and chicken in separate shallow dishes or bowls and season with salt and pepper. Divide the dressing between the bowls and turn the fish and chicken to coat evenly. Skewer the fish and chicken on metal skewers. Grill the fish for 6 to 8 minutes and the chicken for 10 to 12 minutes or until firm and the juices run clear, turning the kebabs frequently.

Drain the orzo and combine in a mixing bowl with the onions, parsley, feta, olives, tomatoes, cucumbers, pine nuts, the juice of 1 lemon, $\frac{1}{4}$ cup of the EVOO, and salt and pepper. Serve the orzo salad with 3 pieces each of chicken and fish alongside. Garnish each plate with a couple of hot peppers.

# Mom's Baked Stuffed Sole

My mom makes this for me on my birthday every few years and sometimes we have it on Christmas Eve or New Year's Eve. It's a gift on any night.

8 tablespoons (1 stick) **butter**

1 medium **onion**, finely chopped

2 **garlic cloves**, finely chopped

2 **celery ribs**, finely chopped

¼ **red bell pepper**, finely chopped

4 thin slices **white sandwich bread**, toasted
**Salt** and **black pepper**

¼ teaspoon **ground thyme**

1 cup (8 ounces) **lump crabmeat**, picked through for any stray shells or cartilage

1 tablespoon fresh **flat-leaf parsley** leaves, chopped

4 (8-ounce) **sole fillets**
Juice of 1 **lemon**

1 package **rice pilaf**, such as Near East brand

1 **shallot**, grated or finely chopped

2 tablespoons all-purpose **flour**

½ cup **dry white wine**

1 cup **seafood or chicken stock**

½ cup **heavy cream**
**Cayenne pepper**

Preheat the oven to 400°F.

Melt 2 tablespoons of the butter in a skillet over medium heat. Add the onions, garlic, celery, and bell pepper and cook for 4 to 5 minutes, stirring occasionally. Butter the toasted bread with about 1 tablespoon of the butter and chop it fine, then add the bread to the vegetables. Season the stuffing with salt, pepper, and thyme. Mix to combine thoroughly. Gently fold in the crabmeat and sprinkle with the parsley.

Rinse the sole fillets and pat dry. Squeeze some fresh lemon juice on the fillets. Butter a baking dish with 1 tablespoon of the butter. Arrange the sole with its darker side facing up. Pile the stuffing onto the sole fillets and fold the fish up over the mounded stuffing. Transfer the fish packages to the prepared baking dish and dot each package with a dab of softened butter so it will brown. The stuffing can poke out the sides of the stuffed sole; it's pretty to see and it gets a crusty finish to it. Bake the fish rolls for 20 minutes.

When the fish goes into the oven, prepare the rice pilaf according to package directions.

Once the rice is going, melt the remaining 2 tablespoons of butter in a small pot over medium heat. Add the shallot and cook for 2 to 3 minutes, then add the flour and cook for 2 minutes more. Whisk in the wine, then the stock, and cook until thick, a couple of minutes. Stir in the cream and a couple pinches of cayenne pepper. Serve the stuffed sole packages with the sauce ladled over them and the pilaf alongside.

# Swordfish Rolls and Spaghetti Squash with Spicy Greens and Arrabbiata Sauce

This is a tribute to my mother's side of the family. It seems like all Sicilians know that you deserve a beautiful dinner like this every once in a while; I'm here to help you get what you deserve without breaking a sweat.

- 1 large **spaghetti squash**
- 6 tablespoons **EVOO** (extra-virgin olive oil), plus some for drizzling
- 7 **garlic cloves**, cracked away from their skins
- 1 teaspoon **red pepper flakes**
- 1 (28-ounce) can whole **plum tomatoes**, preferably San Marzano
  **Salt** and **black pepper**
- 1 **lemon**
- ½ cup fresh **flat-leaf parsley** leaves
- 1 **orange**
- ½ cup fresh **basil leaves**, 10 to 12 leaves, thinly sliced
- ¾ cup pitted **black olives**, coarsely chopped
- 3 tablespoons **capers**, coarsely chopped
- 2½ pounds **thin swordfish steaks**, ½ inch thick
- 1 bunch of **watercress** or arugula, tough stems removed, coarsely chopped
- 1 cup grated **Parmigiano-Reggiano** cheese

Preheat the oven to 400°F.

Cut the spaghetti squash in half and scrape out the seeds. Drizzle a baking sheet with some EVOO then drizzle EVOO over the squash itself. Place the squash on the sheet, cut side down, and roast for 45 minutes or until tender.

In a small saucepot, heat 3 tablespoons of the EVOO over medium-low heat. Grate in 3 garlic cloves, add the red pepper flakes, and cook together for a couple of minutes. Stir in the tomatoes, crushing them in your hand as you drop them into the pot. Season with salt and pepper, cover, and simmer over low heat until ready to serve.

Grate the zest of the lemon onto a cutting board. Chop the remaining 4 garlic cloves and the parsley, then add the lemon zest and continue working your knife through them until all are finely chopped and combined well. You'll use this gremolata mixture to season your fish.

In a small bowl, combine the zest of the orange with the basil leaves, olives, and capers. This will be the stuffing mixture.

Remove the skin from the swordfish as well as any very dark tissue from along the bloodline of the fish. Gently pound the fish between 2 layers of wax paper or plastic wrap to ⅛ inch thickness. Remove the wax paper or plastic wrap and cut the fish into 3-inch-wide strips no more than 5 inches long. You should have a minimum of 12 strips. Dust the fish strips with salt, pepper, and gremolata. Top each strip of fish with a portion of the stuffing mixture. Roll up the strips tight and set aside, seam side down.

Heat the remaining 3 tablespoons of EVOO in a large nonstick skillet over medium to medium-high heat. Add the fish rolls, seam side down, and cook until deeply golden on all sides and cooked through, 8 to 10 minutes. Squeeze the juice of ½ orange and ½ lemon over the top of the rolls and turn off the heat.

Take the squash out of the oven and, holding the squash in an oven mitt, use a fork to shred the squash right in the shell. Dress the squash with a drizzle of EVOO, salt, and pepper and add the chopped greens and cheese. Pile the squash on dinner plates and top with the spicy red sauce. Serve 3 swordfish rolls alongside the squash.

# Shrimp and Bread Bowls and Olive-Pesto Dressed Tomatoes

One of the many dishes my Grandpa Emmanuel used to make to bring his ten kids running to the dinner table was shrimp in garlic oil. He made it in a huge pot, a big, bubbling cast-iron cauldron full of garlic and oil and pounds of shrimp. The kids would fight each other, jockeying for room at the pot's edge so they could be the first to jam their big, crusty chunk of bread down into the oil and juices—the best part! This dish has all of that going for it—in less than 15 minutes.

- 1 loaf **semolina or chewy bread**, torn into large pieces
- ½ cup **EVOO** (extra-virgin olive oil)
- 2 teaspoons **anchovy paste**
- 2 pounds large **shrimp**, peeled and deveined
- 6 **garlic cloves**, grated or chopped
- 1 teaspoon **red pepper flakes**
  **Salt** and **black pepper**
- 3 tablespoons **capers**
- ½ cup **dry white wine** (eyeball it)
- 1 cup **seafood stock**, clam juice, or chicken stock
  Juice of 1 **lemon**
- 2 tablespoons cold **butter**
  A generous handful of fresh **flat-leaf parsley**, chopped
- 6 **plum tomatoes**, sliced
- 1 small **red onion**, thinly sliced
- ¼ cup **olive tapenade**
- ¼ cup **store-bought pesto**

Preheat the oven to 375°F.

Arrange the bread on a baking sheet and toast until crusty all over, about 10 minutes.

Heat about ¼ cup of the EVOO in a large skillet over medium-high to high heat. Stir in the anchovy paste until it dissolves into the oil. Add the shrimp and cook for 1 to 2 minutes, then add the garlic, red pepper flakes, salt, pepper, and capers. Cook for 3 to 4 minutes more. Add the wine and cook for a minute to reduce. Add the stock and bring to a bubble, then add the lemon juice, butter, and parsley and stir for 1 minute to incorporate.

While the shrimp cook, arrange the tomatoes on a large plate or platter and scatter the onion slices on top. Stir together the tapenade and pesto and drizzle over the tomatoes and red onions.

Place some of the bread chunks in each of 4 serving bowls and drizzle with the remaining ¼ cup of EVOO. Top with the shrimp and pan juices. Put an empty bowl on the table to collect tails, and serve the salad on the side.

six

# Who You Callin' Chicken?

## The Best of the Bird, from Drumsticks to Turkey and Eggs

(continued)

# The number one protein—chicken.

Every cook strives to keep reinventing the perfect chicken dinner and a good friend to any quick cook is boneless, skinless breasts that we all reach for once a week or more. If you've only got 15 minutes, why not turn them into the fastest lemon poppy chicken with couscous ever known to man? Another day mix it up with some ground chicken or turkey, boneless thighs, or chicken sausages—you've got plenty of choices in every category. You can even make a roast bird in under an hour. Okay, sure, it's a Cornish hen, but you'll still be putting on the kind of Norman Rockwell Sunday dinner spread that you thought had to take all day, and believe me, once it gets going in the oven, you'll have plenty of time to watch *60 Minutes*. And if you need a dose of Thanksgiving in March, have no fear, it's only 30 minutes away. Trust me, they're going to flock to the table for these.

# Polenta Egg Bake and Roasted Sausages with Vinegar and Grapes

The eggs here are a new version of bird in a nest—the nest being polenta. The sausage part of the dish dates back to Columbus. It's an oldie but goodie and is better than ever when served with these eggs.

Softened **butter**, for greasing the muffin tins
¾ cup **milk**
¾ cup **chicken stock**
4 **sweet Italian sausages**
4 **hot Italian sausages**
1 pound seedless **black or red grapes**
3 tablespoons **EVOO** (extra-virgin olive oil), plus some for drizzling
**Black pepper**
1 cup good-quality aged **balsamic vinegar**—you don't have to go too pricey
½ cup **quick-cooking** polenta
1 cup shredded **Asiago** cheese
**Salt**
6 **eggs**
6 ounces **arugula**
½ cup fresh **basil**, about 10 leaves, torn
Juice of 1 **lemon**

Preheat the oven to 425°F.

Butter a nonstick regular-size muffin tin, the 6-cupper.

In a medium stockpot bring the milk and stock to a boil over medium heat.

While the milk and stock are coming to a bubble, prick the sausages in several places with a fork. Place the sausages and grapes in a baking dish and drizzle with 2 tablespoons of the EVOO, then season with pepper. Pour the balsamic over the dish and pop the sausages into the oven to roast for 20 to 25 minutes.

Slowly whisk the polenta into the bubbling milk and stock, and continue whisking until it begins to thicken and resemble hot oatmeal, about 3 minutes. Turn off the heat and stir in the cheese. Season with salt and pepper.

Divide the polenta among the muffin cups, filling them only halfway. Form a well in each by using the back of a spoon to push the polenta up the side of the cup until it reaches the top rim. Crack an egg into each nest of polenta. Bake for 18 to 20 minutes; the yolk will still be a little runny. Remove the muffin tin from the oven and let the nests sit for a couple of minutes.

Toss the arugula and basil with the lemon juice and remaining tablespoon of EVOO to coat lightly, then season with salt and pepper.

To serve, run a small butter knife around the edges of each polenta nest to loosen from the muffin tin. Gently help them out of the muffin tin with a fork.

Serve 2 sausages per person, 1 each hot and sweet, with some grapes and thickened balsamic drippings spooned over the top. Place one or two egg nests and some of the greens alongside.

## tidbit

Muffin tins hold 6 portions so if you're serving 4, 2 people will get 2 egg nests while 2 get 1, or everyone gets 1½—your call. I could eat 4 all by myself, easy!

# Omelet Calzone

Eggs? Cheese? 'Nuf said—I'm there! Note this serves 1.

2 tablespoons **EVOO** (extra-virgin olive oil), twice around the pan
1 **garlic clove**, peeled and crushed
¼ cup **ricotta cheese**
1 tablespoon fresh **flat-leaf parsley**, chopped
1 teaspoon grated **lemon zest**
2 whole **eggs** plus 2 **egg whites**
Splash of **milk**
**Salt** and **black pepper**
¼ cup shredded **mozzarella** or **provolone** cheese

Preheat a 6-inch skillet over medium heat with the EVOO. Add the garlic and cook until lightly browned, about 2 minutes. Remove the garlic clove and discard; you want the flavor, not the clove, in your calzone.

Meanwhile, mix together the ricotta, parsley, and lemon zest.

Whisk together the whole eggs, milk, salt, and pepper. Beat the egg whites until they form soft peaks. Gently stir the whites into the egg mixture and pour into the warm garlic oil.

Using a heat-proof rubber spatula, stir the eggs, letting the uncooked part settle to the bottom of the pan, until they firm up, 3 to 4 minutes. To flip the omelet, place a plate larger than the skillet over the skillet and invert both together. Lift off the skillet and slide the omelet from the plate back into the skillet to brown the second side. Spread the ricotta cheese mixture over the entire omelet, and sprinkle one half with the mozzarella. Gently fold over to create a half-moon, or calzone, shape. Cover the skillet with a lid or foil and heat for a minute or so to melt the cheese. Serve immediately.

# Lemon Poppy Chicken with Mint and Green Pea Couscous

Huge flavors! This menu turns any night into springtime.

- ¼ cup **EVOO** (extra-virgin olive oil), 4 times around the pan
- 1½ pounds thin **chicken breast cutlets**, cut into bite-size dice
  **Flour**, for dredging
  **Salt** and **black pepper**
  Zest of 2 **lemons**
- 2 tablespoons **poppy seeds**, a couple of palmfuls
- 3 cups **chicken stock**
  Juice of 1 **lemon**
- 2 tablespoons **butter**
- 1½ cups **couscous**
- 1 (10-ounce) package **frozen petite peas**
- ½ cup **fresh basil**, 10 to 12 leaves, chopped or torn
- ¼ cup **fresh mint leaves**, a generous handful, chopped

Heat the EVOO in large shallow skillet over medium-high heat until the oil ripples. Dredge the chicken lightly in the flour, add to the skillet, and season liberally with salt and pepper. Brown for a couple of minutes on one side, then turn the chicken pieces and add the lemon zest to the skillet and sprinkle in the poppy seeds. Continue to cook until the chicken is evenly golden brown in color, 6 to 7 minutes. In the last minute or two of cooking, stir in 1½ cups of the chicken stock, the lemon juice, and 1 tablespoon of the butter.

While the chicken cooks, bring the remaining 1½ cups of chicken stock and 1 tablespoon of butter to a boil in a saucepot. Add the couscous and peas, stir, cover the pot, and turn off the heat. Let stand for 5 minutes, then fluff with a fork and mix in the basil and mint. Serve the lemon poppy chicken on a bed of the couscous.

WHO YOU CALLIN' CHICKEN?

# Grilled Chicken Sausages with Pumpkin Polenta

Use any flavor sausage you like best, such as sun-dried tomato–basil or wild mushroom; just make sure they are the type that come fully cooked.

- 8 **chicken sausages**, heat-and-serve variety
- 3 tablespoons **EVOO** (extra-virgin olive oil)
- 2 cups **chicken stock**
- 2½ cups **whole milk**
- 2 tablespoons **butter**
- 1½ cups **quick-cooking polenta**
- ½ cup grated **Asiago** cheese, a couple of generous handfuls
- 1 (14-ounce) can **pumpkin puree** or 1 (10-ounce) package frozen butternut squash, defrosted
- ¼ teaspoon freshly grated **nutmeg** (eyeball it)
  Pinch of ground **cinnamon**
  Lots of **salt** and **black pepper**
- 3 tablespoons **honey**
- 1 head of **radicchio**, cored and shredded
- 2 heads of **Belgian endive**, shredded
- 1 cup **arugula**, chopped
- ½ small **red onion**, thinly sliced
  Juice of 1 **lemon**

Prick the skins of the sausages in several places with a fork. Place them in a large skillet and add ½ to ¾ inch water and 1 tablespoon of the EVOO, once around the pan. Place the skillet over high heat and bring to a boil, then reduce the heat to medium high and cook until the water has cooked off. Continue to cook until the casings crisp. The water will boil away and heat sausages through in about 7 to 8 minutes; the casings will crisp in just a minute or two longer.

Combine the stock, milk, and butter in a medium saucepot. Cover and bring to a boil, then reduce the heat to a simmer. Whisk in the polenta and cook until it forms a mass, 3 to 4 minutes, stirring often. When it begins to really thicken up, stir in the grated cheese, pumpkin, nutmeg, cinnamon, salt, pepper, and honey. Cook for 2 minutes more to heat through, stirring once or twice.

In a salad bowl, toss the radicchio, endive, arugula, and onions together with the lemon juice and the remaining 2 tablespoons of EVOO, and salt and pepper to taste. Serve the sausages, 2 per person, with a mound of greens and creamy-smooth piles of polenta alongside.

# Ham-and-Cheese–Stuffed Chicken Cutlets

Cordon bleu lightens up.

4 (6-ounce) boneless, skinless **chicken breasts**
3 tablespoons **EVOO** (extra-virgin olive oil), plus more for drizzling
5 to 6 fresh **thyme sprigs**, leaves stripped and chopped
1 **lemon**, zested and halved
¼ cup fresh **flat-leaf parsley**, a generous handful, chopped
4 slices **prosciutto cotto** or rosemary ham (Citerio makes a good one)
4 slices **Fontina** cheese, about 4 ounces
   **Salt** and **black pepper**
½ cup **dry white wine**
1 pound **asparagus**, trimmed

Line up the chicken breast pieces on a work surface with the pointed ends closest to you. Place your hand flat across the top of each breast and use a sharp knife to cut horizontally into the meat, working your way down to the tip end; do not cut all the way through. You just want to be able to open up the breast like a book. Cover the butterflied breasts with plastic or wax paper and gently pound out to ¼ inch with a small skillet; a couple of gentle whacks will do it.

Preheat a large skillet over medium-high heat with 3 tablespoons of EVOO, 3 times around the pan.

Combine the chopped thyme with a couple of teaspoons of lemon zest and the parsley. Sprinkle the inside of each chicken breast with the thyme–lemon zest–parsley mixture. Add a folded slice of prosciutto cotto or rosemary ham and Fontina cheese to each, then fold up the breasts again. Season the stuffed chicken on both sides with salt and pepper.

Add the seasoned stuffed chicken to the hot skillet and brown for 5 minutes. Carefully flip the chicken over, add the wine, and cook for 3 to 4 minutes more.

While chicken cooks, bring 1 inch of water to a boil in a skillet. Salt the water and cook the asparagus for 3 to 4 minutes, until just tender. Drain and dress with the juice of ½ lemon and a drizzle of EVOO.

Arrange a few spears of asparagus on each dinner plate and top with a stuffed chicken breast. Spoon some of the pan juices over each serving.

# Balsamic Chicken with Pesto Gravy and Bitter Greens

This was my very first 15-minute meal. Response was so great, I challenged myself to write more; the rest is history.

2 tablespoons **balsamic vinegar**
4 tablespoons **EVOO** (extra-virgin olive oil)
**Salt** and **black pepper**
4 small boneless, skinless **chicken breasts**
About 6 cups **arugula**, thoroughly washed and dried
Juice of 1 **lemon**
2 tablespoons **butter**
2 tablespoons all-purpose **flour**
1½ cups **chicken stock**
⅓ cup **heavy cream** or half-and-half (eyeball it)
¼ cup **store-bought pesto**
**Parmigiano-Reggiano** shavings, made with a vegetable peeler

In a bowl, combine the vinegar, 2 tablespoons of the EVOO, and salt and pepper to taste. Add the chicken and turn to coat.

Heat a large skillet over medium-high heat with 1 tablespoon of the EVOO. Add the chicken and cook for 5 minutes on each side.

While the chicken is cooking, in a large bowl combine the arugula, lemon juice, a healthy drizzle of EVOO, and salt and pepper to taste.

Remove the chicken to a cutting board. Add the butter to the skillet, and when it has melted, add the flour and cook for a minute or so. Whisk in the chicken stock and cream and bring up to a simmer to thicken. Remove from the heat and stir in the pesto.

Slice the chicken and arrange on dinner plates. Pour the pesto gravy over the chicken, then top with the arugula and cheese shavings.

# Walnut Chicken with Sherry and Rice Pilaf with Chives

This looks like take-out food, but you'll do a double take on the sophisticated taste in this dish.

tidbit

Serve the chicken with a little rice spooned on top. Mix the rice in as you eat the dish so it doesn't bloat and absorb all the sauce.

1 package **rice pilaf mix** such as Near East brand

2 **leeks**

3 tablespoons **vegetable** or peanut oil

1½ to 2 pounds boneless, skinless **chicken**, all white meat or a combination of white and dark

    2-inch piece of fresh **ginger**, peeled and grated

3 large **garlic cloves**, grated or finely chopped

2 red **bell peppers**, seeded and cut into bite-size cubes

1 (8-ounce) can sliced **water chestnuts**, drained

    **Black pepper**

½ cup **dry sherry** (eyeball it)

¼ to ⅓ cup **tamari** (aged soy sauce)

1 cup **walnut halves**, toasted

3 to 4 tablespoons chopped or snipped fresh **chives**

Cook the rice according to the package directions, about 20 minutes.

Trim the leeks of rough tops and root ends. Cut the leeks lengthwise, then slice into ½-inch-thick half-moons. Swish the leeks in a large bowl of ice water, then dry on a kitchen towel.

Heat the oil in a large skillet over high heat. Add the chicken and brown the meat on all sides, 4 to 5 minutes. Add the ginger, garlic, leeks, and bell peppers and sauté for another 3 to 4 minutes, tossing frequently. Add the water chestnuts, black pepper, and sherry and cook for a minute to reduce the sherry, then add tamari to taste and the walnuts. Season with black pepper.

Fluff the pilaf with a fork and stir in the chives. Serve with the chicken.

# Chicken à la Queen

The queen I had in mind when I dreamed up this recipe is Barbara Walters, an absolute queen of television journalism. Sadly, a scheduling conflict kept her from tasting it, but this one is for you, BW. Long live the queen!

8 frozen **puff pastry shells**, such as Pepperidge Farm brand

2 tablespoons **EVOO** (extra-virgin olive oil), twice around the pan

4 **celery ribs** from the heart with leafy tops, thinly sliced on an angle

1 large **onion**, chopped

4 medium **carrots**, thinly sliced on an angle

1 fresh or dried **bay leaf**
**Salt** and **black pepper**

½ red **bell pepper**, halved lengthwise then thinly sliced

3 tablespoons **butter**

3 tablespoons all-purpose **flour**

½ cup **white wine**

1 quart (4 cups) **chicken stock**

1½ pounds boneless, skinless **chicken breasts** or tenderloins, cut into bite-size pieces

½ pound thin **asparagus**, trimmed, then cut into 1-inch pieces on an angle

1 cup **heavy cream**

1 cup frozen **petite peas**

5 to 6 fresh **tarragon sprigs**, leaves stripped and chopped

Preheat the oven for the puff pastry shells according to the package directions. Arrange the shells on a nonstick baking sheet and bake until golden. Let cool.

Meanwhile, place a large deep-sided skillet over medium-high heat with the EVOO. Add the celery, onions, carrots, and bay leaf and season with salt and pepper. Cook the vegetables, stirring frequently, for 6 to 7 minutes, until they become tender. Add the bell pepper and continue to cook for an additional 2 minutes. Scoot the veggies over to the sides of the pan and add the butter to the center. Once the butter has melted, add the flour and cook for about a minute. Whisk in the wine, cook for 30 seconds to reduce it a bit, then whisk in the chicken stock. Bring the liquid up to a bubble, reduce the heat to simmer, and add the chicken. Poach the chicken pieces for 7 to 8 minutes, then add the asparagus and simmer for 2 minutes more. Stir in the cream. Add the peas and tarragon and stir to combine. Discard the bay leaf. Adjust the salt and pepper to taste.

Place 2 shells on each dinner plate and ladle the chicken mixture over the tops. Garnish with the pastry lids and serve. Dinner fit for a queen!

# Piquillo Pepper Chicken with Spanish Rice

Say "piquillo pepper" ten times fast. It doesn't take much longer than that to make this simple Spanish dish.

**tidbit**
Piquillo peppers are native to Spain. You can find them in jars on the imported food aisle or with the Latin foods. Piquillos have a more elongated shape than regular roasted red peppers, but they can be used interchangeably.

3 cups **chicken stock**
Pinch of **saffron threads** or 1 envelope saffron powder
½ teaspoon **ground turmeric**
A small handful of **golden raisins**
3 tablespoons **EVOO** (extra-virgin olive oil)
1½ cups **white rice**
4 boneless, skinless **chicken breasts**
**Salt** and **black pepper**
1 jar red **roasted piquillo peppers**, drained well and sliced
½ cup **dry sherry**
2 tablespoons **butter**, cut into small pieces
½ cup chopped fresh **flat-leaf parsley**
A handful of sliced **almonds**, lightly toasted

Place the stock, saffron, turmeric, raisins, and a tablespoon of the EVOO in a saucepot and bring to a boil. Add the rice, stir, and cover the pot, then simmer until tender, about 18 minutes.

While the rice cooks, heat the remaining 2 tablespoons of EVOO, twice around the pan, in a large skillet over medium-high heat. Season the chicken liberally with salt and pepper and cook for 6 minutes on each side, until lightly browned. Remove the chicken to a plate. Add the piquillo peppers to the pan and heat them through for a minute, then stir in the sherry and cook for a minute or two. Add the butter and half the parsley and turn off the heat, stirring to melt the butter. Spoon the peppers and sauce over the chicken.

Add the remaining parsley and almonds to the rice and fluff with a fork. Serve the rice alongside the chicken.

# Ginger-Garlic Chicken Stir-Fry with Soy-Sesame Noodles

Face it, your kitchen drawer has enough of those duck sauce and mustard packets. It's time to make your own take-out! That way you leave out all the extra oil and MSG and get more of the good stuff, in about the same time.

Salt
1 pound **spaghetti**
3 tablespoons **vegetable oil** (eyeball it)
¾ pound **chicken cutlets**, cut into very thin strips
2-inch piece of fresh **ginger**, peeled and grated
6 **garlic cloves**, finely chopped
10 or 12 **shiitake mushrooms**, stemmed and thinly sliced
1 small head or ½ large head of **napa cabbage**, shredded
1 bunch of **scallions**, trimmed and chopped into 2-inch pieces
1 teaspoon **coarse black pepper**, ⅓ palmful
⅓ cup **tamari** (aged soy sauce), eyeball it
2 tablespoons **sesame oil**
2 tablespoons **toasted sesame seeds**

Bring a large pot of water to a boil and salt it. Add the spaghetti and cook it al dente.

While the pasta cooks, heat the vegetable oil in a large nonstick skillet over high heat until the oil ripples. Add the chicken and stir-fry until golden, 3 to 4 minutes. Add the ginger, garlic, shiitakes, cabbage, and scallions and stir-fry for another 2 to 3 minutes. Season the stir-fry with salt and lots of black pepper and turn off the heat.

Place the tamari and sesame oil in a bowl and add the hot pasta. Toss to coat the pasta, then sprinkle with the sesame seeds. Divide the pasta among 4 shallow bowls and top each serving with some of the stir-fry.

WHO YOU CALLIN' CHICKEN?

# Tarragon-Cream Chicken and Polenta Pot Pies

Honestly, chicken pot pie has gotta be in the comfort-food hall of fame. Here, our old friend quick-cooking polenta gets us that famous pot-pie comfort just as soon as we need it!

2 tablespoons **EVOO** (extra-virgin olive oil), twice around the pan

1½ pounds **chicken tenders**, chopped

2 **carrots**, chopped

1 **onion**, chopped

2 **celery ribs** with leafy tops, chopped

**Salt** and **black pepper**

1 cup **frozen peas**

3 cups **chicken stock**

1 cup **heavy cream**

½ cup **quick-cooking polenta**

1 cup grated **Gruyère** cheese

5 tablespoons **butter**

2 tablespoons all-purpose **flour**

2 teaspoons **Dijon mustard**

6 fresh **tarragon sprigs**, leaves stripped and chopped, 3 to 4 tablespoons

In a deep skillet heat the EVOO over medium-high heat. Add the chicken and lightly brown, about 3 minutes, then add the carrots, onions, and celery and season with salt and pepper. Cook for 10 to 12 minutes to soften. Add the peas and stir for a minute to heat through.

Preheat the broiler. Set the rack in the middle of the oven.

Bring 1 cup of the chicken stock and ½ cup of the cream to a boil. Stir in the polenta and whisk until it masses in the center of the pot, about 3 minutes. (See Tidbit.) Turn the heat to low, stir in the Gruyère cheese, and keep warm.

Scoot the chicken and veggies off to the side of the skillet and add the butter to the pan. When it melts, stir in the flour and cook for 1 minute. Whisk in the remaining 2 cups of stock and combine, then stir in the remaining $\frac{1}{2}$ cup of cream and bring to a bubble, stirring the chicken and vegetables back into the sauce. Stir in the Dijon and tarragon, adjust the salt and pepper, and divide the mixture among 4 ovenproof soup bowls.

Set the soup bowls into a baking dish. Pour the polenta and cheese mixture over the creamy chicken filling and smooth the tops. Slide under the broiler to brown for 2 to 3 minutes.

## tidbit

If the mouths of your bowls are very wide, you may need to increase the polenta to $\frac{3}{4}$ cup or even 1 cup, adding another $\frac{1}{2}$ to 1 cup of stock, to completely cover your pot pies.

# Spanish Chicken Cutlets and Olive Rice with Artichokes and Piquillo Peppers

Another great use for piquillo peppers, my new fave!

- 3 cups **chicken stock**
- 1½ cups **long-grain white rice**
- 7 tablespoons **EVOO** (extra-virgin olive oil)
- 1½ cups **blanched almonds**
- ½ cup **bread crumbs**

  A generous handful of fresh **flat-leaf parsley** leaves
- 1 cup all-purpose **flour**

  **Salt** and **black pepper**
- 2 teaspoons **sweet smoked paprika**
- 2 **eggs**
- 4 (6-ounce) boneless, skinless **chicken breasts**
- 1 (9-ounce) package **frozen artichoke hearts**
- ½ cup pitted **Spanish green olives**, chopped
- 4 jarred **piquillo peppers**, chopped, or 2 roasted red peppers
- ⅓ cup **dry sherry** (eyeball it)
- 2 tablespoons cold **butter**, cut into pieces

Preheat the oven to 375°F.

Bring the stock to a boil and stir in the rice and 1 tablespoon of the EVOO. Cover the pot and reduce the heat to low. Cook for 18 minutes. Keep an eye on the clock: you will be adding more ingredients after the rice has cooked for 12 to 13 minutes.

Combine the almonds, bread crumbs, and parsley in a food processor and pulse on and off until the mixture has the consistency of bread crumbs. Pour the nut mixture onto a plate. Put the flour in a shallow dish and season with salt, pepper, and paprika. Beat the eggs with a splash of water in a second shallow dish.

Place each chicken breast on a cutting board with the flatter side down and the smoother, more rounded side up. Holding the knife parallel to the board, cut into and across but not all the way through the breast meat and butterfly the breast open. Season the chicken with salt and pepper on both sides. Coat each butterflied breast first in the flour, shaking off the excess, then in the egg, and finally in the nut mixture.

Heat about 3 tablespoons of the EVOO, 3 times around the pan, in each of two large skillets over medium to medium-high heat. When the oil ripples, add 2 chicken breasts to each skillet and cook for 10 to 12 minutes, turning once, or until deeply golden.

Five minutes before the rice is done, add the artichokes, olives, and peppers and stir to combine. Cook for 5 minutes more, then turn off the heat and fluff with a fork.

Add the sherry to one of the skillets in which the chicken was cooked and cook for 1 minute, then stir in the butter. Spoon the pan sauce over the chicken and serve with the rice alongside.

# Rummy Grilled Chicken with Brown Rice and Red Onions and Green Peas

A huge shout-out to my girlfriend with lotsa flavor Vicki Filiaci, for this fantastic, easy, groovalicious menu.

- 4 bone-in, skin-on **chicken breasts**
- 4 bone-in, skin-on **chicken legs** and thighs
- 2 tablespoons **grill seasoning** blend, such as McCormick's Montreal Steak Seasoning
- 1 cup **light rum**
  Zest and juice of 1 **orange**
- 1 cup fresh **basil**, 20 leaves, shredded
- 1 quart (4 cups) **chicken stock**
- 2 tablespoons **EVOO** (extra-virgin olive oil)
- 2 cups **brown rice**
- 1 small **red onion**, chopped
- 1 (16-ounce) bag frozen **peas**
  **Salt** and **black pepper**

Place the chicken in a shallow dish. Season the meat liberally on both sides with grill seasoning. Add the rum, orange zest and juice, and basil to the dish; turn the chicken to coat and combine. Let stand for 15 minutes.

Preheat an outdoor grill or grill pan to medium-high.

While the chicken is marinating, place 3 cups of the stock and 1 tablespoon of the EVOO in a medium saucepot with the brown rice. Bring to a boil uncovered, then cover, reduce the heat to low, and cook at a simmer for 25 minutes. Turn off the heat and let stand for 10 minutes longer.

While the rice cooks, grill the chicken for 20 to 25 minutes, turning occasionally, until the juices run clear. Ten minutes before the chicken comes off the grill, heat 1 tablespoon of the EVOO over medium heat in a medium skillet. Add the onions and cook for 5 to 6 minutes to soften. Add the peas and the remaining cup of chicken stock and cook to heat through, 3 to 4 minutes. Season the onions and peas with salt and pepper.

Fluff the rice with a fork and serve with the grilled chicken and peas.

# Grilled Chicken Shawarma

Tired of wondering if you're pronouncing *shawarma* the right way when you're calling the delivery guy? When you make your own take-out, you can say it however you please and giggle all you want! Plus, you get to control the quality of the ingredients going in without the questionable cleanliness of the street-meat cart you normally buy it from.

| | |
|---|---|
| 1 | tablespoon plus ½ teaspoon **ground cumin** |
| 1 | tablespoon **ground coriander**, a palmful |
| 1 | tablespoon **ground cardamom**, a palmful |
| 1 | tablespoon **chili powder**, a palmful |
| 1 | teaspoon **smoked sweet paprika** |
| 1 | tablespoon **grill seasoning**, such as McCormick's Montreal Steak Seasoning |
| 1½ | **lemons** |
| 6 | tablespoons **EVOO** (extra-virgin olive oil), plus a drizzle |
| 1 | large **garlic clove**, grated or finely chopped |
| 4 | boneless, skinless **chicken breasts** or 12 chicken tenders |
| 1 | red **bell pepper**, seeded and sliced |
| 1 | yellow **bell pepper**, seeded and sliced |
| 1 | large **red onion**, sliced |
| ¼ | cup **sesame tahini paste**, available in the refrigerated case near the hummus |
| 1½ | to 2 cups **Greek-style plain yogurt** |
| | **Salt** |
| 8 | **pita breads** |
| 1 | cup fresh **flat-leaf parsley** tops |
| ½ | cup **hot banana pepper rings** (optional) |

Preheat a grill pan or outdoor grill to medium-high.

Combine the tablespoon of cumin, the coriander, cardamom, chili powder, paprika, and grill seasoning in a mixing bowl. Stir in the juice of ½ lemon, ¼ cup of the EVOO, and the garlic. Add the chicken and turn it in the spices; let stand for 15 minutes. Grill the chicken until marked and cooked through, 12 minutes for breasts, 8 to 10 for tenders. Chop or slice the chicken into bite-size pieces.

While the chicken is cooking, heat the remaining 2 tablespoons of EVOO, 2 times around the pan, in a skillet over medium-high heat. Add the bell peppers and onions and sauté until they become tender, 10 minutes.

In a small bowl combine the juice of the remaining lemon with the tahini, yogurt, the remaining ½ teaspoon cumin, a drizzle of EVOO, and salt to taste. Stir in about 3 tablespoons of water, or just enough to make a spoonable sauce.

Toast the pita breads in the grill pan or on the grill until lightly charred. Fill each pita with chicken, peppers and onions, some parsley leaves, and hot pepper rings, and top with tahini.

## tidbit

Triple or quadruple the shawarma spice mixture to sprinkle on chicken or lamb whenever you grill. It will keep in your pantry for up to 3 months.

# Chicken Marsala Masala with Peach–Watermelon Rind Chutney

Here's a clever mash-up of two of the world's classic chicken dishes, one from Italy and one from India. It's the best of both worlds!

- 1 quart (4 cups) **chicken stock**
- 2 tablespoons **butter**
- 1 fresh or dried **bay leaf**
- 1½ cups **long-grain rice**
- 4 tablespoons **EVOO** (extra-virgin olive oil)
- 1½ pounds **chicken breast cutlets**, thinly sliced into ⅛- to ¼-inch strips
   **Salt** and **black pepper**
- 1 **red onion**, quartered lengthwise, then thinly sliced
- 4 **garlic cloves**, grated or thinly sliced
- 3 **portobello mushroom caps**, thinly sliced
- 8 ounces **shiitake mushrooms**, stems removed, thinly sliced
- 2 tablespoons **curry powder**, a couple of palmfuls
- 2 teaspoons **garam masala**, ⅔ palmful
- ¼ to ⅓ cup **Marsala wine** (eyeball it)

### Chutney

- 1 tablespoon **butter**
- 2 **peaches**, pitted and chopped
   1-inch piece of fresh **ginger**, peeled and grated
- 2 tablespoons **cider vinegar**
- 2 tablespoons **light or dark brown sugar**
- ½ cup **pickled watermelon rind**, chopped
- ½ cup chopped **macadamia nuts**, toasted
   A handful of fresh **flat-leaf parsley** or cilantro, chopped
- 4 **scallions**, white and green parts, finely chopped

Bring 2 cups of the chicken stock, 1 cup water, the butter, and the bay leaf to a boil in a medium pot with a tight-fitting lid. Add the rice, stir, and cover. Reduce the heat and cook for 18 minutes, or until tender.

Heat 2 tablespoons of the EVOO, 2 times around the pan, in a large skillet over medium-high to high heat. Add the chicken, season with salt and pepper, and brown for 6 to 7 minutes. Remove the chicken to a plate, add the remaining 2 tablespoons of EVOO to the pan, and turn the heat down a bit. When the oil ripples, add the red onions, garlic, and mushrooms. Cook until the mushrooms are dark and tender, 6 to 7 minutes, then season with salt and pepper. Return the chicken to the pan and season with the curry powder and garam masala. Add the Marsala and stir to deglaze the skillet, scraping up all the bits from the bottom of the pan, then add the 2 remaining cups of chicken stock. Reduce the heat and simmer for a few minutes to combine the flavors.

To make the chutney, melt the butter in a small pan over medium-high heat. Add the peaches to the pan and season with the ginger, salt, and pepper. Cook the peaches for 3 to 4 minutes. Add the vinegar and brown sugar and stir to glaze the fruit, then stir in the watermelon rind, nuts, parsley, and scallions. Remove from the heat.

Fluff the rice with a fork. Serve the chicken on a bed of rice with chutney on top to garnish. Yum-o!

## tidbit

Garam masala is widely available in large supermarkets in the spice section. If your store does not carry it, raid your spice cabinet to make your own. Mix together a combo of however many of these spices you have on hand: ground cinnamon, ground cloves, ground mace, ground cardamom, black pepper, ground cumin, ground coriander, ground fennel, nutmeg, and chili powder.

# Hot Pepper Chicken Under a Brick

Cooking your chicken under a brick might seem silly, but there is nothing silly about the flavor you end up with here. It is seriously tasty. Try it and see!

4 large **chicken legs and thighs** or 4 chicken breasts
   **Salt** and **black pepper**
1 teaspoon **red pepper flakes**
1 rounded tablespoon **Dijon mustard**
5 tablespoons **EVOO** (extra-virgin olive oil), plus more for drizzling the bread
2 to 3 tablespoons **banana pepper rings**, finely chopped, plus
   2 tablespoons of the juice from the jar
   A handful of chopped fresh **flat-leaf parsley leaves**
1 tablespoon **orange marmalade**
1 teaspoon **poppy seeds**
2 tablespoons **red wine vinegar**
½ **seedless cucumber**, thinly sliced
4 **plum tomatoes**, thinly sliced
1 bunch **arugula** or watercress, cleaned and chopped
   Loaf of **crusty bread**, for mopping
1 **garlic clove**, peeled and halved

Season the chicken with salt and black pepper. Combine the red pepper flakes, mustard, and about 2 tablespoons of the oil in a small dish. Slather the mixture all over the skin of the chicken. Place the chicken skin side down in a large nonstick skillet. Set a sheet of foil on top of the chicken, then place a plate or smaller pan on top and weight it with a brick or some heavy cans. Place the skillet over medium to medium-high heat and cook for 17 to 18 minutes. Remove the weight, turn the chicken over, and reduce the heat to medium-low. Replace the brick and cook the chicken for another 2 minutes. When the chicken is cooked through, sprinkle it with the chopped hot peppers, douse with the pepper juice, and top with the parsley.

While the chicken cooks, stir together the marmalade, poppy seeds, and vinegar, then whisk in the remaining 3 tablespoons of EVOO, adding it in a slow stream. Toss the cucumbers, tomatoes, and greens with the dressing and season with salt and pepper.

Preheat the broiler.

Cut the bread into 1- to 2-inch-thick slices and broil until charred, a couple of minutes. Rub the bread with the cut side of the garlic clove and drizzle with EVOO. Transfer the chicken to 4 dinner plates, then press the bread slices into the pan juices, swishing them around to pick up as much juice as possible.

Serve the chicken with the salad and bread.

# Grilled Chipotle-Rubbed Whole Chicken Legs with Corn and Scallion Polenta

This is one hot-legged chick! You won't be able keep your hands off 'er.

- 2 tablespoons **ground chipotle powder**
- 1 tablespoon **grill seasoning**, such as McCormick's Montreal Steak Seasoning
- 2 teaspoons **ground coriander**, ⅔ palmful
- 2 teaspoons **paprika**, ⅔ palmful
- 1 teaspoon **ground cumin**, ⅓ palmful
- 4 large bone-in, skin-on **chicken leg** and **thigh quarters**
  **EVOO** (extra-virgin olive oil), for liberal drizzling
- 2 cups **chicken stock**
- 1 cup **whole milk**
- 1 cup **quick-cooking polenta**, found in Italian markets or the specialty foods aisle
- 1 (10-ounce) box **frozen corn**, defrosted
- 2 to 3 tablespoons **honey**
- 4 **scallions**, white and green parts, thinly sliced
- 4 tablespoons (½ stick) cold **butter**, cut into pieces
  **Salt**
- 1 pound **green beans**, trimmed

Preheat a grill pan or outdoor grill to medium.

In a bowl combine the chipotle powder, grill seasoning, coriander, paprika, and cumin. Put the chicken legs in a shallow dish and coat with the chipotle mixture, rubbing it into the legs. Let them hang out for 20 minutes.

When you are ready to cook the chicken, drizzle the pieces liberally with EVOO and place on the grill. Cook the chicken, turning frequently, for about 20 minutes, until the juices run clear. When the leg can be wiggled freely from the thigh, the chicken is done. Remove to a platter and cover loosely with foil. Let the chicken rest for 5 to 10 minutes before serving.

While the legs are grilling, start the polenta: In a medium-size saucepot, bring the chicken stock and milk to a boil over high heat. If you're cooking outside, you can place the pot right on the grill, or make it inside once the meat has cooked and is resting. Once the liquids are at a boil, pour in the polenta in a slow, steady stream while whisking constantly. Add the corn and pour in the honey to taste, then cook until thick, 2 to 3 minutes. Remove from the heat and stir in the scallions and butter until well combined.

While the polenta liquid is heating, bring an inch of water to boil in a skillet. Add salt and the green beans and cook until just tender, 4 to 5 minutes.

Serve the chicken legs with the polenta and beans alongside.

## tidbit

If you can't find chipotle powder, use 2 tablespoons chili powder and substitute smoked paprika for the paprika.

# Buffalo Baked Chicken with Blue Cheese, Celery, and Carrot Slaw

Long for your glory days of beer and bar food? You'll be happy to see that Buffalo wings can grow up and fly right—right into an irresistible entrée that's perfect for game night.

6 tablespoons (¾ stick) **butter**

¾ cup **hot sauce**, such as Frank's Red Hot

4 bone-in, skin-on **chicken breasts**, halved crosswise

4 **chicken drumsticks**
   **Salt** and **black pepper**

1 cup **blue cheese crumbles**
   Juice of 2 **lemons**

⅓ to ½ cup **mayonnaise**

6 to 8 **celery ribs** from the heart with greens, thinly sliced on an angle

2 cups shredded **carrots**

6 **scallions**, white and green parts, thinly sliced

½ head of **red cabbage**, cored and shredded

3 cups **salad croutons**, ground into crumbs in a food processor

¼ cup fresh **flat-leaf parsley** leaves, a generous handful, finely chopped

Preheat the oven to 400°F.

Melt the butter over low heat in a small pot and combine with the hot sauce. Place the chicken in a large bowl, season with salt and pepper, then toss to coat in the Buffalo sauce. Let stand for 10 minutes.

In a bowl combine the blue cheese, lemon juice, mayonnaise, salt, and pepper. Add the celery, shredded carrots, scallions, and red cabbage. Toss to combine.

Arrange the crushed croutons in a shallow dish, add the parsley, and mix with your fingers to combine. Press the sauce-coated chicken into the bread-crumb mixture to coat evenly, and set onto a nonstick baking sheet. Bake the chicken for 40 minutes, or until cooked through and golden brown.

Remove the chicken from the oven and serve alongside the blue cheese, celery, and carrot slaw.

## tidbit
If your baking sheet is not non-stick, you can line a rimmed baking sheet with parchment paper to prevent the chicken from sticking.

# Paprika Chicken Stew
# with Potato Pierogies

Stew on this Hungarian-Polish comfort food when the weather is cold and the kitchen is warm and welcoming; you won't walk away from this one hungry.

3 tablespoons **EVOO** (extra-virgin olive oil)

½ pound smoky, good-quality **bacon**, chopped into ½-inch pieces

2 pounds boneless, skinless **chicken breasts and thighs**, cut into chunks
 **Salt** and **black pepper**

1 large **onion**, chopped

2 **carrots**, peeled and grated or finely chopped

3 **garlic cloves**, chopped

2 tablespoons **sweet paprika**

1 tablespoon **ground cumin**

½ teaspoon dried **marjoram** or oregano

1 fresh or dried **bay leaf**

2 tablespoons all-purpose **flour**

½ cup **white wine**

2 cups **chicken stock**

1 (15-ounce) can **crushed tomatoes**

½ cup **sour cream**

12 **frozen potato pierogies**

2 tablespoons **butter**

¼ cup chopped or snipped fresh **chives**
 Zest of 1 **lemon**

¼ cup fresh **flat-leaf parsley**, chopped

Place a large pot of water over high heat and bring up to a boil for the pierogies.

Place a large, deep skillet over medium-high heat with 1 tablespoon of the EVOO, once around the pan. Add the bacon and cook until brown and crisp, 3 to 4 minutes. Season the chicken with salt and pepper, add to the skillet with the bacon, and brown all sides, 7 to 8 minutes. Add the onions, carrots, garlic, paprika, cumin, marjoram, and bay leaf and cook for 5 to 6 minutes, until the veggies are just tender.

Make a well in the middle of the pan and add the remaining 2 tablespoons of EVOO. Add the flour to the EVOO and mix to form a paste. Add the white wine, scraping up all of the brown bits on the bottom of the pan. Add the chicken stock and tomatoes and cook for about 20 minutes, until the stew has thickened. Stir in the sour cream and remove from the heat.

While the stew is cooking, cook the pierogies in boiling water according to the package directions. Heat a medium skillet over medium-high heat, add the butter and cook until the butter turns slightly brown and gives off a nutty aroma. Drain the cooked pierogies, add them to the pan, and cook until slightly browned on both sides, about 2 minutes per side. Add the chives and turn the pierogies to coat.

Serve the stew in large bowls, sprinkled with lemon zest and parsley. Arrange 3 pierogies on top of each bowl of stew.

# Vinegar and Honey Chicken with Creamy Dijon Smashed Potatoes

A good ol' square meal on a round plate, and probably my 5,783rd way to cook chicken. Enjoy!

6 tablespoons **EVOO** (extra-virgin olive oil)
4 bone-in, skin-on **chicken breasts** or 4 fat thighs and drumsticks, your choice
**Salt** and **black pepper**
3 large **onions**, thinly sliced
3 tablespoons **thyme leaves**, from 7 to 8 sprigs, chopped
¼ cup **honey** (eyeball it)
4 large **garlic cloves**, chopped
1 cup **apple cider vinegar**
2 cups **chicken stock**
6 **russet potatoes**, peeled and cut into chunks
⅓ to ½ cup **half-and-half**
3 tablespoons **Dijon mustard**
3 tablespoons fresh snipped or chopped **chives**
2 **Belgian endives**, thinly sliced
2 cups **watercress**, tough stems removed
1 **lemon**

Preheat a deep skillet or Dutch oven over medium-high heat with 2 tablespoons of the EVOO, twice around the pan. Season the chicken liberally with salt and pepper, and add to the hot oil, skin side down. Brown the chicken, about 5 minutes on the first side and 2 to 3 minutes on the second. Remove the chicken to a plate and reserve. Add another 2 tablespoons of the EVOO to the skillet, along with the onions, thyme, honey, and garlic. Season the onions with salt and pepper and cook, stirring frequently, for about 20 minutes or until the onions are really brown.

Add the vinegar to the pan with the onions, scraping up all the brown bits on the bottom of the pan with a wooden spoon. Add the chicken stock and bring up to a bubble. Once the mixture is at a simmer, return the chicken to the pot. Place a lid on the pot, turn the heat down to medium, and simmer for about 15 minutes, flipping the chicken over in the sauce about halfway through. Remove the lid, turn the heat up to high, and simmer until the sauce thickens slightly, 4 to 5 minutes.

While the chicken simmers, place the potatoes in a medium pot with cold water to cover. Bring the water to a boil and salt the water. Cook until tender, about 15 minutes. In the last few minutes of the chicken's cooking time, drain the potatoes and add them back to the hot pot. Smash the potatoes with the half-and-half, mustard, chives, and salt and pepper. Adjust the seasonings to taste.

Dress the greens with the lemon juice, the remaining 2 tablespoons of EVOO, and salt and pepper.

Serve the chicken and sauce alongside the smashed potatoes with a little of the bitter green salad.

# Casablanca Chicken and Yellow Rice

This is the start of a beautiful dinner. So exotic and flavorful, you'll want to *make it* again, Sam.

- 5 tablespoons **EVOO** (extra-virgin olive oil)
- 3 tablespoons **curry powder**, 3 palmfuls
- 1 cup all-purpose **flour** (eyeball it)
- 1 whole **chicken**, cut into 8 pieces: 2 thighs, 2 drumsticks, each breast cut into 2 pieces
- **Salt** and **black pepper**
- 2 large **onions**, chopped
- 1 large **carrot**, peeled and grated
- 1 3-inch piece of **fresh ginger**, peeled and grated
- 4 large **garlic cloves**, chopped or grated
- ½ tablespoon **ground cumin**, ½ palmful
- ½ tablespoon **ground coriander**, ½ palmful
- ½ tablespoon **paprika**, ½ palmful
- ½ teaspoon **cayenne pepper**
- ½ teaspoon **ground cinnamon**
- ½ cup **golden raisins**, a couple of handfuls
- 1 cup large pitted good-quality **green olives**
- 2 quarts (8 cups) **chicken stock**
- 1½ cups **white rice**
- 1 fresh or dried **bay leaf**
- 1 teaspoon **ground turmeric**
- Zest of 2 **lemons**
- ½ cup fresh **flat-leaf parsley** leaves, a couple of handfuls, coarsely chopped
- ¼ cup fresh **cilantro leaves**, a handful, coarsely chopped

Place a large Dutch oven or similar pot over medium-high heat with 3 tablespoons of the EVOO, 3 times around the pan. While the oil is heating, combine the curry powder and the flour in a shallow dish. Season the chicken with salt and pepper and then dredge in the flour mixture, shaking off the excess. Brown the chicken working in 2 batches, about 3 to 4 minutes on each side. Reserve the browned chicken on a plate.

To the pot add the onions, carrot, ginger, garlic, cumin, coriander, paprika, cayenne pepper, and cinnamon. Cook for 3 to 4 minutes, stirring frequently. Add the raisins, olives, 5 cups of the chicken stock, and the browned chicken pieces. Cover with a lid and bring up to a bubble, then simmer for 10 minutes. Remove the lid and simmer for 10 to 15 minutes longer, or until the chicken is cooked through and the liquid in the pan is reduced by half.

While the chicken cooks, place a medium-size saucepot over medium-high heat with the remaining 2 tablespoons of EVOO, twice around the pan. Add the rice to the pot and stir to coat with the oil, then add the remaining 3 cups of chicken stock and the bay leaf. Bring up to a bubble, stir in the turmeric, then cover the pot, turn the heat down to medium, and cook for about 18 minutes or until the rice is tender. Remove the bay leaf.

Add the lemon zest, parsley, and cilantro to the chicken and stir to combine. Fluff the rice with a fork. Mound the rice on a platter and top with the chicken and some of the sauce. Pass the remaining sauce at the table.

# Braised Indian Chicken and Potatoes

Get your spice on with this succulent one-pot meal.

6 tablespoons **EVOO** (extra-virgin olive oil)
1 **chicken**, cut into 8 serving pieces (a family pack)
**Salt** and **black pepper**
1 pound red or white **boiling potatoes**, cut in quarters
1 large **onion**, $\frac{1}{2}$ thinly sliced and $\frac{1}{2}$ finely chopped
4 large **garlic cloves**, 3 chopped or grated, 1 crushed and left whole
3 **celery ribs**, thinly sliced
1 cup shredded **carrots**
$\frac{1}{3}$ to $\frac{1}{2}$ cup **mild curry paste** (eyeball it)
1 **Granny Smith apple**, cored and thinly sliced
2 heaping tablespoons all-purpose **flour**
1 quart plus 3 cups (7 cups total) **chicken stock**
1 tablespoon **ground coriander**, a palmful
$1\frac{1}{2}$ cups **white rice**
1 (10-ounce) box **frozen peas**
$\frac{1}{4}$ cup fresh **cilantro leaves**, a generous handful, coarsely chopped
$\frac{1}{4}$ cup fresh **flat-leaf parsley**, a generous handful, coarsely chopped
1 cup **whole-milk plain yogurt**, look for Greek-style yogurt
**Hot sauce**, to pass at the table
**Mango chutney**, to pass at the table
4 **pita breads**, warmed, to pass at the table

In a large, heavy-bottomed pot heat 3 tablespoons of the EVOO, 3 times around the pan, over medium-high heat. Season the chicken liberally with salt and pepper and add to the hot pan in 2 batches, cooking until brown on all sides, 4 to 5 minutes per batch. Remove the browned chicken to a plate and reserve while browning the second batch.

Once you have the first batch of chicken browning, place a large nonstick skillet over medium-high heat with 2 more tablespoons of the EVOO. Add the potatoes, season with salt and pepper, and brown on all sides for 10 minutes.

When the second batch of chicken is browned, remove it to the plate with the first batch and add the sliced onions, chopped garlic, celery, carrots, curry paste, apple, and some salt and pepper to the skillet. Cook for 5 minutes, stirring frequently. Add the flour and stir and cook for 1 minute, then add 1 quart (4 cups) of the chicken stock and bring it up to a bubble. Add the browned chicken and potatoes to the pot and bring everything back up to a simmer. Cover the pot with a lid, turn the heat down to medium-low, and braise for 20 minutes, or until the chicken is cooked through.

Once the chicken is simmering, prepare the rice. Heat the remaining tablespoon of EVOO in a medium saucepot over medium-high heat. Add the chopped onion, crushed garlic clove, and coriander and cook for 2 to 3 minutes, stirring frequently. Season with salt and pepper, add the rice, and stir for a minute to coat the rice in the oil and combine with the onions. Add the remaining 3 cups of chicken stock and bring up to a bubble. When it boils, cover the pot, turn down the heat to medium, and cook until the rice is tender, about 18 minutes. Once it is cooked, fluff the rice with a fork. Discard the garlic.

Just before you're ready to serve, add the peas to the chicken and cook for 2 minutes to heat through. Add the cilantro, parsley, and yogurt to the pot, and stir to combine.

To serve, divide the curry among 4 shallow bowls. Top each serving with rice or serve it alongside. Pass the hot sauce, mango chutney, and warm pita breads at the table.

# tidbit

To save time, buy a family pack of chicken rather than buying a whole chicken and cutting it into serving pieces yourself. Each family pack contains 2 breasts, 2 wings, 2 thighs, and 2 drumsticks.

# Tarragon Roast Chicken with Fennel and Boursin Smashed Potatoes

Take a trip to the French countryside without leaving the kitchen. Here's a beautiful Sunday dinner that's quick enough for any night of the week. *C'est magnifique, n'est ce pas?*

1 large **fennel bulb**, cored and sliced

1 large **onion**, sliced

4 fresh or dried **bay leaves**

6 **parsnips**, peeled and cut on an angle into large chunks

6 tablespoons **EVOO** (extra-virgin olive oil)
   **Salt** and **black pepper**

8 fresh **tarragon stems**, leaves stripped

1 cup fresh **flat-leaf parsley** leaves, loosely packed, a small bunch

6 **garlic cloves**, gently cracked from their skins

2 **lemons**

4 skin-on, bone-in **chicken breasts** of average size (too big will be too tough)

4 **chicken drumsticks**

½ to ¾ cup **dry white wine**

2½ pounds large **russet potatoes**, 5 or 6, peeled and cut into chunks

1 (5.2-ounce) package **Boursin cheese**

⅓ to ½ cup **half-and-half** or whole milk

¾ cup **chicken stock**

Preheat the oven to 425°F.

Arrange the fennel, onions, bay leaves, and parsnips in a roasting pan or large, deep casserole. Drizzle the vegetables with 2 tablespoons of the EVOO and toss to coat, then season with salt and pepper. Chop the tarragon and parsley and place it in a bowl. Grate the garlic and lemon zest into the bowl. Stir in the remaining ¼ cup EVOO (eyeball it). Cut the chicken breasts in half across. Arrange the chicken pieces on top of the vegetables and slather with the herb and oil mixture. Season the chicken liberally with salt and pepper. Add wine to the dish and roast in the oven for about 45 minutes, or until the juices run clear. Discard the bay leaves.

Halfway through the cooking time, place the potatoes in a pot, cover with water, and bring to a boil. Salt the water and cook the potatoes until tender, 15 minutes. Drain the potatoes and return them to the pot. Add the cheese, half-and-half or milk, and salt and pepper and mash to your preferred consistency.

Transer the chicken and veggies to a platter and keep warm. Add the chicken stock to the roasting pan and stir over medium heat to deglaze the pan and reduce slightly, 2 or 3 minutes.

Serve up the roast chicken, allowing 2 pieces of breast meat and 1 drumstick per person, with some roast veggies and mashed potatoes alongside. Drizzle the pan juices over the meat and vegetables.

# Cornish Hens and Citrus-Scented Roasted Vegetables

Hens so tender all your friends will squawk about it!

- 2 pounds **baby potatoes**
- 3 **leeks**, trimmed of 3 to 4 inches of rough greens and roots
- 3 **carrots**
- 1 **fennel bulb**
- 1 **lemon**, zested and halved
- 1 **orange**, zested and halved
- ⅓ cup **EVOO** (extra-virgin olive oil)
  **Salt** and **black pepper**
- 2 to 3 fresh or dried **bay leaves**
- 2 **Cornish hens**, split lengthwise, cleaned and dried
- 6 to 7 fresh **thyme sprigs**, leaves stripped and chopped
  **Crusty bread** to pass at the table (whole-grain baguette is tasty with this meal)

Preheat the oven to 425°F.

Slice the potatoes crosswise into thirds and place in a roasting pan. Halve the leeks lengthwise and slice into ½-inch half-moons. Wash the leek slices in a large bowl of water or by tossing vigorously in a colander under cold running water. Separate the layers to free the grit. Wrap the leeks in a towel to dry them, then toss in with the potatoes. Peel the carrots and slice them ½ inch thick on an angle. Trim off the tops of the fennel bulb and chop and reserve a few fronds. Quarter the bulb, cut away the core, and slice the bulb thin. Add the fennel to the roasting pan. Add a tablespoon or so each of the lemon zest and orange zest to the mix and coat the vegetables in about ¼ cup of the EVOO (eyeball it). Season the vegetables liberally with salt and pepper and toss in the bay leaves.

Coat the hens in a couple more tablespoons of the EVOO and season with salt, pepper, and the thyme. Set the birds on top of the vegetables, skin side up, and roast for 15 minutes. After 15 minutes, reduce the heat to 375°F and roast the hens for another 30 minutes. Squeeze the juice of 1 lemon half and 1 orange half over the hens and vegetables when you remove them from the oven. Serve the birds and roasted veggies directly from the roaster. Pass some bread for mopping up the pan juices.

Tarragon-Tomato Chicken and Bread Stoup
(page 271)
Chicken in Creamy Mushroom Sauce with Chive
Egg Noodles (page 272)

# Poached Chicken and Vegetables

This is the base for both dinners. Try one dish tonight:
between the poaching and the preparation you'll spend
45 minutes to 1 hour. Then, store the remaining 4 cooled
chicken breasts in the cooled chicken poaching liquid in
the refrigerator for up to 4 days. The next night's dinner
will be whipped up in minutes!

6 cups **chicken stock**
4 **carrots**, peeled and cut in half
4 **celery ribs** from the heart with leafy tops, cut in half
1 fresh or dried **bay leaf**
2 small **onions**, peeled, roots trimmed, onions left whole
8 (6-ounce) boneless, skinless **chicken breasts**

In a large, high-sided skillet with a tight-fitting lid, place the
chicken stock and bring up to a boil. Once it is boiling, add the carrots, celery, bay leaf, onions, and chicken breasts. Shake the pan to
nestle everything into the stock. Place the lid on the skillet and
bring back up to a boil, then turn the heat down to simmer the
chicken for 15 minutes, until it is firm but not tough.

Remove the chicken and the bay leaf from the poaching liquid and
let it cool; reserve the poaching liquid. Reserve the vegetables for
the Tarragon-Tomato Chicken and Bread Stoup.

# Night One: Tarragon-Tomato Chicken and Bread Stoup

If you loved tomato soup from a can as a kid, try this pot of grown-up tomato flavor and you'll never can-it again!

5 tablespoons **EVOO** (extra-virgin olive oil)
3 **garlic cloves**, crushed
Zest of 1 **lemon**
1 loaf **French bread**
**Veggies** from chicken poaching liquid (see page 270)
1 (28-ounce) can **crushed tomatoes**
2 cups **chicken poaching liquid** (see page 270)
4 **poached chicken breasts** (see page 270)
3 tablespoons chopped **fresh tarragon**, 5 to 6 sprigs
**Salt** and **black pepper**

Preheat the broiler.

Place about ¼ cup of the EVOO in a small saucepot and add 2 of the garlic cloves and the lemon zest. Place over low heat and gently cook for 3 to 4 minutes. Remove from the heat and reserve. Split the French bread open lengthwise, brush both sides liberally with the garlic-lemon oil, and then place under the broiler to toast until golden brown. Remove and chop the bread into large bite-size pieces.

Cut the poached vegetables into large bite-size pieces.

Place a large skillet over medium-high heat with the remaining tablespoon of EVOO. Add the remaining garlic clove and cook for about 1 minute. Add the crushed tomatoes, poached vegetables, and the chicken poaching liquid. Bring the mixture up to a simmer.

(recipe continues)

While it is heating, chop the chicken breasts into chunks. Once the liquids are simmering, add the chunked chicken and the tarragon and season with salt and pepper. Simmer until the chicken is heated through, 3 to 4 minutes.

Divide the bread cubes among 4 shallow bowls, top with the tomato-tarragon chicken, and serve.

# Night Two: Chicken in Creamy Mushroom Sauce with Chive Egg Noodles

This is one I come back to again and again. It's a comfort meal that'll get you feeling cozy quickly; trust me.

- ½ pound **wide egg noodles**
- 4 tablespoons (½ stick) **butter**
- 3 tablespoons chopped or snipped fresh **chives**
  **Salt** and **black pepper**
- 2 tablespoons **EVOO** (extra-virgin olive oil)
- 2 large **shallots**, thinly sliced
- 1 pound **button mushrooms**, thinly sliced
- ½ teaspoon **ground thyme**
- 2 tablespoons all-purpose **flour**
- ½ cup **dry white wine**
- 2 cups **chicken poaching liquid** (see page 270)
- ½ cup **heavy cream** or half-and-half
  Freshly grated **nutmeg**, 5 or 6 strokes over your grater, or to taste
- 4 **poached chicken breasts** (see page 270)

Place a large pot of water over high heat and bring to a boil to cook the egg noodles. Cook the noodles according to package directions. Drain and then return to the pot and add 2 tablespoons of the butter and the chopped chives. Season with some salt and pepper and toss to coat.

While the water is coming up to a boil to cook the egg noodles, start the mushrooms. Place a large skillet over medium-high heat with the remaining 2 tablespoons of butter and the EVOO, add the shallots, and cook, stirring frequently, for 2 minutes. Add the sliced mushrooms and continue to cook for 5 more minutes or until they are tender and barely golden in color. Season the mushrooms with a little salt and pepper and the ground thyme. Add the flour and continue to cook for 1 minute, then whisk in the wine and then the chicken poaching liquid and the cream. Season with a little nutmeg and bring up to a simmer.

Slice the poached chicken breasts on an angle, slide into the creamy mushroom sauce, and simmer until the chicken is heated through again. Add more of the poaching liquid if the sauce becomes too thick.

Divide the buttered chive egg noodles among 4 dinner plates and top each serving with sliced chicken and creamy mushroom sauce.

# First Night: Poached Chicken with Creamy Mushrooms, Fennel, and Potatoes

The ease of leftovers with the "wow" of show-stoppers. This reminds me, I should come up with some more of these!

- 2 quarts (8 cups) **chicken stock**
- 8 (6-ounce) boneless, skinless **chicken breasts**
- ¼ cup **EVOO** (extra-virgin olive oil), 4 times around the pan
- 1½ pounds **cremini mushrooms**, cut in half
- 4 sprigs fresh **rosemary**, leaves stripped and chopped
- 4 **garlic cloves**, grated
- 1 large **yellow onion**, thinly sliced
- 1 **fennel bulb**, cored and thinly sliced
- ¾ pound **red potatoes**, cut in half and then thinly sliced into half-moons
- 1 teaspoon **red pepper flakes**
  **Salt** and **black pepper**
- ½ cup **heavy cream**
- 1 cup fresh **basil**, about 20 leaves, chopped
- ½ cup pitted **Sicilian green olives**, coarsely chopped
- ½ cup grated **Parmigiano-Reggiano** cheese
  **Crusty bread**, to pass at the table

Place the chicken stock in a large soup pot with a tight-fitting lid. Bring to a boil over high heat. Add the chicken breasts, bring back to a simmer, and reduce the heat to medium-low. Replace the lid and poach the chicken for 15 minutes, or until cooked through.

While the chicken is poaching, heat a large skillet over medium-high heat with the EVOO. Add the mushrooms and rosemary to the skillet and brown for 8 to 10 minutes. Add the garlic, toss to combine, then add the onions, fennel, potatoes, and red pepper flakes and season with salt and pepper. Cook, stirring frequently, for 10 minutes more. Add 1½ cups of the chicken poaching liquid and cook for 5 minutes more. Stir in the cream and heat for a minute or two. Turn off the heat and stir in the basil, olives, and cheese.

Slice 4 of the poached chicken breasts. Arrange each poached breast in a shallow bowl and top with one fourth of the creamy mushroom, fennel, and potatoes. Pass crusty bread for mopping.

Cool and reserve the poaching liquid and chicken for another dinner later in the week.

# Second Night: Chicken, Corn, and Tomatillo Lasagna

- 4 poached **chicken breasts** and their poaching liquid (see page 274)
- 2 tablespoons **butter**
- 2 tablespoons all-purpose **flour**
- 1½ cups **milk** (eyeball it)
- 1 cup **tomatillo salsa** (eyeball it)
- 2 cups shredded **white Cheddar cheese**
- 1 (10-ounce) box frozen **corn kernels**, defrosted
- ¼ cup fresh **cilantro leaves**, coarsely chopped
  Juice of **1 lime**
  **Salt** and **black pepper**
  A drizzle of **EVOO** (extra-virgin olive oil)
- 5 (8-inch) **flour tortillas**

Preheat the oven to 375°F.

Chop the chicken into bite-size pieces and place in a large bowl.

Place a medium-size saucepot over medium-high heat and melt the butter. Once it is melted, add the flour and cook for 1 minute.

(recipe continues)

Whisk in the milk, 1 cup of the chicken poaching liquid, and the tomatillo salsa. Bring up to a bubble and let it thicken. Add the cheese and stir until melted; reserve the sauce.

Add the corn, cilantro, and lime juice to the chopped chicken and season with salt and pepper. Coat the bottom of an 8 x 8-inch baking dish with a little EVOO. Add a flour tortilla and coat with a few large spoonfuls of the cheese sauce, then top with one quarter of the chicken-corn mixture. Top with another flour tortilla and continue until all of the chicken mixture has been used. Top the last layer of chicken with the remaining flour tortilla and the remaining sauce.

Bake the lasagna for 25 minutes, or until warm through and deeply browned on top.

# Soprano Chicken Cigars

Here's a cigar that Carm wouldn't mind Tony enjoying.

- 4 tablespoons **EVOO** (extra-virgin olive oil)
- 1 medium **onion**
- 4 **garlic cloves**, grated or finely chopped
- 1½ to 2 pounds **ground chicken breast**, 2 packages
- ½ cup **sun-dried tomatoes**, chopped
- 1 cup, about 20 leaves, **fresh basil**, chopped
- 1 teaspoon dried **oregano**, ⅓ palmful
- 2 tablespoons **fennel seeds**, 2 palmfuls
- 2 teaspoons **red pepper flakes**, ⅔ palmful
- ½ cup grated **Parmigiano-Reggiano**, a couple of generous palmfuls
  **Salt** and **black pepper**
- 8 sheets **phyllo dough**
- 1 stick of **butter**, melted
- 2 hearts of **romaine lettuce**, chopped
  Juice of 1 **lemon**

Preheat the oven to 425°F.

Heat a medium skillet with 2 tablespoons of the EVOO over medium high heat. Add the onions and garlic and cook until soft, about 6 to 7 minutes. Let the mixture cool in a medium mixing bowl. Add the chicken to the bowl with the sun-dried tomatoes, basil, oregano, fennel, pepper flakes, cheese, salt, and black pepper and combine

Brush a sheet of phyllo dough with some of the melted butter. Top with a second sheet of phyllo and brush again. Form ¼ of the chicken mixture into a 1-inch thick log as long as the phyllo sheet. Cut the roll into 3 "cigars" and brush with a dab more butter. Repeat to make a total of 12 "cigars." Bake for 16 to 18 minutes, until golden brown.

Toss the lettuce with the lemon juice and the remaining EVOO, and season with salt and pepper. Serve 4 chicken cigars per person.

# Turkey Tetrazzini

This is my tribute to football hero and ballroom dance champ Emmitt Smith. It's so tasty it's a touchdown every time, and so easy it'll have you dancing around the kitchen.

**Salt**
½ pound **extra-wide egg noodles** or papardelle pasta
1 pound **turkey cutlets**
3 tablespoons **EVOO** (extra-virgin olive oil)
**Black pepper**
2 teaspoons **poultry seasoning**
4 tablespoons (½ stick) **butter**
2 **shallots**, thinly sliced
3 tablespoons all-purpose **flour**
1 cup **dry white wine**
2 cups **chicken or turkey stock** (both are now available in resealable cartons)
1 cup **sour cream**
Freshly **grated nutmeg**
½ cup **fresh bread crumbs**
¼ cup grated **Parmigiano-Reggiano**, a generous handful
¼ cup fresh **flat-leaf parsley** leaves, chopped
8 **cornichons** or 6 baby gherkins, finely chopped

Place a large pot of water over high heat and bring to a boil. Once it is boiling, add some salt and the egg noodles and cook according to package directions until al dente.

While the water comes to a boil, place the turkey cutlets between two pieces of plastic wrap. Smack the cutlets a few times with a small heavy-bottomed skillet to make them a bit thinner, about ¼ inch thick.

Heat a large skillet with 2 tablespoons of the EVOO, twice around the pan, over high heat. Season the turkey with a little salt, pepper, and poultry seasoning, and brown them for 2 to 3 minutes on each side, working in batches to avoid overcrowding the pan.

Once all of the turkey has been browned, add 2 tablespoons of the butter to the skillet and melt over medium heat. Once melted, add the shallots and cook for 2 minutes. Sprinkle the skillet with the flour and cook for 1 minute, stirring constantly. Whisk in the white wine, cook and stir for 1 minute, then add the stock. Raise the heat a bit and when the sauce comes to a bubble, stir in the sour cream. Thinly slice or chop the turkey into bite-size pieces and slide them into the sauce.

In a small hot skillet melt the remaining 2 tablespoons of butter, then add the bread crumbs and toss and stir until they are nice and toasty. Mix in the grated cheese, remove from the heat, and add the chopped parsley.

Add the drained noodles to the turkey and sauce and stir to coat with the sauce. Dish up the turkey Tetrazzini and sprinkle each serving with the bread-crumb mixture and chopped cornichons.

## tidbit

To make 1 cup of fresh bread crumbs, whir about 3 slices of bread in a food processor until chopped into large crumbs. You can remove the crusts if you prefer but it's not necessary.

# Square Meal: Turkey Chili Meatballs, Fire-Roasted BBQ Sauce, Sour Cream Smashed Potatoes, and Broccolini

This is just pure satisfaction from top to bottom. Dig into these savory turkey chili meatballs and then put out the fire with decadent smashed potatoes. De-lish!

2 pounds **new potatoes** or baby Yukon Gold potatoes

3 tablespoons **butter**

**Salt** and **black pepper**

½ to ¾ cup **sour cream** (eyeball it)

3 to 4 tablespoons snipped or chopped fresh **chives**

1¼ pounds **ground turkey breast** (the average weight of a package)

1 **onion**, peeled

4 large **garlic cloves**, grated or finely chopped

1 tablespoon **chili powder**, a palmful

2 cups shredded **Pepper Jack** cheese

¼ cup fresh **cilantro or flat-leaf parsley** leaves, a handful, coarsely chopped

2 tablespoons **EVOO** (extra-virgin olive oil), 2 times around the pan, plus some for drizzling

¼ cup **molasses** (eyeball it)

½ cup **cider vinegar** (eyeball it)

¼ cup **light or dark brown sugar** (eyeball it)

1 (28-ounce) can crushed **fire-roasted tomatoes**

1 pound **broccolini**, stem ends trimmed

Preheat the oven to 400°F.

Cut larger potatoes in half, leave smaller baby potatoes whole and place them in a saucepot. Add water to cover by about 1 inch, cover with the lid, and bring to a boil over high heat. Remove the lid and simmer the potatoes until tender, 12 to 15 minutes. Drain and return the potatoes to their pot, then add 2 tablespoons of the butter, some salt and pepper, and the sour cream and chives. Smash with a fork or potato masher until your preferred consistency is achieved.

While the potatoes are coming up to a boil, place the turkey in a mixing bowl. Grate half of the onion into the meat along with half of the garlic, the chili powder, shredded cheese, cilantro or parsley, and salt and pepper. Form the mixture into 1½-inch-round meatballs and arrange on a nonstick baking sheet. Drizzle the meatballs with a little EVOO and roast in the oven for 12 minutes, or until they are golden and the juices run clear.

Once you have the meatballs in the oven, start the barbecue sauce. Place a large skillet over medium-high heat with the 2 tablespoons of EVOO. Chop the remaining half onion, and add it to the center of the skillet along with the remaining garlic and salt and pepper. Cook, stirring frequently, for 3 to 4 minutes. Add the molasses, cider vinegar, and brown sugar; stir to combine; then stir in the fire-roasted tomatoes. Bring up to a bubble and simmer the sauce over low heat until you are ready to eat.

Place about 1 inch of water in a high-sided skillet over high heat, put a lid on it, and bring up to a simmer. Add some salt and the broccolini and cook for 3 to 4 minutes, keeping the broccolini on the crunchy side. Drain and return to the skillet, season with salt and pepper and add the remaining tablespoon of butter; stir until the butter has melted and coated all the broccolini.

Remove the meatballs from the oven and add to the skillet with the barbecue sauce. Toss to coat with the sauce. Plate up the meatballs with a little more sauce on top and serve with the smashed potatoes and the broccolini alongside.

# A Mediterranean-Style Everyday Thanksgiving: Turkey Saltimbocca, Creamy Polenta, and Braised Kale

I like to give thanks throughout the year for my favorite earthly pleasure: food! You'll be grateful for every bit of this one.

5 tablespoons **EVOO** (extra-virgin olive oil)
8 **turkey breast cutlets**, pounded out between plastic to $\frac{1}{8}$- to $\frac{1}{4}$-inch thickness
**Salt** and **black pepper**
16 fresh **sage leaves**
8 slices **prosciutto di Parma**
3 cups **chicken stock**
$\frac{1}{4}$ cup **parsley**, a handful, chopped
4 tablespoons ($\frac{1}{2}$ stick) **butter**
$1\frac{1}{2}$ cups **whole milk**
1 cup **quick-cooking polenta**
$\frac{1}{2}$ cup grated **Asiago** cheese, a couple of handfuls
Freshly **grated nutmeg**
$\frac{1}{4}$ pound **pancetta**, chopped
1 medium **onion**, chopped
2 **garlic cloves**, chopped
$1\frac{1}{2}$ pounds **kale**, stemmed and coarsely chopped
1 tablespoon **sugar**
2 tablespoons **red wine vinegar**

Preheat a large nonstick skillet over high heat with 2 tablespoons of the EVOO, twice around the pan.

Lay out the turkey cutlets on a cutting board and season liberally with salt and pepper. Place 2 sage leaves in the center of each cutlet, then top with a slice of prosciutto. Roll each cutlet up on a diagonal angle, making long, skinny rolls. Add the turkey rolls to the hot pan seam side down and brown on all sides. Once the rolls are brown, turn the heat to medium and continue to cook until cooked through, 7 to 8 minutes. Remove the rolls to a plate and add 1 cup of the stock to the skillet, scraping up any of the brown bits with a wooden spoon. Bring up to a bubble and cook for about 2 minutes until somewhat reduced. Add the parsley and 2 tablespoons of the butter, stirring and shaking the skillet until the butter has melted. Set the rolls back in the pan and turn off heat.

While the turkey cooks, bring $1\frac{1}{2}$ cups of the chicken stock and the milk to a boil in a saucepan. Once the liquid comes to a boil, stir in the polenta with a wooden spoon and cook until it all comes together. Stir in the remaining butter and the cheese and season with nutmeg, salt, and pepper.

While the liquids come to a boil for the polenta, heat the remaining 3 tablespoons EVOO in a large skillet. Add the chopped pancetta and cook until crispy, 2 to 3 minutes. Add the onions and garlic and cook until soft, 3 to 4 minutes. Add the kale and wilt it down, tossing and turning frequently. Sprinkle in the sugar, toss again, then deglaze the pan with the vinegar. Add the remaining $\frac{1}{2}$ cup stock, reduce the heat to low, and let the kale mellow for a few minutes.

Serve 2 turkey rolls per portion, spooning the sauce over each serving. Mound some polenta and kale generously alongside.

# Another Everyday Thanksgiving:

Gravy-Soaked Turkey over Sausage Stuffing and Peas
with Sweetened Cranberries

   2  tablespoons **EVOO** (extra-virgin olive oil)

  ¾  pound **bulk sweet Italian sausage** or maple breakfast sausage
      removed from casing

   4  **celery ribs** with leafy tops, chopped

   1  medium to large **onion**, chopped

   1  **bay leaf**, fresh or dried

   5  to 6 fresh **sage** sprigs, chopped; a couple of tablespoons

   5  to 6 fresh **thyme** sprigs, leaves stripped and chopped; a couple of
      tablespoons

      **Salt** and **black pepper**

   4  slices **white or whole-wheat bread**

   5  tablespoons **butter**, softened

   1  quart (4 cups) **chicken or turkey stock**

   2  tablespoons all-purpose **flour**

  ½  cup fresh **flat-leaf parsley** leaves, a couple of handfuls, chopped

1½  pounds thickly **sliced roasted turkey breast** from a good-quality deli
      counter

  ½  cup sweetened **dried cranberries**

   2  (10-ounce) boxes **frozen peas**

For the stuffing, preheat a large skillet over medium-high heat with
1 tablespoon of the EVOO, once around the pan. Add the sausage
and break it up using the back of a wooden spoon. Cook until well
browned, 5 minutes. Add the celery, onions, bay leaf, sage, thyme,
and some salt and pepper. Continue to cook until the veggies are
soft, 7 to 8 minutes.

Toast the bread, then spread it with 2 tablespoons of the butter. Chop it into small cubes and add to the sausage and veggies. Toss to combine and moisten with a cup or so of the stock. Cover the skillet and keep warm until ready to serve. (Remove the bay leaf just before serving.)

Over medium heat, combine 2 tablespoons of the butter and the remaining tablespoon of EVOO in another large skillet. Once the butter has melted, add the flour and cook, stirring frequently, for 1 minute. Whisk in 2 cups of the stock, season with salt and pepper, and cook until thickened, about 2 minutes. Stir in the parsley, and then add the turkey and simmer until it is heated through, 1 to 2 minutes.

For the peas, place the remaining cup of stock in a medium-size saucepot or skillet and add the sweetened dried cranberries. Turn the heat up to medium-high and bring up to a simmer. Once it is simmering, cook for 2 to 3 minutes, then add the frozen peas and season with salt and pepper. Cook until heated through. Add the remaining tablespoon of butter and stir to melt.

Serve a mound of stuffing topped with gravy-soaked turkey, and spoon some cran-peas alongside.

seven

# Mmmm, Beefy!

## Steaks, Chops, Cutlets, and Tenderloins

(continued)

Most of the time I'm perfectly happy with a 30-Minute Meal—hey, how much time does any of us really want to spend in the kitchen anyway—but some cold, rainy, snowy, or otherwise lazy days all I really want is a big pot of stew or nice roast making the house smell amazing while we cozy up by the fire and watch some DVDs. In this chapter you'll find plenty of speed-em-up dinners that will please your most ravenous carnivores, plus a big bunch of slow-it-down dinners that take a little more time getting to the table but won't stick you in the kitchen for a minute longer then absolutely necessary. And because roasts retain their flavor and juiciness really well, they make great leftovers, so I've given you some great Double Duty and Rollover recipes that let you cook once, eat twice with very little effort.

# Skillet Tamale Pie

Yes, your kids will eat this . . . if you don't eat it all first.
This one is dedicated to Dr. Phil, who loves to eat meat
right out of the skillet!

1 tablespoon **EVOO** (extra-virgin olive oil), once around the pan

1 quart (4 cups) **chicken stock**

2 cups **whole milk** or half-and-half

2 **bacon slices**, chopped

¾ pound **ground beef**

¾ pound **ground pork**

1 medium **onion**, chopped

1 small red or green **bell pepper**, seeded and chopped

1 **jalapeño pepper**, seeded and thinly sliced

3 to 4 **garlic cloves**, chopped

1 tablespoon **chili powder,** a palmful

2 teaspoons **ground cumin**, ⅔ palmful

Pinch of **ground cinnamon**

**Salt** and **black pepper**

1 (15-ounce) can **tomato sauce**

2 cups **quick-cooking polenta**

A handful of fresh **cilantro** or parsley, finely chopped

1 cup shredded **Cheddar** or Monterey Jack cheese

Preheat the broiler to high and place the oven rack 1 rung beneath
the highest level of your oven.

In a large skillet, heat the EVOO over medium-high to high heat.
Combine the chicken stock and milk or half-in-half in a pot to bring
to a boil over medium heat.

Add the bacon to the hot EVOO and cook for 2 minutes or until crisp, then add the ground meats, raise the heat to high, and cook until they are browned, 3 to 4 minutes. Add the onions, bell pepper, jalapeño, and garlic and season with the chili powder, cumin, cinnamon, salt, and pepper. Cook for 5 minutes to soften the vegetables, then stir in the tomato sauce and heat through, 1 minute more.

While the meat cooks, whisk the polenta into the simmering stock and milk. Stir for 5 minutes, or until the polenta is thick and masses together in the pot. Fold in the cilantro or parsley. Use a rubber spatula to spread the polenta over the meat mixture and top with the cheese. Place the skillet under the hot broiler to brown the cheese and set the polenta, about 1 minute. Serve directly from the skillet.

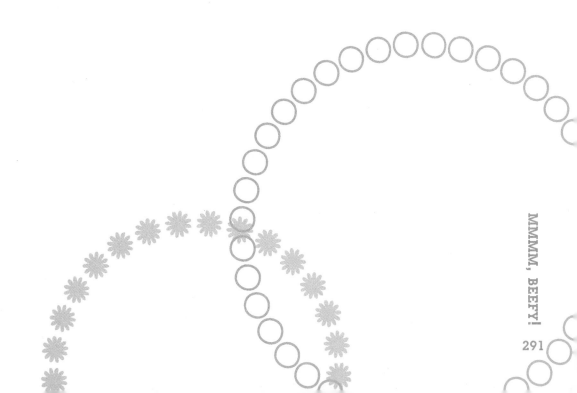

# Southern-Style Shepherd's Pie

So good, yo momma will think she invented it, and with pork and sweet potatoes in it, it's so Southern, y'all will be drawlin' by the time you eat the last yummy bite.

3 pounds **sweet potatoes**, peeled and cut into chunks
4 tablespoons (½ stick) **butter**
1 **banana**, sliced
  Zest and juice of 1 **orange**
½ cup **heavy cream**
  **Grated nutmeg** to taste, about ¼ teaspoon
  **Salt** and **black pepper**
2 tablespoons **EVOO** (extra-virgin olive oil), twice around the pan
2 pounds **ground pork** or turkey
1 large **onion**, chopped
2 medium **parsnips** (about 8 ounces), peeled and thinly sliced
3 **celery ribs**, sliced
3 tablespoons **cider vinegar**
1 tablespoon **dark or light brown sugar**
2 tablespoons all-purpose **flour**
1 bunch of **Swiss chard**, stemmed and chopped
2½ cups **chicken stock**
1 cup **frozen peas**
¼ cup fresh **flat-leaf parsley**, a generous handful, chopped

Preheat the oven to 400°F.

Bring a pot of water to a boil over high heat for the sweet potatoes. Add the sweet potatoes and cook until tender, 15 minutes. Drain the potatoes and reserve. Return the pot to the stovetop over medium heat. Add the butter and sliced banana to the pot. Cook the banana in the butter for 5 minutes, then add the orange zest and juice. Return the sweet potatoes to the pot and mash with the cream. Season with the nutmeg, and salt and pepper to taste. Keep warm.

While the potatoes cook, heat the EVOO in a large skillet over medium-high heat. Add the meat and cook, breaking it up into small bits with the back of a spoon, until well browned, 7 to 8 minutes. Add the onions, parsnips, and celery and cook for another 10 minutes, stirring every now and then. Add the cider vinegar and brown sugar, and stir. Sprinkle the mixture with the flour, and stir again for another 2 minutes so the flour cooks a little. Add the Swiss chard and stir until it is wilted, then add the chicken stock. Bring up to a bubble, then simmer for a few minutes until the mixture is cooked and has thickened. Remove from the heat.

Add the peas and parsley to the meat and veggie mixture, and stir to combine. Pour into a medium casserole or 8- or 9-inch square baking dish. Top with the mashed sweet potatoes and spread them out evenly. Transfer the dish to the oven and bake until the top of the potatoes is lightly browned, 15 to 20 minutes.

# Baked Stuffed Potatoes Topped with Saucy Ground Meat Sauce

This is like an upside-down shepherd's pie.

4 large starchy **potatoes**, such as russet, scrubbed
**EVOO** (extra-virgin olive oil) for drizzling, plus 2 tablespoons
**Salt**
1½ pounds **ground beef** or lamb
**Black pepper**
2 **carrots**, shredded on the large side of a box grater
2 medium **onions**, grated or chopped
1 fresh or dried **bay leaf**
1 tablespoon **Worcestershire sauce**
1 bottle of **dark ale**, such as Guinness
½ cup **heavy cream** or half-and-half
1½ cups shredded **white extra-sharp Cheddar cheese**
Freshly grated **nutmeg**
Finely chopped **flat-leaf parsley**, a palmful

Preheat the oven to 425°F. Rub the potatoes with a little EVOO and season with salt. Place on a rack in the upper half of the oven and roast for 40 minutes.

While the potatoes roast, heat 2 tablespoons of EVOO, twice around the pan, in a deep skillet over medium-high heat. Season the meat with salt and pepper and add it to the skillet. Brown the meat for 7 to 8 minutes, then add the vegetables and bay leaf and cook for another 8 to 10 minutes. Add the Worcestershire sauce and ale and deglaze the pan, using a wooden spoon to scrape up all the pan drippings. Adjust the salt and pepper and reduce the heat to low. Discard the bay leaf before serving.

Remove the potatoes from the oven and switch on the broiler. Cut the potatoes in half lengthwise. Hold the potato halves in a clean towel and scrape the flesh into a bowl, leaving a thin layer in the skin for stability. Set the potato skins onto a baking sheet. Mash the reserved potatoes with a little cream or half-and-half and the cheese. Season the cheesy potatoes with salt, pepper, and nutmeg. Refill the skins and slide under the broiler to brown the tops.

Place two potato halves on each serving plate and ladle some of the meat sauce over the tops. Sprinkle with the chopped parsley.

# Sliced Steak Stroganoff in French Bread and Dill Relish Dressed Salad

Serious guy food that's also good for girls with guy-size appetites.

    1   crusty **baguette**
    5   tablespoons **EVOO** (extra-virgin olive oil)
    2   tablespoons **butter**
1¼   pounds inch-thick **sirloin** or strip steak, very thinly sliced
        (¼ inch or less)
        **Salt** and **black pepper**
    1   cup all-purpose **flour**
    1   small **onion**, peeled
1½   cups **beef stock**
    ⅓   cup **sour cream**
    2   tablespoons fresh **lemon juice**
    2   to 3 tablespoons chopped fresh **dill**
    2   teaspoons **Dijon mustard**
    1   tablespoon **white wine or cider vinegar** (eyeball it)
    2   rounded spoonfuls **dill pickle relish**
    3   or 4 **radishes**, sliced
    1   head of **green leaf lettuce** or other lettuce of choice, chopped
        **Pickled onions** for garnish (optional)
    1   bunch of **watercress**, washed and tough stems removed, chopped

Cut the baguette into 4 pieces and split almost all the way through but do not separate. In a large skillet heat 2 tablespoons of the EVOO, twice around the pan, and the butter over medium to medium-high heat until very hot.

Pat the sliced meat dry with paper towels. Season with salt and pepper and dip in the flour to coat. Shake off the excess flour, then add to the very hot pan. Grate the onion directly onto the meat. Cook the meat for 5 to 6 minutes, turning occasionally. Add the stock to the pan and cook until thickened, 1 minute. Stir in the sour cream, a tablespoon of the lemon juice, and the dill. Season with pepper and remove from the heat.

While the meat cooks, combine the mustard, the remaining tablespoon of lemon juice, and the vinegar in the bottom of a salad bowl and mix with a fork or a whisk. Beat in the remaining 3 tablespoons of EVOO, then stir in the relish. Add the radishes, lettuce, and pickled onions if using and toss to combine. Season with salt and pepper to taste.

Pile the meat onto the cut baguette pieces, top with some of the chopped watercress, and serve with the salad.

# Beef Tips with Mushrooms, Almond-Citrus Rice, and Barcelona Bean Salad

The sun also sets . . . and when it does, this Spanish supper will heat you up!

- 1 tablespoon **butter**
- ¼ cup slivered or sliced **almonds**
- 1 cup **white rice**

  Zest and juice of 1 **orange**

  Zest and juice of 1 **lemon**
- 2 cups **chicken stock**

  **Salt**
- 1 pound trimmed fresh **green beans** or a mix of yellow wax and green beans, coarsely chopped on an angle
- 1 tablespoon **Tabasco** or other hot sauce
- 6 tablespoons **EVOO** (extra-virgin olive oil)

  **Black pepper**
- 1½ pounds **beef tenderloin** or sirloin tips, cut in bite-size pieces
- 1 pound **cremini or white mushroom caps**, brushed clean and halved
- 3 **garlic cloves**, finely chopped
- ½ cup **dry Spanish sherry**
- ½ cup **beef stock**

Melt the butter in a saucepot over medium heat. Add the almonds and stir for 3 to 4 minutes to toast. Add the rice and the orange and lemon zests, then turn the rice to coat in the butter and cook for 1 minute. Add the stock and bring to a boil, then reduce to a simmer, cover the pot, and cook the rice for 17 to 18 minutes.

Add an inch of water to a medium skillet and bring it to a simmer. Salt the water liberally, then add the beans and cook for 3 to 4 minutes, until just tender. Drain and cool under cold running water.

Whisk the orange and lemon juices together with the hot sauce in the bottom of a shallow bowl. Stream in 3 tablespoons of the EVOO, whisking constantly. Add the beans and toss to coat. Season the beans with salt and pepper to taste.

Heat a large shallow skillet over medium-high heat with 1 tablespoon of the EVOO, once around the pan. Pat the meat dry. When the oil ripples and begins to smoke, add the beef and brown for 3 minutes on each side. Remove when evenly deep brown and reserve on a plate.

Heat the remaining 2 tablespoons of EVOO in the same skillet until the oil ripples. Add the mushrooms and brown for 7 to 8 minutes, adding the garlic after the mushrooms have cooked for a few minutes. Season the mushrooms with salt and pepper, then add the sherry. Cook for 1 minute to reduce the sherry, then add the beef stock and browned beef tips and any juices that have accumulated. Reduce the heat and cook for 3 to 4 minutes more. Turn off the heat.

Fluff the rice with a fork.

Serve the beef and mushrooms over the rice with the bean salad alongside.

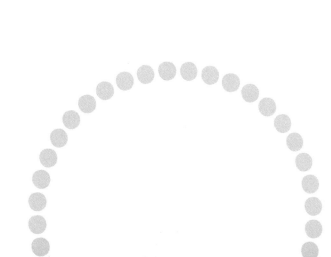

# Sliced Steak, Mushrooms, and Green Onions with Warm Dijon Potato Salad

This one is elegant enough to entertain with but so easy that you could even entertain yourself with it when you're flying solo! Don't worry if you don't polish it all off; whatever's left over will be great hot or cold the next day.

4 **strip steaks**, 1 inch thick
   **Salt**
2 pounds **baby red-skin potatoes**, halved
4 tablespoons **EVOO** (extra-virgin olive oil), plus some for drizzling
4 slices **thick-cut bacon**, chopped
3 **shallots**, thinly sliced
3 tablespoons **white wine vinegar**
6 tablespoons **grainy Dijon mustard**
   A generous handful of fresh **flat-leaf parsley**, chopped
   **Black pepper** or grill seasoning blend for steak
¾ pound **cremini** mushrooms, quartered
1 bunch of **scallions**, white and green parts chopped separately
½ cup **white wine** (eyeball it)
2 tablespoons **butter**, cut into pieces
   A handful of fresh **flat-leaf parsley**, chopped

Remove the steaks from the fridge so they can rest at room temperature.

Bring water to a boil for the potatoes, season the water with salt, and cook the potatoes until tender, 12 to 15 minutes. Drain and return to the hot pot to evaporate the excess water.

Preheat a grill pan over high heat.

While the potatoes cook, heat a skillet over medium to medium-high heat. Add 2 tablespoons of the EVOO, twice around the pan, then the bacon. Cook until almost crisp, then add the shallots, lower the heat a bit, and cook for 6 to 7 minutes, until very tender. Add the vinegar and deglaze the pan, then whisk in the Dijon mustard. Add the potatoes and parsley to the skillet and turn to coat evenly, allowing the potatoes to absorb the flavors and dressing.

While the shallots are working, drizzle the steaks with EVOO and season both sides with salt and pepper or grill seasoning. Place the meat on the grill pan and cook for 7 to 8 minutes for rare meat or up to 12 minutes for medium well, turning the steaks once. Let the meat rest for 5 minutes before slicing. While the steaks cook, heat the remaining 2 tablespoons of EVOO in a medium skillet over medium-high heat. Add the mushrooms and the white parts of the scallions and cook until the mushrooms are dark and tender, 7 to 8 minutes. Add the wine and reduce for 1 minute. Add the butter in small bits and turn off the heat. Slice the steaks against the grain and top with the mushrooms, then scatter the parsley and scallion greens across the top. Serve the warm Dijon potato salad alongside.

# Gorgonzola and Herb Tenderloin Steaks and Pasta with Roasted Garlic and Grape Tomatoes

I made this garlic-centric meal for my in-laws, who are not normally fans of garlic, and they cleaned their plates! My husband was so happy to see his parents FINALLY embrace garlic (his first love; I'm number three, behind that and Scotch) that he literally cried about it later that night!

**Salt**
1 pound **penne pasta**
2 pints **grape tomatoes**
6 **garlic cloves** cracked but left in their skins, plus 1 garlic clove peeled and halved
3 to 4 tablespoons **EVOO** (extra-virgin olive oil) plus some for drizzling
**Black pepper**
4 **beef tenderloin steaks**, about 1¼ inch thick
2 **scallions**, white and green parts, chopped
8 to 10 fresh **sage leaves**, thinly sliced
A handful of fresh **flat-leaf parsley** leaves, finely chopped
1 cup crumbled **Gorgonzola** cheese
1 cup grated **Parmigiano-Reggiano** cheese, a few generous handfuls
1 cup fresh **basil**, 20 leaves, torn or shredded
2 cups **arugula** leaves, coarsely chopped

Preheat the oven to 450°F.

Bring a large pot of water to a boil. Salt the water, add the pasta, and cook to just shy of al dente. It needs to have a real bite left to it because it will sit in the sauce for 2 minutes later on and continue to cook. Heads up: you will need to set aside about 1½ cups of the starchy cooking water before you drain the pasta.

Place the grape tomatoes on a rimmed baking sheet with the cracked garlic and coat the tomatoes and garlic with 3 to 4 tablespoons of the EVOO. Season with lots of salt and pepper. Roast in the oven for 20 minutes.

Season the steaks with salt and pepper and rub both sides with the halved garlic clove. Drizzle the steaks lightly on both sides with EVOO. Combine the scallions, sage, and parsley with the Gorgonzola crumbles.

When the tomatoes are just about done, heat an ovenproof skillet over high heat. Add the steaks and sear the meat on both sides; 90 seconds per side should do it. Leave the steaks in the skillet.

Take the tomatoes out of the oven and turn the oven off. Top the meat with the Gorgonzola mixture and transfer the skillet with the steaks to the oven. Let the meat sit in the hot oven for 4 to 5 minutes. The Gorgonzola will melt down over the meat and the steaks will be tender and pale pink inside.

Slip the roasted garlic cloves from the skins and mash into a paste with the side of your knife. Scrape the garlic paste into a pasta bowl. Using a fork, mix the garlic into the reserved pasta cooking water. Add the tomatoes to the bowl and mash them with a potato masher until a sauce forms and the tomatoes are well combined with the garlic broth. Add the drained penne, grated Parm, basil, and arugula, and toss for a minute or two to allow the pasta to soak up the flavors.

Serve the steaks with the pasta alongside.

# Elsa's Cider Beef with Smashed Cheddar Potatoes

Mama knows best! Here again, my mama, Elsa, proves she's top chef!

- 2 tablespoons **EVOO** (extra-virgin olive oil)
- 3 tablespoons **butter**
- 2 pounds **top sirloin**, trimmed and cut into 1½-inch cubes
  **Salt** and **black pepper**
- 1 large **onion**, chopped
- 2 medium **carrots**, peeled and chopped
- 1 pound **turnips**, peeled and chopped
- 4 tablespoons all-purpose **flour**
- 2 cups good-quality **apple cider**—go dark and cloudy
- 1 (15-ounce) can **beef stock**
- 3 pounds **Idaho potatoes**, peeled and chopped
- ½ cup **milk**
- ½ cup **sour cream**
- 2 cups shredded **sharp white Cheddar cheese**
- 3 tablespoons chopped or snipped **chives**

Preheat the oven to 425°F.

Place a large stew pot or Dutch oven with a lid over medium-high heat. Add the EVOO and butter. When the butter melts, season the beef with salt and pepper and add to the pot. Brown on all sides, 7 to 8 minutes total. Add the onions, carrots, and turnips, and cook for 5 minutes. Sprinkle the vegetables with the flour and stir to combine and coat, 1 minute. Stir in the apple cider and the beef stock, bring to a boil, cover the pan, and transfer to the oven. Braise the beef for 45 minutes.

Once the beef has been in the oven for about 15 minutes, place the potatoes in a large saucepot with water to cover by at least 1 to 2 inches. Bring to a boil over high heat, then reduce the heat a bit, add some salt, and cook the potatoes until tender, about 15 minutes.

When the potatoes are tender, drain them and return them to the pot. Add the milk, sour cream, and cheese. Use a potato masher to smash them to your preferred consistency. Season with salt and pepper and add the chives. Cover and keep warm until the beef is done.

To serve, ladle the stew into shallow serving bowls. Make a well in the center and fill with the potatoes. (It should be noted, however, that there are members of our family—like my brother—who would fill a bowl with potatoes instead, leaving a small well in the center to hold a few bites of stew.)

# Forest Beef Stew

Who needs a Crock-Pot? Here you get all the slow-cooked, earthy flavor of an all-day stew—without the all-day commitment.

- 2 tablespoons **EVOO** (extra-virgin olive oil), twice around the pan
- 2 pounds **sirloin shell steak**, trimmed and chopped into bite-size pieces
  **Salt** and **black pepper**
- 2 **carrots**, peeled and sliced on an angle
- 4 **parsnips**, peeled and sliced on an angle
- 4 **shallots**, peeled and quartered
- 2 fresh or dried **bay leaves**
- 12 **dried apricots**, coarsely chopped
- 8 **dried figs**, coarsely chopped
  A handful of **dried cranberries**
- 1 tablespoon **Worcestershire sauce**
- 1 quart (4 cups) **beef stock**
- 8 fresh **sage** leaves, finely chopped
- ¼ teaspoon **ground allspice** (eyeball it)
- ¼ cup chopped fresh **flat-leaf parsley**, a generous handful
- 3 tablespoons fresh **chives**, snipped or chopped
- ½ cup **smoked almonds**, chopped
  Toasted **whole-grain bread** or rolls
  Softened **butter**

Heat the EVOO in a large, deep skillet or stew pot over high heat. When the oil ripples, add the beef and brown it all over, 6 to 7 minutes. Season liberally with salt and pepper, then add the vegetables and bay leaves to the pot. Reduce the heat to medium-high and cook for 5 minutes to begin to soften the vegetables. Add the dried fruits, Worcestershire, and beef stock. Mix well, then stir in the sage and allspice. Reduce the heat to a simmer and cook for 20 minutes, or until the dried fruits are plump and the vegetables tender. Adjust the salt and pepper to taste and remove the bay leaves. Serve the stew in shallow bowls and top with the parsley, chives, and smoked almonds. Pass bread and butter at the table.

# Lamb Meatballs in Tomato Mint Sauce with Pine Nut Couscous

By Zeus! This meatball supper is fit for a whole pantheon of Greek gods! Better yet, it's so hearty and healthy you'll be ready to climb Mount Olympus when you're finished.

- 4 cups **crusty bread**, torn into small pieces
- 1 cup **milk**
- 1 pound **ground lamb**
- 1 **egg**
- ½ cup grated **Parmigiano-Reggiano** cheese, a couple of handfuls
  **Salt** and **black pepper**
- 2 pinches of **ground allspice**
- 2 teaspoons grated **lemon zest**
- 4 **garlic cloves**, minced
- 1 small **onion**, peeled
- 3 tablespoons **EVOO** (extra-virgin olive oil), 3 times around the pan
- 1 (28-ounce) can **crushed Italian tomatoes**
- 2 cups **chicken stock**
- ¼ cup fresh **flat-leaf parsley**, a generous handful, finely chopped
- ¼ cup fresh **mint sprigs**, a generous handful, finely chopped
- 2 tablespoons **butter**
- 1½ cups **couscous**
- ¼ cup **pine nuts**, a generous handful

Soak the bread in the milk for a few minutes, then squeeze the bread to wring out the excess moisture. Place the bread in a food processor and pulse to grind it up. Transfer to a mixing bowl and add the lamb, egg, cheese, salt, pepper, allspice, lemon zest, and 1 minced garlic clove. Use a grater to grate about 2 tablespoons of onion into the lamb. Use your hands to combine the meatball mix, then roll into balls the size of walnuts; you should have about 20 balls.

Heat the EVOO in a deep skillet over medium heat. Add the remaining garlic and grate the remaining onion into the EVOO. Sauté the garlic and onion for a few minutes, then stir in the tomatoes and $\frac{1}{2}$ cup of the chicken stock. When the sauce bubbles, add the meatballs and simmer for 7 to 8 minutes to cook through. Stir in the parsley and mint and season the sauce with salt and pepper.

While the meatballs cook, bring the remaining $1\frac{1}{2}$ cups of stock and the butter to a simmer in a saucepot. Add the couscous, turn off the heat, and cover. Let the couscous stand for 5 minutes. Toast the pine nuts in a dry skillet over medium-high heat for 3 minutes, or until light golden. Add the pine nuts to the couscous and fluff with a fork.

Serve the meatballs and sauce on a bed of the couscous.

# Moroccan Chili and 10,000 Grains of Sand

If you're a spice-aholic, you can use half the spice cabinet in this exotic take on chili.

- 2 tablespoons **EVOO** (extra-virgin olive oil), twice around the pan
- 2 pounds **ground lamb**
  **Salt** and **black pepper**
- 2 tablespoons **chili powder**, a couple of palmfuls
- ½ tablespoon **ground cumin** (½ palmful)
- ½ tablespoon **sweet paprika** (½ palmful)
- 1 tablespoon **ground coriander** (a palmful)
- ¼ teaspoon **ground cinnamon** (eyeball it in your palm)
- 1 **bay leaf**
- 1 large **onion**, chopped
- 1 green **bell pepper**, seeded and chopped
- 2 **garlic cloves**, finely chopped
  Zest and juice of 1 **lemon**
- 2 tablespoons **Worcestershire sauce** (eyeball it)
- 1 (15-ounce) can **tomato sauce**
- 4 **pita breads**
- 2 tablespoons **butter**
- 1¾ cups **chicken stock**
  A handful of **golden raisins**, chopped
- 4 to 5 **dried apricots**, chopped
- 1½ cups **couscous**
- 3 to 4 tablespoons toasted **pine nuts**
  A handful of fresh **flat-leaf parsley**, chopped
  A handful of fresh **mint**, chopped
- 3 tablespoons finely chopped **chives**

Preheat the oven to 400°F.

Heat the EVOO in a skillet over medium-high to high heat. When it's hot, add the meat and brown, turning and breaking up with a wooden spoon until it's no longer pink, 3 to 4 minutes. Season the meat with salt, pepper, the chili powder, cumin, paprika, coriander, and cinnamon. Add the bay leaf, onions, bell pepper, and garlic to the pan and cook until the onions are soft, about 8 minutes. Stir in the lemon zest, Worcestershire, and tomato sauce, and reduce the heat to a simmer.

Separate each pita into 2 layers, then pile the layers together and cut them into quarters. Spread the pita "chips" out on a large baking sheet and toast until evenly golden, 8 minutes.

In a pot with a tight-fitting lid, combine the butter, stock, and dried fruit and bring to a boil. Add the couscous, stir, then turn off heat and cover. Let stand for 5 minutes. Add the nuts, herbs, and lemon juice and fluff with a fork.

Remove the bay leaf from the chili and discard. Ladle the chili into shallow bowls and top with a small mound of couscous "sand." Serve with pita chips for scooping up Mo' chili! (Hey, Moroccans don't use silverware; why should you?)

# Lamb Chops with Roasted Tomato Gravy and Green Olive Couscous

I've been using roasted tomatoes a ton recently, because they contribute so much flavor and intensity to a dish with virtually no work. You'll find this gravy works on any chop.

- 1 pint **grape tomatoes**
- 5 tablespoons **EVOO** (extra-virgin olive oil), plus some for drizzling
  **Salt** and **black pepper**
- 1 large **shallot**, finely chopped
- 2 to 3 large **garlic cloves**, finely chopped
- 2 tablespoons all-purpose **flour**
- 1 cup **dry white wine**
- 3 cups **chicken stock**
- 8 **loin lamb chops**, about 1½ pounds total
- 2 cups **couscous**
- ½ cup **Sicilian green olives**, chopped
  A handful of fresh **flat-leaf parsley**, finely chopped
- 3 to 4 tablespoons fresh **mint leaves**, a generous handful, finely chopped

Preheat the oven to 400°F.

On a rimmed baking sheet, toss the tomatoes with 2 tablespoons of the EVOO, plus salt and pepper to taste. Roast the tomatoes for 20 minutes.

In a medium skillet or saucepot heat 2 tablespoons of the EVOO, twice around the pan, over medium heat. Add the shallots and garlic and cook for 2 to 3 minutes, then sprinkle in the flour and cook for a minute more. Whisk in the wine and cook until reduced by half, a minute or two, then whisk in 1 cup of the chicken stock and season with salt and pepper. Reduce the heat to low and simmer until thick.

In another small or medium saucepot with a tight-fitting lid, bring the remaining 2 cups stock to a boil.

While the stock comes up to a boil, heat the remaining 1 tablespoon EVOO in a skillet over medium-high heat. Season the chops with salt and pepper and cook for 4 minutes on each side for medium.

Crush the roasted tomatoes with a potato masher and then stir into the gravy.

Add a drizzle of EVOO and the couscous to the boiling stock and stir. Add the olives and parsley, stir again, and turn off the heat. Cover the pot and let stand for 5 minutes.

Just before serving, stir the mint into the tomato gravy, and fluff the couscous with a fork.

Serve the chops and couscous covered with the tomato gravy.

# Italian Pork and Beans

This is stick-to-your-ribs fare in just 15 minutes!

3 tablespoons **EVOO** (extra-virgin olive oil), 3 times around the pan
⅓-pound chunk of **pancetta**, cut into ¼-inch dice
1 medium **onion**, finely chopped
1 **carrot**, peeled and grated
2 **celery ribs** with leafy tops, finely chopped
2 to 3 **garlic cloves**, chopped
1 fresh or dried **bay leaf**
2 (15-ounce) cans **white beans**, drained
  **Salt** and **black pepper**
1 cup **chicken stock**
2 cups **tomato sauce**
  **Crusty bread**, for mopping

Heat the EVOO in a deep skillet over medium-high heat. Add the
pancetta and cook for 5 minutes or until crisp. Add the onions, carrot, celery, garlic, and bay leaf and cook for 5 minutes more. Add
the white beans and season liberally with salt and pepper, then stir
in the stock and tomato sauce and cook until heated through, 2 to
3 minutes. Remove the bay leaf and serve the pork and beans in
shallow bowls with the bread.

# Five-Spice Barbecued Pork Chops with Asian-Style Succotash

This is your classic East-meets-West barbecue love story, and the marriage of flavors will bring a tear to your eye!

- 4 **center-cut boneless pork chops**
- 1 teaspoon **five-spice powder**
- 2 teaspoons **grill seasoning blend**, such as McCormick's Montreal Steak Seasoning
- 4 tablespoons **vegetable oil**
- ¼ cup **hoisin sauce**, found on the Asian foods aisle
- 3 **garlic cloves**, chopped
- 1 red **bell pepper**, seeded and chopped
- 2 generous handfuls of **snow pea pods**, coarsely chopped
- 2 cups **frozen corn**
- 4 **scallions**, chopped
  Juice of 1 **lime**
- 2 teaspoons **hot sauce**

Season the chops liberally on both sides with the five-spice powder and grill seasoning. Heat 2 tablespoons of the vegetable oil in a nonstick skillet over medium-high heat. Cook the chops for 6 minutes on each side, then add the hoisin sauce to the pan. Heat through and turn the chops to coat in the sauce. Turn off the heat.

While the chops cook, heat the remaining 2 tablespoons of oil in a second skillet over medium-high heat. Add the garlic and bell peppers, cook for 2 minutes, then add the pea pods, corn, and scallions and cook for 3 minutes more. Toss the succotash with the lime juice and hot sauce to combine.

Serve the chops with succotash alongside.

MMMM, BEEFY!

# Sweet 'n' Spicy Red-Eye Ham Steaks, Cheese Grits, and Seared Chard

This one I wrote for my friends in Enterprise, Alabama, who asked me to develop a more Winn-Dixie–type menu—a basic square meal that can be shopped for in a small-town market.

    3  tablespoons **butter**
    1  large **ham steak**, 1¼ to 1½ pounds
    ¼  to ⅓ cup strong **coffee**
    ¼  cup **maple syrup**
    3  tablespoons **grainy mustard**
    1¼ cups **milk**
    ½  cup **hominy grits**
    1  cup grated **Cheddar cheese**
       Dash of **granulated garlic**
    2  to 3 dashes of **hot sauce**
    ½  teaspoon **paprika**
    1  tablespoon **EVOO** (extra-virgin olive oil), once around the pan
    2  **bacon slices**, chopped
    1  small **red onion**, thinly sliced
    1  pound **Swiss chard** or red Swiss chard, stemmed and coarsely chopped
    2  to 3 tablespoons **cider or wine vinegar**
    1  teaspoon **sugar**
       **Salt** and **black pepper**

Preheat the oven to 375°F.

In an ovenproof skillet melt 1 tablespoonof the butter over medium to medium-high heat. Add the ham steak and brown for a couple of minutes on each side. Combine the coffee, maple syrup, and mustard in a measuring cup and pour into the pan. Turn the ham to coat with the sauce and allow the sauce to caramelize for a minute or two, then transfer to the oven and bake for 10 minutes, turning once.

Combine 1 cup water with the milk in a saucepot and bring to a boil. Add the grits and simmer for 12 to 14 minutes, stirring now and then. Stir in the remaining 2 tablespoons butter, the cheese, granulated garlic, hot sauce, and paprika.

While the cheese grits cooks, heat the EVOO in a skillet over medium-high to high heat until it ripples. Add the bacon and cook until crisp, 2 to 3 minutes, then add the onions and greens. Sear, tossing constantly, for 3 to 4 minutes. Douse the greens with the vinegar and season with the sugar, salt, and pepper. Lower the heat and keep warm while you finish up the grits and plate the ham.

Cut the steak into 4 servings, removing the bone. Pour the pan juices over each portion of ham, and serve with the cheese grits and greens.

# First Night: Roasted Pork Loin and Gravy with Roasted Veggies and Potatoes

This is a classic pork dish that you can spin into two more daring dinners as you go (see pages 320–321). It's a great way to save time *and* learn a new dish!

- 1 5-pound boneless **pork loin roast**
- 1 cup **EVOO** (extra-virgin olive oil)
  **Salt** and **black pepper**
- 10 to 12 fresh **thyme sprigs**, leaves removed and chopped
- 8 **baking potatoes**, peeled and chopped into bite-size cubes
- 2 pounds **baby carrots**
- 2 small or 1 large head of **cauliflower**, trimmed into florets (halve larger florets)
- 3 tablespoons **butter**
- 2 **garlic cloves**
- 3 tablespoons all-purpose **flour**
- 1 quart (4 cups) **chicken stock**
- ½ cup fresh **flat-leaf parsley** leaves, chopped
- 4 **scallions**, green and white parts, finely chopped
  Zest of 1 **orange**

Heads up: you need 3 rimmed baking sheets and a roasting pan to make this recipe. Buy disposables for what you do not have in your cabinets.

Preheat the oven to 425°F.

Place the pork roast in a roasting pan or on a rimmed baking sheet. Drizzle thoroughly with some EVOO, about ¼ cup; season liberally with salt and pepper and sprinkle with the chopped thyme. Transfer to the oven and roast for 45 to 55 minutes, or until the internal temperature is 145°F. Remove from the oven and let the roast rest.

Coat the potatoes with ¼ cup of the EVOO, season with salt and pepper, and roast on a baking sheet for 40 minutes or until deeply golden. Place the baking sheet in the oven lengthwise alongside the roasting pan.

Coat the carrots with a couple of tablespoons of EVOO and season with salt and pepper. Arrange on a baking sheet. Do the same with the cauliflower. Transfer to the oven about 30 minutes before you are ready to remove the pork roast. Place the baking sheets in the oven lengthwise so they fit next to each other.

For the gravy, place the butter in a medium-size saucepot over medium-high heat and melt it. Once it is melted, add the garlic, grating it right into the pot, and cook for 1 minute. Add the flour and whisk together for 1 minute. Whisk in the chicken stock, bring up to a bubble, and cook until thickened, 7 to 8 minutes. Reserve covered until ready to serve.

Combine the parsley, scallions, and orange zest in a bowl and reserve.

Transfer half of the veggies and potatoes to a serving platter; reserve the other half to cool and store for a rollover supper later in the week, Indian Curry Vegetables with Spiced Rice (page 320).

Slice just over half of the pork roast, 8 ½-inch-thick pieces, and arrange it next to the vegetables. Reserve the remainder of the pork roast for a second rollover supper later in the week, Roasted Pork and Black Bean Chili (page 321).

Measure 3 cups of the gravy and reserve. Once cool, cover and refrigerate to roll over into the chili later in the week. Serve the sliced pork with the vegetables and potatoes alongside. Pour the remaining cup of gravy over the pork and potatoes. Sprinkle the parsley-scallion-orange mixture over the entire dinner plate.

# Second Night: Indian Curry Vegetables with Spiced Rice

Roll from classic American fare into vegetarian Indian on night two.

**tidbit**
I put the rice on top to prevent it from drawing all the liquids away from the vegetables.

1 quart (4 cups) **chicken stock**
4 tablespoons **EVOO** (extra-virgin olive oil)
1 tablespoon **ground coriander**, a palmful
1 teaspoon **ground turmeric**
1 fresh or dried **bay leaf**
1½ cups **white rice**
  **Salt** and **black pepper**
2 **garlic cloves**
1 medium **onion**, peeled
  **Leftover roasted vegetables** from night 1 (page 318)
2 rounded tablespoons **mild curry paste**
1 (14.5-ounce) can **chickpeas**, drained
1 (28-ounce) can **diced fire-roasted tomatoes**

Heat a medium saucepot over medium heat with 3 cups of the chicken stock and 2 tablespoons of the EVOO, twice around the pan. Add the coriander, turmeric, bay leaf, rice, and salt and pepper. Stir it all together, cover, bring to a boil, then reduce the heat to a simmer and cook for 18 minutes, or until the rice is tender.

While the rice is working, heat a large skillet with high sides over medium-high heat with the remaining 2 tablespoons of EVOO. Grate the garlic and onion into the pot and cook for 2 minutes, then add the leftover roasted vegetables, curry paste, chickpeas, tomatoes, and about a cup of the chicken stock. Bring to a bubble, reduce the heat, and simmer until the rice is done. Discard the bay leaf.

Serve shallow bowls of the vegetables topped with a healthy portion of the spiced rice.

# Third Night: Roasted Pork and Black Bean Chili

Roll into serious Tex-Mexville on the third night of your rollover supper.

2 tablespoons **EVOO** (extra-virgin olive oil), twice around the pan
1 large **onion**, chopped
3 **garlic cloves**, chopped
1 **red bell pepper**, chopped
  **Salt** and **black pepper**
2 tablespoons **chili powder**
1 tablespoon **ground cumin**
1 **bay leaf**
½ bottle **beer**, about 1 cup
3 cups **leftover gravy**
2 (15-ounce) cans **black beans**, drained
5 to 6 cups **cooked pork** chopped into bite-size pieces
  Zest and juice of 1 **lime**
2 cups crushed yellow or white **corn tortilla chips**
  **Sour cream**, for garnish (optional)

Heat a large pot over medium-high heat with the EVOO. Add the onions, garlic, and bell pepper and season with salt and pepper, the chili powder, cumin, and bay leaf. Cook, stirring frequently, for 5 minutes or until the veggies start to get tender, then add the beer and cook for a minute more. Stir in the leftover gravy and the black beans and bring it up to a simmer. Add the cooked pork and cook to heat it through, 7 to 8 minutes. Add the lime zest and juice and stir to combine. Discard the bay leaf. Serve up the chili and top with some of the crushed tortillas and a dollop of sour cream.

# First Night: Roast Pork Tenderloins with Green Onion Smashed Potatoes and Roasted Green Beans

The first night, it's another square meal: meat, potatoes, and a simple vegetable. The next night, sammies so tasty that the kids and the adults will argue over who likes them more.

2 to 2½ pounds **starchy potatoes**, such as russet, peeled and cut into chunks
   **Salt**
4½ pounds **pork tenderloins**, 2 packages with 2 tenderloins in each package
4 tablespoons **EVOO** (extra-virgin olive oil)
4 tablespoons **grill seasoning** or a blend of coarse salt and black pepper
1 pound **green beans**, stems trimmed
1 medium **onion**, chopped
2 large **garlic cloves**, finely chopped
3 tablespoons **butter**
1 tablespoon all-purpose **flour**
¼ cup of your favorite **barbecue sauce**
1½ cups **chicken stock**
½ cup **milk**
4 **scallions**, white and green parts, thinly sliced

Preheat the oven to 500°F.

Place the potatoes in a large saucepot, cover with water, and place over high heat to bring up to a boil. Once it is boiling, salt the water and cook until the potatoes are tender, about 15 minutes.

While the water comes up to a boil, trim the silver skin or connective tissue off the tenderloins with a very sharp, thin knife. Place the tenderloins on a rimmed nonstick baking sheet. Coat the tenderloins with 2 tablespoons of the EVOO, then sprinkle with the grill seasoning or salt and pepper and transfer to the oven. Roast for 25 to 30 minutes, to an internal temperature of 145°F. Remove the meat from the oven and let it rest under a foil tent.

Once you remove the pork from the oven, reduce the temperature to 400°F. Place the green beans and half the chopped onion on a rimmed baking sheet and drizzle with 1 tablespoon of the EVOO, and season with salt and pepper. Toss to coat evenly and then transfer to the oven to roast for 10 to 12 minutes. Give them a toss about 5 minutes into the roasting time.

For the barbecue pan gravy, heat a medium skillet with the remaining tablespoon of EVOO, once around the pan, over medium-high heat. Add the remaining onion, the garlic, and a little salt and pepper and cook, stirring frequently, for 5 minutes, or until the onions start to get tender. Melt in 1 tablespoon of the butter, then add the flour and cook for 1 minute. Add the barbecue sauce and whisk in the chicken stock. Bring up to a bubble and then turn down the heat and let the pan sauce cook until thick, a couple of minutes.

Once the potatoes are tender, drain and return to the pot. Add the milk and the remaining 2 tablespoons of butter; season with salt and pepper and add the scallions. Smash with a potato masher or the back of a fork to the desired consistency.

To serve, thinly slice 2 of the roasted pork tenderloins. Platter it up and drizzle with the barbecue pan sauce, and serve alongside the green onion smashed potatoes and the roasted green beans.

Cool the other tenderloins, then wrap and store in the fridge.

# Second Night: Cheddar-Smothered Pork and Apple Sauce Sammies

2 roasted **pork tenderloins** (see page 322)

2 tablespoons **butter**, plus some for spreading on sandwich-size English muffins

2 **Golden Delicious apples**, peeled, cored, and sliced

4 sprigs of fresh **thyme**, leaves removed and coarsely chopped

2 tablespoons **brown sugar**

4 tablespoons **cider vinegar**

4 sandwich-size **English muffins**, split

½ pound aged **white Cheddar cheese**, sliced

2 tablespoons **honey**
  **Salt** and **black pepper**

3 tablespoons **EVOO** (extra-virgin olive oil)

4 cups **watercress**, trimmed of thick stems, 2 bunches

Preheat your broiler. Thickly slice the roasted pork tenderloins on a slight angle and reserve.

Heat a medium-size skillet over medium heat with the 2 table-spoons of butter. Once the butter melts, add the apples, thyme, brown sugar, and about 2 tablespoons of the cider vinegar. Cook, stirring frequently, for 5 to 7 minutes. Add the sliced pork and toss to combine and heat up the pork slightly, a minute or two.

While the apple sauce and pork are cooking, toast the English muffins until they are golden, remove from the toaster, and spread lightly with butter.

To assemble, divide the pork among the 8 toasted muffin halves, top each one with some of the apple sauce, and then top that with a slice of the Cheddar cheese. Transfer to the oven or broiler for a few minutes to melt the cheese.

While the cheese is melting, in the bottom of a salad bowl combine the remaining 2 tablesoons of cider vinegar with the honey. Whisk in the EVOO in a slow, steady stream, season with salt and pepper, then add the watercress and toss to coat.

Serve the open-faced pork and apple sammies, 2 halves per person, alongside the cress salad.

# Maple-Glazed Pork Chops with Scallion Smashed Potatoes and Escarole

This one's so simple and so elegant. You can entertain with this or cook it for your family any old day of the week!

2½ pounds small **potatoes**, such as baby Yukon Gold or small red-skin potatoes, halved
   **Salt**
4 (1½-inch-thick) boneless **pork loin chops**
   **Black pepper**
6 tablespoons **EVOO** (extra-virgin olive oil)
1 heaping tablespoon **grainy mustard** (eyeball it)
2 tablespoons **white wine vinegar** (eyeball it)
1 cup **chicken stock**
6 fresh **thyme sprigs**, leaves stripped and chopped
¼ cup **maple syrup** (eyeball it)
   Zest and juice of 1 **lemon**
½ cup **milk** or half-and-half (eyeball it)
3 tablespoons **butter**
4 **scallions**, white and green parts, thinly sliced
1 large head of **escarole**, cored and the leaves torn into bite-size pieces

Place the potatoes in a medium saucepot with water to cover by about 1 inch. Bring to a boil over high heat, add some salt, and cook for 12 to 15 minutes, until tender.

Season the pork chops with salt and pepper. Preheat a large skillet over medium-high to high heat with 2 tablespoons of the EVOO, twice around the pan. When the oil begins to ripple, add the pork chops and sear for 2 minutes on each side, then turn the heat down to medium and cook for another 5 to 6 minutes.

While the chops cook, stir together the grainy mustard, a little salt and pepper, and the vinegar in the bottom of a salad bowl. Whisk in the remaining ¼ cup of EVOO, pouring it in a slow, steady stream.

Transfer the pork chops to a plate and cover loosely with foil to keep warm. Add the chicken stock, thyme, maple syrup, 2 teaspoons of the lemon zest, and the lemon juice to the skillet. Bring up to a bubble and simmer until lightly thickened, a couple of minutes.

Drain the potatoes and return them to the hot pot. Add the milk, butter, scallions, and some salt and pepper and mash the potatoes to your preferred consistency.

Return the pork chops to the pan with the glaze and flip around to coat them well. Place the chops on dinner plates; drizzle with any remaining glaze from the skillet. Toss the escarole with the dressing to coat and serve alongside each pork chop with a pile of smashed potatoes.

# Hazelnut-Crusted Veal Scallopini with Cognac Tarragon Sauce and Fennel Salad

Why pay $30 for something you can make in 30 minutes? Another fancy fake-out for friends or family!

- 1 tablespoon **Dijon mustard**
- 2 tablespoons **aged balsamic vinegar**
  **Salt** and **black pepper**
- ½ cup plus 1 tablespoon **EVOO** (extra-virgin olive oil)
- 1 large **fennel bulb**, cut in half lengthwise, cored, and then thinly sliced
- 3 cups peeled whole **hazelnuts**
- 2 cups all-purpose **flour** (eyeball it)
- 2 **eggs**
- 1½ pounds **veal** scallopini
- 4 **shallots**, thinly sliced
- 1 **garlic clove**, grated or finely chopped
- 1 shot **cognac** (look for a nip, or small airplane-serving bottle, if you don't want to invest in a larger bottle)
- 2 cups **chicken stock** (eyeball it)
- 3 tablespoons cold **butter**
- 2 fresh **tarragon sprigs**, leaves stripped and chopped
- 4 to 5 cups **arugula leaves**
  **Parmigiano-Reggiano** cheese, for shaving

Preheat the oven to 250°F.

In the bottom of a salad bowl combine the mustard with the balsamic vinegar. Add a little salt and pepper, then whisk in about ¼ cup of the EVOO, pouring it in a slow, steady stream. Add the sliced fennel and set the bowl aside.

Place the hazelnuts in a food processor and pulse on and off to grind the nuts into very fine bits, almost as fine as bread crumbs. Transfer to a shallow dish. Place the flour in another shallow dish, then beat the eggs with a splash of water in a third shallow dish.

Season the veal scallopini liberally with salt and pepper. Working in batches, coat the veal in flour and shake off the excess, then coat in egg and finally in the ground nuts. Repeat until all of the scallopini is coated. Place a large skillet over medium-high heat and coat the bottom of the pan in a thin layer of EVOO, about 2 tablespoons. Once you see a ripple in the oil, add half the scallopini. Cook for 5 minutes, turning once. Transfer the cooked scallopini to a plate and set in the oven to keep warm. Wipe any dark nuts out of the skillet and repeat with the remaining oil and scallopini.

While the scallopini cook, place a medium skillet over medium heat with the remaining tablespoon of EVOO, once around the pan. When the oil is hot, add the shallots and garlic and cook for 2 to 3 minutes. Remove the skillet from the heat. Stand back to add the cognac, then carefully ignite it. Return to the heat and cook for 1 minute or until the flame dies out, then add the chicken stock and bring up to a bubble. Simmer for 5 minutes, until only ½ cup of liquid remains in the skillet. Add the cold butter and the tarragon to the warm cognac sauce; stir until the butter has completely melted. Turn the heat off.

Add the arugula to the salad bowl with the fennel. Use a vegetable peeler to add about ⅓ cup Parmigiano shavings to the bowl, and toss to combine.

Divide the scallopini among 4 serving plates. Drizzle with some of the sauce and serve the salad alongside.

# index